DANCING ON AIR

MY LIFE WITH RAI PURDY
BY
VERITY SWEENY PURDY

PIONEERING RADIO AND TELEVISION
BROADCASTING IN CANADA, THE UNITED
STATES AND SCOTLAND

CANADIAN CATALOGUING IN PUBLICATION DATA

Purdy, Verity Sweeny, 1922 -
        Dancing on air: my life with Rai Purdy / by Verity
Sweeny Purdy.

ISBN 978-1-896238-07-4

        1. Purdy, Rai, 1910-1990. 2. Television producers and
directors–Canada–Biography. 3. Radio producers and
directors–Canada–Biography. I. Title.

PN1992.4.P86P86 2008   791.4502′32092   C2008-903830-4

TWIN EAGLES
PUBLISHING
Box 2031
Sechelt BC
V0N 3A0
pblakey@telus.net
604 885 7503

Acknowledgements

I would very much like to thank Betty C. Keller of Quintessential Literary Services for having been the true, warm-hearted task master I needed to pull together my first two books: The Luckiest Girl in the World *and* As Luck Would Have It.

Now W. Paul Blakey, of Twin Eagles Publishing, honours my third memoir, Dancing On Air, My life with Rai Purdy.

Also for knowing–and caring about, my life as a Dancer: Peter Watson and Pip Wedge are special.

Thank you my friends. Thank you.

Verity Purdy, 2008

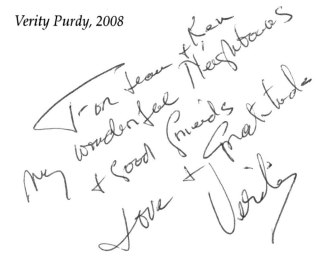

Contents

Foreword

I am honoured to have been asked to write a foreword to *Dancing on Air, My life with Rai Purdy*, Verity's third memoir. It is the candid, honest, portrayal of her life with husband Rai, through the difficult but rewarding years following WW II. This story is about two highly creative and talented people who met while with the Canadian Army Show, were married after the war and, working as a team, created a rare dance of life filled with challenges and risks; what Verity calls 'Fancy Dancing'. She writes that their lives were "One after another Purdy Productions".

Following his early days as a stage and radio actor and head of drama with CFRB in Toronto, Rai joined the Army as a producer with the Canadian Army Shows. After the war he went back to radio broadcasting in Toronto. However, even before it was established in Canada, Rai became enchanted with television and headed for New York. With a bit of 'Fancy Dancing', he landed a seven year contract with CBS-TV as a producer/director. His next adventure was in Glasgow as programme director for Scottish Television.

Three years later, with the opening of the major market private television stations across Canada, the Purdy's came home. First to Toronto, where in 1960, Rai, as program director, helped launch CFTO Toronto. Next, he re-opened Purdy Productions in Vancouver. For Verity, it was returning to her roots, and a new beginning; for Rai, it was the opportunity to bring his expertise and experience to the newly launched Vancouver station CHAN-TV.

A couple of 'Fancy Dancers' ourselves, Ray Peters and I were solo performers at the time we met Verity and Rai and joined their dance. Ray, having help run a successful private television station in Hamilton had also returned to his Vancouver roots to manage the new station, CHAN-TV. Just home from England, I got a job at the station where I met Ray. We were married in 1966.

During the early years of private television broadcasting in Vancouver, Ray and his team at CHAN-TV worked with Purdy Productions to produce 'People in Conflict', 'Magistrate's Court' and other special programs for the CTV Television Network. Rai also produced Variety Club telethons for CHAN as well as for other stations across Canada. I joined Purdy Productions where I honed my television skills as Rai's production assistant, just one of scores of young people he taught and encouraged over his many years in the industry. He was highly professional and respected by all the production personnel with whom he worked.

Verity, very much part of all that Rai did, was integral to Purdy Productions. But in addition, she always made sure the hard working crews were properly nourished. We started a life-long friendship. The Purdy's lived in the British Properties at the time, one of at least twelve domiciles in the West where they hosted wonderful gatherings. Many we enjoyed with them over the years. I don't know if they ever counted all the places they lived together but this wonderful memoir certainly paints a picture.

Rai Purdy was a true pioneer, an innovator and entrepreneur who helped develop, and contributed to, the success of private radio and television broadcasting. In 1990, we were sad to say goodbye to our dear friend, but have been refreshed by memories of many happy times together.

The Canadian Association of Broadcasters honours individuals involved in the industry for outstanding achievements and contributions to private broadcasting, and to Canada. In 2007, Rai Purdy was posthumously inducted into the CAB Broadcast Hall of Fame. An honour well deserved.

Over almost 50 years, Verity and I have shared the inner and outer landscapes of our lives, our sorrows and joys, our hearts. She has become a mentor of extraordinary lightness and sensitivity. Her artistic talents are for all of us to share. Her friendship is treasured.

Thank you, Verity, for offering me the privilege to add these movements to your dance!

Heidi Freya Peters (nee Sohnel)

Preface

To some, the term *fancy dancing* might conjure a vision of Radio City Rockettes wowing the crowd with their perfect high kicks, or it might bring to mind the demanding pirouettes of classical ballet. Certainly Cossacks who leap and spin are fancy dancers as are the performers of the Hawaiian hula, the Irish jig and our own west coast First Nations' "Fancy Dance." But my particular concept of fancy dancing has none of this brilliance. To me, the term *fancy dancing* means using one's wits to avoid life's pitfalls and managing to succeed without disclosing one's lack of knowledge. Fancy dancers usually come to their careers by way of a difficult childhood.

As a team, we two "Fancy Dancers" put our heads into some pretty magical "Purdy Productions."

CHAPTER 1

The Young Rai Purdy

Born in England in November 1910, Horatio John (Rai) Purdy, the fifth child of Lionel and Emily Purdy, was a blonde and delicate toddler of three when his family, along with his mother's sister Maude, left London to make their home in Toronto. Horatio's father was a self-educated man. Coming from deep poverty, he had taught himself to write and read and had come to believe in astrology. Since the chart he drew up for his infant son indicated a life of no value before the age of twenty, Horatio was allowed a kind of freedom seldom offered any child, particularly a child from a struggling immigrant family. His father's employment was sporadic, so the family was constantly on the move, but the six months they spent in a grand old house by a ravine in Rosedale was every boy's dream. Despite having to mow the lawns surrounding the house, water the vegetable garden and sometimes wax floors, Horatio could often escape to totally private places among the tall trees. One elm in particular he called his own. When he wanted to be alone, he would climb to its topmost branches. Perched there, feeling like a king, he dreamt of one day reigning over a kingdom sparkling with celebrities.

Despite Lionel's dismal prognostication for the boy, Emily adored him, smothered and pampered him, allowing him to

The Purdy family

Horatio John Purdy and older brother Tim, 1917

eat only what pleased him (mostly white bread and jam), let him go to bed without brushing his teeth and get up when he chose. When he started school at age six, she let him stay home on days that were "not good for him," that is, days not good according to the astrological chart Lionel had prepared for him. This delighted Horatio, who hated having to sit at a school desk because his legs and what he called his hams itched so much he couldn't stay still. As a consequence, he was often sent to the corner for fidgeting. He couldn't concentrate nor did he learn anything, but his parents didn't concern themselves. Horatio wouldn't amount to much before he was twenty, anyway.

Although Canada never provided the environment for it, neither Emily nor her husband ever lost their ambition to join the social "upper crust," if not for themselves, at least for their five children. Coming from a once well-to-do background, Emily's schooling had been good and she played the piano with determination. Her sister Maude had graduated with honours from the Royal Academy of Dramatic Art. In fact, their whole family had involved themselves in amateur theatrics, writing plays, making costumes, singing and dancing, and these were the gifts Emily gave to her own children. Wherever they lived, and despite the Great Depression, she encouraged her children and all the neighbour's children by making herself the theatrical centre of the community. On winter evenings their house was usually filled with amateur artists making props and costumes or rehearsing plays that they performed in church basements. Lionel kept order by closing down festivities precisely at midnight when he played "God Save The King" on the wind-up gramophone.

Though Kathleen, Horatio's favourite sister, spoke with a lisp, she loved words and used them with great enthusiasm to write scripts for her younger brother who spoke particularly well, articulating clearly with a completely Royal Academy accent, thanks to Auntie Maude's coaching. However, when the Depression was at its worst, Horatio left high school to become a bicycle messenger boy, thereby bringing home enough money to contribute the odd bag of coal. By this time he had

11

also memorized quite a repertoire of poems, songs and comedy sketches and earned a few dollars performing them at evening banquets or church concerts. When asked by his audiences where he came from, he would say, sort of proudly, "Born wivin the saund a' Bow Boweus. Oim a reeoo Cockney." But no one could have guessed. At fifteen, the budding thespian was also quoting Shakespeare, and he carried a spear as an extra when Sir Martin Harvey's travelling company came to town.

Though he grew wiry by cycling about the city every day, he remained skinny. (His mother said he was "not thin, just cadaverous," which she thought meant suave or elegant.) His father definitely did not believe in doctors, so it was not until Horatio was eighteen that a friend convinced him to see a doctor who explained anaemia to him. Mega-iron injections quickly took the pallor from his cheeks.

In 1929, following several years in amateur theatrics, Horatio's gaunt but aristocratic features and deep, rich voice got him into the University of Toronto's Hart House Theatre Company. Probably because of his cultured manner of speaking, people assumed he was enrolled at the U of T. Already a *fancy dancer,* he didn't bother to correct them. As well as having an agile body, he acted with much confidence, and with his talent for mimicry and for memorizing lines, he could play a part with conviction without even having read the whole script. Once he was safely into his twenties, the well-known actress Dora Mavor Moore befriended him. Her son Mavor and John Drainie of Vancouver were also benefiting from her mentorship at that time. Soon Horatio became head of the Dickens Fellowship and for several years took plays to the Ontario Drama Festival where they always did very well. When his friend Edgar Stone, one of Toronto's earliest radio technicians, invited the young actor to apprentice with him, Horatio learned the magical capabilities of the carbon microphone and how to use it. In 1931 Stone encouraged his prodigy to audition for Harry Sedgewick, the manager of radio station CFRB (Canadian Federation of Radio Broadcasters) in Toronto. This station was the brainchild of

Horatio Purdy on stage at the Hart House Theatre

Horatio the dandy

Edward "Ted" Rogers Sr., the inventor of the world's first successful alternating current radio tube, which made it possible to dispense with batteries in radios and operate them instead off household electricity. To sell his new tubes, Rogers produced the *Rogers' Batteryless Radio*, which quickly became a commercial success. He followed this with the creation of CFRB.

When Harry Sedgewick offered Horatio his first job as a broadcaster, he made two stipulations: he must drop the English accent Aunt Maude had so carefully polished and choose a new name. And that was why, by taking three letters from his given name, Horatio Purdy began his broadcasting life as "Rai" Purdy. His pay was $25 a week. Though ignorant of French, the new announcer recorded interviews with such celebrities as Dr. Allan Dafoe and the famous Dionne Quintuplet family. Then, with no clue about science, he questioned Professor Albert Einstein who gave him a revealing interview and played for him on his violin.

Rai's career blossomed when Sedgewick made him head of CFRB's drama department, and the company built Rai his own studio, big enough for a small audience and complete with a music and sound effects booth. He was allowed to hire and train two of his friends, Dick Fonger as music librarian and Irvin Teitle as sound effects operator, and together Rai and Dick set up the original CFRB music library. While his main acting strength still lay in his exceptional dramatic abilities, Rai was also a comic. Teamed up with Alan Savage, the two captured a major part of the Ontario lunch-time radio audience with a rollicking broadcast called Treasure Trail, a fast, slap-happy show which stayed on the air for several years and got them weekly bags of fan mail.

Meanwhile, back in 1935, the then gallant "Horatio", still virginal and pure, had rescued Frances, a Little Theatre actress, from her fraught family situation. Fran's gentle father, a landscape gardener, lived under the critical eye of his domineering wife who, having tried it once, had very definite ideas about the evils of sex and the dangers of childbirth. Rai married Fran and took her to live on the top floor of his parents' home on Nina Avenue, but because of the frightening way her mother had described childbirth, Rai as well as Fran were destined to go through traumatic experiences during Fran's only pregnancy. After four hysterical months of being terrified about what was happening to her, she tried to abort the fetus by throwing herself down a staircase. In due course and without undue physical difficulty, their healthy son Brian was born in 1937, but Fran collapsed emotionally, even refusing to allow Rai to visit her during the weeks she lay in hospital. There was nothing he could do except advertise for a kindly household helper who didn't need a lot of money. The woman who came to his rescue was Deanie, a Christian Science practitioner, who not only brought Fran out of her despair but, during the two years she stayed with them, convinced Fran to become a Christian Scientist. This was difficult for Rai who, though he tried to comply with the women's wishes, simply couldn't accept this faith for himself.

During this period Rai had become widely known for a weekly mystery drama series called *Out of The Night* for which he wrote and regularly read the creepy opening: "Out of the night there comes a mist which shrouds the thoughts of day and opens up a world to us of things that live a different way. But do they live? Or are they just the figment of a tortured mind distorted by an arduous day?" The scripts for this series came from the pen of his sister Kathleen. Rai not only produced and directed this regional network phenomenon but also, using his flexible voice and many accents, played multiple roles in each drama. Soon the show's Canadian ratings were higher than those for the US broadcast sponsored by Ivory Soap that was offered on another station at the same hour.

When CFRB began to pay him a decent salary, Rai made the down payment on a small house in a new development called Leaside. He also bought a white piano and Tovy, a Russian wolfhound. But as he went on to success after success with CFRB as interviewer, actor and producer, he had less and less time for his wife and their growing son, and after Deanie left them, Fran became lonely and depressed. Perhaps if they had another child, Rai suggested, and perhaps if he tried to

15

get home more, her life would be fuller. When Fran refused to consider another pregnancy, they made plans to adopt a daughter. Later Rai would admit that the agency had been wrong ever to consider them as adoptive parents while their relationship was so unstable. "But," he confessed, "because I was well known, they never questioned us." His son Brian was two when nine-months-old Brenda came to join the family.

Throughout these years Rai maintained a close relationship with his parents and siblings, telephoning his mother every day and lunching with his aging parents at least once a week. Lionel, who had by now given up trying to cope, completely relied on his children for financial support, and Rai managed to pay a generous share of that support from his increasing income. With some of his extra earnings he bought an Austin and began taking his parents for drives on the weekends. This may not have pleased Fran.

At home, Rai added a white bar to his recreation room and bought a safe old half-Arab gelding (which he boarded where he bought it at a Don Valley stable), a riding outfit for himself and a Dalmatian as a companion for his wolfhound. Although he hadn't ridden before, after only a few lessons he rode well enough to explore the valley trails with his dogs each morning before driving to CFRB at seven to put the station on the air for the day. When on occasion Rai brought home a noisy crowd of theatrical friends such as John Drainie, Mavor Moore, Alan Savage, Cy Mack and Herb May–usually at a late hour–to drink at the white bar and sing around the white piano, his wife was not happy. As a result, instead of spending more time at home, Rai stayed away more and more. Later he would tell hair-raising stories of dare-devil driving down Yonge Street in the small hours while well lubricated, dodging lamp posts and skidding on icy streetcar tracks; he joked about having been stopped by a cop who said, "Oh, it's you, Rai. Go get some sleep."

In May 1939 CFRB's principal owner, Ted Rogers Sr. died suddenly, and ownership of the station fell into the hands of the remaining shareholders. Rai took this opportunity to leave the station's employ, and with Harry Sedgewick's blessing,

16

became an independent producer. Rai Purdy Productions opened for business in the same building on Bloor street as CFRB but just down the hall. As his many radio fans idolized him, he never had a problem finding excellent secretarial help, and from the applicants who answered his first ad he chose Vi Webb, a mature, cheery "Girl Friday" who instantly became his right hand and on whom he was to rely for many years. Around the same time he engaged as his coproducer American-born Robert L. Simpson (father-to-be of the Globe and Mail's political columnist Jeffrey Simpson). Robert, always conscious of his tall, dark good looks, handled his audiences with the smug superiority of an "ad agency" man. From the new offices Rai created and directed shows for CFRB in which he also acted. He also leased CFRB's studios to produce his own commercial shows. During the next three years he produced and directed *Howie Wing, Hollywood Gossip, The Circle K Club, Double or Nothing, This Day, Musical Beauty-Box, Voice of Victor, The Canadian Theatre of The Air, The O'Keefe Show, Penny's Diary, Flying for Freedom* and the highly successful soap, *George's Wife*, which in 1939 when Canada went to war became Soldier's Wife.

By 1941, despite his popularity and the secure position of his company, Rai's continuing conflict at home precipitated a radical change in his life. Seeing an overseas posting as an acceptable way out of this discomfort, he decided to leave RP Productions in the hands of Vi Webb and Bob Simpson, with his sister Kathleen's husband, Ernie Edge, as overseer. Then with his friends Dick Fonger and Irvin Teitle, he attempted to enlist in the Air Force. Fonger and Teitle were promptly accepted but, because he only weighed 135 pounds, the Air Force wouldn't take Rai. A few months later, however, when the Canadian Army announced plans to broadcast a patriotic radio show, Rai was the obvious candidate to produce it. This time, when the 31-year-old volunteered, even though he was so slightly built and had received little formal education, the Army grabbed him. And his high IQ meant that he was whisked off to Trois Rivieres for officer's training. Because his acting career had given him good, strong lungs and taught him to move quickly, he suffered less during army training than many others did. Soft professionals such as doctors and dentists had more difficulties, and one of them died because of the army's requirement that officer-cadets run everywhere they go, even in zero temperatures. But Rai survived three months of this training and returned to Toronto with the rank of lieutenant to join the military broadcast unit. Shortly after that he moved into army quarters.

The new unit was commanded by then Captain W. Victor George, a veteran broadcaster and the managing director of Whitehall Broadcasting of Montreal. It also included musical conductor Captain Geoffrey Waddington and the well-known composer/conductor Captain Robert Farnon, who was arranging scores for a large mixed chorus, for solo vocalist Jimmy Shields and balladeer Raymonde Maranda as well as the comedy team of Frank Shuster and Johnnie Wayne. Many of Canada's top musicians had volunteered to join this unit, some coming from the Toronto Symphony, while others were experienced recording and broadcasting artists. It became Rai's job to produce a weekly radio show for the national network, combining Farnon's music with the sketches and dialogues full of comic and serious propaganda that Shuster and Wayne wrote. From these highly rated 1941/42 radio broadcasts grew the first Canadian Army show (CAS), a full-blown extravaganza produced by the brilliant showman Jack Arthur and choreographed by Aida Broadbent (Canada's ambassadress in Hollywood)–both of whom remained civilians. CAS headquarters was Toronto's old Victoria Theatre on Queen Street East. At this point, while Rai continued as broadcast officer for CAS, he also took on the theatrical duty of assistant to stage-director Romney Brent, a Canadian with a successful Broadway career. A military exercise, later to be performed in the stage production by the Army Show Drill Squad, had already proved an effective publicity asset, and Lieutenant Purdy thoroughly enjoyed his position as officer in charge, strutting his showmanship at the head of an immaculate column when the squad paraded on the streets of Toronto.

Captain Rai Purdy

Army show ready to board ship

Captain Purdy leading the drill squad

CHAPTER 2

CAS On Tour

In addition to the Canadian Army Show's value as a morale booster for both service and civilian populations across the country and as a powerful propaganda tool, the travelling show was designed to sell war bonds and raise funds to establish and operate service canteens. These rest-and-recreational centres for service people were run by local civilians, so it was they who administered revenues from CAS performances. In Vancouver, one of these civilians was my uncle, Richard Bell-Irving.

By the spring of 1943 CAS was on a whirlwind tour, its cast members living aboard their own exclusive train and playing all of the major service camps and big theatres across Canada. They were entertained royally at every stop. Lieutenant Rai Purdy took full advantage of the comparative freedom given to officers, who often returned to the parked train long after "lights out." When they found the doors locked, they climbed into their quarters through an unlocked window via an upturned "honey bucket," one of the slop-pails that were normally placed on the track under the toilets when the train was on a siding.

It so happened that by the time the show reached Vancouver in July of that year the company was in need of a new lead dancer, and my uncle, who was a friend of the commanding officer, arranged an audition for me. Recently returned from Seattle where I had been teaching dance, I performed in the old Hotel Vancouver ballroom for Lieutenant Lineaweaver who was the present lead dancer and, more importantly, the Canadian Womens' Army Corps (CWAC) administrative officer. Also gathered to assess my capabilities were captains Robert Farnon, Romney Brent and Lieutenant Rai Purdy.

At precisely the time I auditioned for these officers, I was awaiting a contract to dance with the American Ballet Theatre. However, I found myself willing to consider putting my classical ballet career on hold when the CO, Victor George, who was by then a major, offered me the position of lead dancer in the Army Show and assistant to choreographer Felicia Sorrel.

"If you accept, you'll have to enlist," he explained.

"I'll let you know very shortly," I answered as calmly as I could.

Three months later, graduated from basic training in Vermilion and wearing the crisp summer uniform of a CWAC, I met Rai Purdy again, this time in Toronto where I attended a CAS production meeting held in his quarters, a suite at the King Edward Hotel. Though Rai was primarily in charge of radio broadcasts, since he was pouring the drinks, I assumed this to be his meeting. Also in the room were the other members of the production staff to which I had been assigned: stage director Romney Brent, departing lead dancer Lisa Lineaweaver, stage manager Jim Hozak, theatre manager Howard Legrow, and music director Robert Farnon. These were all officers or senior noncommissioned officers (NCOs), considerably older than I, and every one of them was a professional show person. Brand new to the production department and only a lance corporal, I was overwhelmed to be treated by everyone there like an "old pro," especially by the fellow in charge who struck me as cheerful and energetic, though a bit of a dandy. Already a radio celebrity in Ontario, Rai Purdy was visibly surprised to learn, as he handed me a rum and Coke and sat beside me on his bed, that I knew nothing about him or his career. I had to explain that, though I was Canadian, I had been dancing in London and the United States for the past ten years.

During the day Rai worked in a studio on the top floor of the Royal York Hotel where he produced the weekly propaganda broadcast featuring the musicians and stars of the Army Show. I saw him only at evening meetings, but looking back, I suspect he had a bit of a crush on me right from the beginning. He was attentive, gentlemanly, self-assured and engagingly enthusiastic about the job he was doing. In fact, he seemed quite pleased with himself. But though the attention he paid me was flattering, I had another man on my mind at the time.

When Romney Brent, who was old enough to retire from the Canadian Army, chose to return to his Broadway career, it became Rai's responsibility, in addition to producing radio shows, to remake, replace and reorder the Canadian Army Show for its second season on the road. From then on, as a member of the production staff, I worked with him every evening, and I was amazed to discover that through his extensive involvement in amateur theatrics, he had developed a capacity for retaining details of an entire show in his head. He could memorize every word and note of music and every lighting and curtain cue. However, well before this new show was ready for its grand opening, I knew that Rai had received top secret information about Ottawa's plans for the company. Privately he told me the show would definitely open in Toronto, though how long it would run he couldn't say. But very soon, those in charge of production were given the facts, and because of the bustle in the scenery workshop, script and music departments, excitement began to run high throughout the whole company.

A single gala performance for Ottawa's top military brass in mid-November 1943 was followed the very next day by a parade of the production department, the cast and stage crew—now 100 plus—in front of our commanding officer, Major George. He told us that Canadian Military Headquarters had decided CAS was to be split into small units suitable for travelling from one military station to another and would, when prepared and equipped, proceed overseas. He assigned higher ranks to those NCOs who would take responsibility for each of the five independent shows to be known as units A to E. My dance partner Ev Staples and I were posted to B unit and I was promoted to sergeant. Also, since choreographer Sorrel (a nonmilitary American) would soon return to New York, I became permanent choreographer. Major George also swore everyone to secrecy about the departure date, a mere four weeks away. "Now," he said, "the real work must begin." Then he handed the meeting over to the production staff.

From then on, with five shows in rehearsal, the Old Victoria Theatre thrummed with activity on stage, in the green room, in every dressing room, office and corridor until only a few days before departure when sets, props, lights, costumes and sound systems had to be crated for shipping. Since there were to be no further army radio shows in Canada, Rai now spent all of his time at the Victoria Theatre. Meanwhile, because of the heavy administrative demands on those officers preparing the show for overseas travel, it was necessary that the new NCOs take charge of their own units. Advised and occasionally supervised by Rai and using as much of the "big show" dance material as Felicia and I could modify, each of the NCOs, already seasoned artists, went to work on his own production.

Romney Brent's return to Broadway opened the way not only for Rai's promotion to stage director but also for his military step up to the rank of captain, which, considering that his total military training had consisted of three months as an officer cadet at Trois-Rivieres, was a heavy responsibility. However, it was one he handled easily. Like everything else he tackled, he took soldiering seriously. But more importantly his move up had placed him in the perfect position to put into action every creative and theatrical skill he had developed for himself as well as those he had borrowed from amateur theatre, Hart House productions, drama festivals and radio broadcasting. He was not the least afraid of handling large crowds of people nor of assigning responsibility where it belonged. In his wisdom, he gathered around himself intelligent, competent and enthusiastic subordinates from whose experience he was eager to learn. Around the Old Victoria, he issued orders with brevity, authority and his own high sense of theatre, enjoying with the entire company the excitement of the project that lay ahead.

But Captain Rai Purdy still had to salute Major Victor George, his commanding officer–though a personal friend for many years–and was obliged to listen carefully to Captain Bill Wren, the unit adjutant. Wren, a liquor salesman in civvy street, had served before that as a permanent force soldier. As a result, he knew "the book" inside out, posted every detail of army regulations and dispensed discipline with sardonic relish. He wasn't always liked, but he certainly set an admirable standard, one that was to stand CAS personnel apart for their good behaviour and to gain the units an enviable reputation under tough field conditions.

When word leaked out that Captain Purdy was headed overseas, the broadcast industry honoured him, presenting him with travelling gifts such as a steamer trunk and a mini-bar. Ladies from his adoring audiences sent him hand-knit wool socks to protect his feet from the roughness of army boots. His mother promised to write to him every day–a promise she kept.

Heading for Halifax on their way overseas, the NCOs and officers of CAS–no longer in their own comfortable train–were assigned extra duties to assure the safe transportation of the bodies in their charge as well as their mountains of theatrical baggage. But aboard the troop ship, a ship I recognized from childhood travelling; the Cunard liner "SS Berengaria," orders were issued by the ship's command and discipline was handled by army provosts. We other ranks, when not stuffed three bunks high and 24 to a cabin, were crowded shoulder to shoulder in the mess halls or lounges of the peacetime luxury liner. Including our CAS personnel, the ship carried 3,200 troops on what proved to be her last safe voyage.

Boarding last made things easier for officers. Only ten were assigned to a cabin of reasonable size, and Rai was able to grab a lower bunk. But the resounding crash as he dumped his haversack on the floor beside it told him to his horror what had happened to 60 ounces of good Canadian rye whisky he had stowed in it. Trying to rescue it, he hit his head on the bunk above, then flopped on the hard mattress moaning over his loss. For the next five days and nights the tantalizing aroma hung around the cabin.

Although the Atlantic wasn't particularly rough, the voyage was not without excitement. Once outside Halifax harbour, Berengaria settled into the centre of a large merchant convoy but, because of her superior speed, she was soon ordered to steam ahead. At dusk she left the motley collection of ships where the maximum speed could only be as fast as the slowest of them. After dinner aboard ship the troops retired and most were probably asleep when suddenly the ship lurched and tipped sideways, rolling much of her human cargo onto the decks. She stayed over for several minutes before righting herself, and though everyone must have been awake by this time, no alarm bells rang. No one shouted orders. After another few minutes, Rai announced to his fellow officers, "Everybody back to bed!" In no time snoring had begun again. When the same thing happened in the opposite direction about twenty minutes later, the occupants clung to the edges of their bunks, and this time most remained attached. But that was not the end of it. In fact, the twisting and turning went on all night and in the morning the word was that Berengaria had been navigating to avoid U-boats. Far from disturbing the troops, the episode excited them as they felt they had begun to participate in the actual conflict.

CHAPTER 3

CAS Overseas

On December 24, 1943, the day the Army Show company arrived in England, quarters in the ancient garrison town of Aldershot were already overcrowded. As a result, CASO (the O was added for overseas) officers and other ranks were billeted in order of rank wherever beds and primitive palliasses (straw-filled sacks) were available to sleep on, some of us finding ourselves with British as well as Canadian fighting units. No facilities for rehearsals had been prepared nor was an appropriate CASO mess hall provided, but with Vic George at the helm plus Bill Wren's military know-how, CASO officers were soon given a mess several miles away in Farnborough.

A short time later Rai signed a barrack damages contract with the British Army to give CASO personnel a crumbling brick compound in the heart of Aldershot for barracks, an orderly room, and rehearsal and mess halls. Although long ago condemned as unsafe, these buildings were still in use. Little did Rai suspect that intrigue lurked beneath the apparently friendly surface of Britain's bristling military town. The first indication of trouble ahead came just a few days later with a memo from the CASO paymaster to the adjutant reporting complaints from "other ranks" about being cheated when cashing pound notes.

During the first couple of weeks in January 1944 the CASO crew put their stamp on the tawdry quarters they had inherited, scrubbing, patching and painting with enthusiasm. Meanwhile, musicians practised, dancers rehearsed and the scene shop whirred with activity as the five units equipped themselves to hit the road. Then for the next six weeks we set out nightly by convoy to entertain troops within a radius of 20 miles of Aldershot.

From the start, everything in England was stressful for the CASO personnel. The noise of air-raids, the grime and crowding, the continuous blackouts and checking, and re-checking to make sure no chink of light showed kept us newcomers on edge, but from Rai's point of view the excitement of the adventure far outweighed any fear of physical danger. As an officer he had privileges that gave him access to London where he contacted many of his Toronto buddies. Both Dick Fonger and Irv Teitle, now RCAF officers, were stationed near there, and one of his closest broadcast friends, John Collingwood-Reid, was now a war correspondent headquartered in London. Rai also visited other officers' messes and, despite regular nighttime bombardment and the consequent disruption of performance schedules, he enjoyed the London theatre, such as it was. The London air raids were so frequent at this time that, except in very heavy raids, most people simply ignored them, stayed away from windows at night and said, "That was a close one," when a bomb burst nearby. The unmanned doodle bombs were harder on the nerves because of their rattling sound and the knowledge that, when their measured fuel ran out and the engine ceased, they could drop upon one instantly. Rai had lots of "close calls" but somehow he nipped safely about in his staff car or on foot with his flashlight, finding the night spots and enjoying the camaraderie. The closest he came to being wounded was when he dislocated a knee playing a game of "shove-ha'penny" not with buttons on a table but, along with other officers in his own mess, well-oiled and feeling no pain, lying on his back on the floor with a living room chair balanced on his feet seeing how far he could toss the thing. Though his staff must have been appalled, no one breathed a word, and Rai signed himself out of hospital on crutches the next day.

Once settled in England, it was Rai who made all the production decisions. As I had taken full charge of choreography and the day-time rehearsals for the five unit shows, during the weeks those units were performing in the Aldershot area, Rai and I were in constant communication and became good friends even though he knew I had become engaged to my prewar British admirer, RAF Squadron Leader Norman Silk. I had properly introduced my fiancé to Captain Rai Purdy at CASO headquarters on the weekend Norman took me north to meet his parents.

By February several more CASO units had been recruited and rehearsed in Toronto, and one by one these shows arrived in Britain where I mothered the CWACs through their initial experiences of night-time bombardment. This addition of new bodies called for much larger living quarters for CASO, and Captain Wren's request to the British Army was answered this time by the assignment of a whole village named Ballydeig on a bit of a hill outside Aldershot. We were delighted to pack our bags and leave our crumbling quarters, and we were literally on board the trucks when word came that they weren't to be moved until barrack damages had been paid. Considering all the work we had done to improve the property, this was a great injustice. Rai was upset when it finally trickled back to him that several hundred pounds had been docked from our pay books, and he readily acknowledged that he should have inspected those quarters before he had so glibly signed for them. However, everyone forgave him when he apologized and said it wouldn't happen again. And it didn't.

Ballydeig had been a landscaped housing development before Aldershot geared up for WW II so it was quite attractive to look at. Each little white house, surrounded by a white picket fence, had four bedrooms with fireplaces, one bathroom, a living-dining room (also with fireplace), a kitchen, and a laundry–meaning a large, round, tub-with-lid built over a coal-burning stove on a slab of cement. Several larger buildings nearby housed an officer's mess, an orderly room and administration offices as well as kitchen and mess hall for other ranks. What had once been a community common had been black-topped to make a small parade square. There was also a substantial, though fenced-off, supply of coke.

Accommodations for other ranks were quite comfortable with only three to a room, but there were unexpected difficulties. Spring was late and the temperature still dropped to freezing at night. As the buildings had been empty for a long time, they were damp. The adjutant, Captain Wren, being from the old school of military procedures, posted orders requiring the outside airing of bedclothes once a week–fog or rain not withstanding– which precipitated hacking coughs and colds among us other ranks, along with chilblains caused by sitting too close to our fireplaces. Once the gate to the coke yard had been opened, the pile diminished rapidly but was not replenished. When he received a demand for more coke from the CWAC orderly room sergeant and from the kitchens and other ranks, Captain Wren berated the lot of us for having exceeded our ration of coke and told us to dig through our dustbins for half-burned cinders. It wasn't surprising–nor was anyone severely reprimanded– when the picket fences in front of the cottages began to disappear. In fact, Rai encouraged his batman to help himself.

Within three months, army life overseas had lost its appeal for two of the senior Army Show officers. Since they were over military age and not obliged to remain abroad, adjutant Bill Wren and CWAC officer Lisa Lineaweaver requested return to Toronto. At the same time, our commanding officer, Vic George, accepted a promotion to become head of Canadian Auxiliary Services in London. This gave Rai his big opportunity: promotion to major and the position of commanding officer of Canadian Army Shows overseas. He quickly found himself a new adjutant, Captain Bob Roberts from CMHQ in London, and he sent Sergeant Audrey Shields (wife of Army Show singer Jimmy Shields) to officers' training in Aldershot so that she could replace Lieutenant Lineaweaver as OC CWACs.

Daily parades, which had always been obligatory, now

Round the clock wardrobe

Lieutenant V. Sweeny

took on a different aura. Always the showman, Rai brought new pizzazz onto the parade square. The rakish angle of his battle-dress beret tipped slightly closer to his right eye and his back straightened just a fraction. As usual, the CWAC platoon assembled and were first to be marched into position on the right hand side of the square where we were ordered to "stand at ease" until the male ranks were ready to take centre stage. When the whole parade was "at attention," the new major received the salute of his new adjutant and proceeded to inspect, with meticulous care, his ever-enlarging company.

Once the first five units, A to E, had played all the nearby stations, they moved out of Ballydeig headquarters to perform in other parts of England. Ev Staples, and I headed out with B unit. For several weeks of performances our unit set out each evening from billets in a baronial castle in Nottingham before moving on to the Barley Mow, a pub near Dorking. As the senior female in our unit I rated a room of my own. Small but cosy, it offered a feather bed with a bed-warmer–such luxury as I shall never forget!

It must have come as a shock to Rai, early in April 1944, to receive a memo saying that B Unit had suffered a casualty in the person of Sergeant Verity Sweeny. During our free time, the casts of travelling shows were expected to exercise and I, while riding a rented horse, had been thrown, badly injured and now lay unconscious in #1 Canadian Neurological Hospital at Basingstoke. Military wheels turned fast and Rai made sure that my mother was informed. When, after ten days on the critical list, I regained consciousness, Lieutenant Lineaweaver, not yet repatriated, and Major Purdy were my first CASO visitors. I could hear them but, as my vision was impaired, I could not see them clearly. They read me get-well-notes and mail that had been gathering. But since I had my British aunt, Doffie, and my very attentive fiancée already looking after me, Lineaweaver and Purdy returned to business as usual at headquarters. After six weeks at Basingstoke, the authorities moved me to Alderbrook Convalescent Hospital which was closer to CASO headquarters.

When orders came for the shipment of shows to Italy, the first to leave was my old unit "B", complete with my replacement, a dancer named Private Alfreda Shepherd. The newer units continued to tour England, returning to HQ every month or so for repairs and new material. This became an increasingly demanding load for Rai who, in spite of his military obligations as commanding officer, also remained the key person in production. He badly needed help in that department, especially as more new units were due to arrive from Canada and since CWAC acting-Lieutenant Audrey Shields, who had become pregnant, would soon leave for home. After six weeks of convalescence I was ready to return to headquarters. Fortunately for Rai, because I'd suffered a head injury, the army's medical authorities confined me to England, thereby solving his help problem. I also soon learned, through a shattering memo from the orderly room, that I was not only confined to England but refused permission to dance in a unit show.

My confidence returned somewhat on becoming Rai's permanent production assistant and rose further as I studied to become a CWAC officer. Despite my theatrical background, I must have convinced the examiner I also knew something about soldiering, and my second lieutenant's pip soon turned up on Rai's desk. That evening we celebrated in the officers' mess, and Rai told me he had requested a bat-woman for me and, more importantly, assigned a CWAC warrant-officer, new to the unit, to ease my administration load. After that, dear Staff Sergeant Mary "Sully" Sullivan took over much of the responsibility for the well-being of the women.

I had been an officer barely three months when Rai brought me the awful news that my fiancé, Norman Silk, was in a RAF hospital at Cosford, suffering from a brain tumour. In my despair, I was grateful for train tickets and passes that Rai signed so I could visit Norman which I did regularly for the next several months. On one occasion Norman produced a package his brother Colin had delivered. In it was my wedding ring. He asked if we could be married right away. Although permission to marry had been requested, it had not yet come through. Even so, I agreed, and he gave me the ring, but he died that December before we could be married.

Norman had filled my need for one very special person in my life, a man with many of the characteristics I had loved and admired in my late father. Our long relationship had blossomed despite separation due to the war, an earlier illness he had suffered while he had been serving in India, and my accident. We had enjoyed an unusually reserved but intensely full and beautiful courtship. Losing him left me empty and aimless.

By early 1945 CASO had again outgrown its quarters. Rai detailed his new and competent "acquisitions officer," Montrealler Maurice Bourque, to locate something better for us, and he discovered a grand estate called Down Place just off the Hog's Back near Guildford in Surrey. Here Rai reigned with confidence over his now 400-strong establishment. The mansion had a separate wing that was used for the officers' mess and the remainder was large enough to house all the CWACs. Being the only female officer, I inherited the master suite. Visible from the officers' mess, half a dozen staff cars were parked across the back of a parade square which had once been the front lawn. Less obvious were a fleet of quarter-ton and half-ton trucks as well as troop-carrying vehicles and several backup 22-KVA diesel generators. (Each unit travelled with one). Behind the mansion, the male ORs were quartered in Nissen huts of various sizes that slept 20, 40 or 80. Rather like enormous corrugated drain pipes with windows on either side and a door on each end, they were constructed of metal arches on concrete slabs, and erected in rows, in rectangles or end-to-end, depending on what they were to be used for: showers, kitchens, mess-halls, rehearsal halls, scene and music shops or orderly rooms. "Transport" used three Nissen huts in a U-formation to surround a motor transport repair pit. "Production" used three in a row for a wardrobe department where Sergeant Helen Gill presided over a genuine costume factory that ultimately operated three eight-hour shifts.

For everyone other than cooks and those on fatigues, reveille was at 06:00 hours. Bed-making, brass polishing and breakfast came before parade at 08:00. Breakfast in the officers' dining room was brief. I blew in and out on my way to inspection of CWAC quarters with Sully. By 07:50 hours she would have the women assembled to march onto the parade square for personal inspection. Accompanied by the adjutant, Rai first inspected the men. Then Sully and I joined him to inspect the platoon of women. Rehearsals began at 09:00 hours by which time musicians, singers and actors had gathered to work out new material and dancers were in practice costume, bundled up in the cold weather with every available woolly.

At Down Place that year life for Rai was intense and strenuous but satisfying. At the height of production he had as many as three shows at home base, all at different stages of rehearsal, with a fourth unit on leave. As many as six units toured England and seven more were further afield. Every weekday Rai met with me regarding rehearsals in progress, and in the evenings we planned new material. We always enjoyed working together and as time went by and I began to overcome my loss, Rai took to calling me by my first name. Much against my conscience at first, he gradually moved into the emptiness left by Norman Silk's death. After an early rebuff from me when he made a physical advance, he was careful not to overstep again, but he was attentive and treated me as his best friend. He certainly respected my enthusiasm for hard work and enjoyed the company of another show person.

One evening the subject of my riding accident came up, and Rai reminisced about riding his own horse in the Don Valley. He told me he intended renting a horse if Maurice Bourque could find a stable nearby and asked if I was ready to try again. "It would be fun," he said, "to visit the local farmers on horseback." Though I was hesitant, the idea appealed and Rai's enthusiasm was catching. "Okay," I said. "Let's find some nags!" Rai suggested we look for a couple of dogs as well. It proved to be the perfect respite from building shows, and on Sundays we enjoyed riding over the lovely Surrey countryside with Rai's English setter, Simon, and my German shepherd, Flicka, running beside us. We met many charming people, all of whom seemed interested in the work we did.

As I was the only female officer in our mess, Rai was attentive to me and invited no other women. Thus I was treated well by the other men who assumed that I was spoken for. Rai even looked to me, as he would to a wife, for advice on entertaining visiting officers, one of whom was my cousin, Budge Bell-Irving, by then a senior Seaforth Highlander who had recently returned to Britain from Italy. Although the other CASO officers probably wrote letters full of promises to their waiting women, as I knew Rai did, some had in the meantime found for themselves temporary replacements–the wives (or widows) of British servicemen. This made me sad for the Canadian women they had left at home, but I naively consoled myself it would all straighten out at war's end.

Meanwhile, despite feelings of guilt, I took full advantage of the benefits Rai offered me: a car and driver whenever I wished, signed passes to London and theatre tickets plus his undivided attention. I suppose it came as no surprise to anyone that over time we became more openly familiar. He became less careful in the mess about using profanity (a habit I also fell into quite easily) and let everyone know he was a woman-watcher, a "leg man." "You've got the god-damndest racy legs, Sweeny," he said in front of the other officers. I enjoyed this kind of attention but sometimes wished his talk was less shallow.

In the beginning, Rai had respected my feelings about Norman. Maybe he had hoped that, lonely and needy, I would one day accept his shoulder to cry on. Now, by the way he acted, he was clearly inviting me to become his mistress, and one day I deliberately let down my guard and replied to one of his sensual personal remarks with enthusiasm. The next time we went to London we had a few drinks and I slept with him.

Norman and I had discussed the subject of sex with both candour and respect, but this experience with Rai was not the kind of gentle and considerate bonding I had come to expect. I wasn't transported. In fact, I found the whole thing rushed and crude, but then it dawned on me that Rai wasn't expecting a virgin. I said to myself, "You asked for this, remember? Now you'll have to play the game or be the laughing stock of the mess."

Back at the mess, when we were alone, each having a drink from our own cache, I encouraged Rai to believe all was well with us. At that time I figured I was lucky to be there and wondered why he was attracted to me. Later I came to understand that he needed a friend as much as I did and, like me, he had also seen dreams fall apart and had pushed his disappointments down. But I kept my true feelings to myself and chided my conscience that I had made my choice, taken a risk and failed. We cared for each other and could still be good friends. At the time I didn't see the other side of the picture: an older man, disillusioned with his marriage, finding pleasure in the company of a fresh young female with some unusual skills. I didn't know then that taking care of a vulnerable younger woman could give a man a sense of power. Unaware how much I depended on him and innocent of the power he had to hold me, I believed our partnership would be short-lived. Looking back, I am sure everyone guessed the truth about us, that we were having an affair, but no gossip ever came back to me.

Following D-Day, June 6, 1944, and during the long months of exceptionally heavy fighting in Europe, the business of providing good entertainment for troops under stress required all the energy we at CASO could muster. The shows returning to England from the battle fronts, their personnel tired from multi-performances, came into camp for quick re-fits and went straight back into the field to boost the morale of exhausted soldiers.

But CASO's finest hour came in answer to difficulties which arose shortly after VE Day, May 8, 1945. Due to enormous losses of troop-carrying liners, thousands of soldiers were obliged to wait in repatriation depots, sometimes for months, before they could be returned to Canada. As a result, Aldershot became a hotbed of trouble. Rai rose to the challenge and submitted his inspired solution to Canadian Military Headquarters in London. His plan was to stage a lavish production under canvas in a field near our headquarters and truck in 2,000 of Aldershot's restless Canadian servicemen per performance. His brilliant idea to counter the unrest got a quick okay plus a giant budget from CMHQ to produce "Rhythm Rodeo," a combination stage-show and stampede. The biggest Army Show either of us would ever tackle, it meant assembling 200 performers and technicians, 36 musicians and 76 horses. Without question it was Rai's idea, but we worked together on it from the start. Although there were times when many of his staunchest supporters doubted Rai could handle the horrendous task he had set himself, leaving Rai and me virtually the only two who really believed in it, all departments pulled together in the end and met the deadlines. That fall and winter "Rhythm Rodeo" played to a total of 40,000 cheering troops in the largest circus tent ever raised in England.

As an opener, the commanding officer of the Canadian Army Show, now Lieutenant Colonel Rai Purdy, followed closely by Lieutenant Colonel "Kit" Carson (head of the rodeo) and six other officers (including me) led a mounted parade into the tent and around the tanbark track which circled the stage, while a full concert orchestra played the wonderful circus music, "Gaily Through The World." Behind the officers came cowboys and Indians, bronc riders, charioteers, Roman riders, chuck-wagons, and a stagecoach with outriders and highwaymen–enough to fill the whole track. Beginning slowly, the parade gathered speed until, after the third time around, the horses raced out of the tent at full gallop. That's when Rai rode back into the spotlight at each performance to greet the audience with: "DOES ANYONE HERE WANT TO GO HOME?" This always evoked a roar of shouting and whistles as Rai galloped out, and their excitement sent spirits flying high.

Lights blazed onto the stage as the gold curtains parted and a crowd of dancers in cute, short, pale-blue, western-style outfits fringed in white, with white Stetsons, white gauntlets and white boots, ran out to fill the stage. While they danced, they spun white lariats and sang "Don't Fence Me In." Then a mess of cowboys rode in from either side, tied their horses to the queen poles and leapt onto the stage to join the girls in a square dance. After a rousing series of calls and a lot of spinning

38

their partners, the men re-mounted to show the girls how they could do the figures on horseback and make their horses bow.

The lighting followed the production numbers, which alternated between the tanbark and the stage. Next on the stage was a comedy ballet done by a platoon of khaki-clad soldiers in boots with fans. They entered noisily via curving staircases which descended from either end of a Bailey Bridge which, high above the stage, supported the 30-piece orchestra. These performers acted deadly serious, but the gyrations they went through were screamingly funny and had the audience in an uproar. It lasted only a couple of minutes before it was followed by chariot-racing in the ring.

"Holland Memory" was a serious and touching picture of young Dutch people as they would have appeared before the horrors of war. For the girls, petticoats and aprons, blonde braids and starched white bonnets, and for the boys, balloon pants, knee socks and clogs. The simple and familiar waltz music and light-hearted songs seemed to invite soldiers to sing along. Between Roman riding, a stage-coach hold-up, a chuck-wagon race and "bucking-out" horses on the tanbark, there was a comedy carrousel with acrobatic "horses" on the lighted glass turntable at centre-stage as well as a sparkling water ballet to Gershwin's Rhapsody in Blue. In a dramatic winter scene, with children throwing snowballs and skaters ice-dancing on the spinning turntable, our glamorous show-girls, riding in silver sleighs drawn by miniature white ponies, were later joined by the entire cast for the finale. Rhythm Rodeo was a stunning success.

In the third week of January 1946 CASO performed Rhythm Rodeo–with a few extra flourishes dreamed up by the cast–for the last time. But after the "after-parties" which followed that last performance, there came a thud of recognition, definitely in the officers' mess and probably throughout the whole company, that an important chunk of our lives had come to an end. If it had not been for the enormous job of dismantling, stock-taking and reporting to CMHQ that required our full attention, we might have mourned, despite our personal preparations for repatriation, the losses we would suffer as, one by one, our names came up for home-going. Kit Carson and his cowboys–all men who had volunteered to stay in England to ride in the show when their regiments were being repatriated–were given a particularly rewarding assignment–breaking and preparing for sale all the Irish-hunter-bucking-broncos we had used in the rodeo. Being true western cowboys, they did this without difficulty, and within a week all the so called "unbreakable" thoroughbreds Captain Bourque had acquired in Ireland were successfully sold at auction to unsuspecting local gentry. After the tents and circus ponies were safely returned to Blackpool and the western gear was on its way to Calgary, orders were posted that everything else connected with the rodeo, including costumes and all equipment–generators, lights, sewing machines, everything–must be inventoried and packed for shipment to London. It was disappointing to learn that even Rai's and my personal riding clothes must also appear on the inventory. I had acquired beautiful black boots, cream britches, snappy white shirts, stocks and gloves, a perfectly fitted black jacket and velvet hunting cap, and my saddle and bridle shone from good care. Dutifully we did as we were ordered. Lorry load after lorry load, all of Rhythm Rodeo's equipment–generators, microphones, wiring, sets, curtains, even the carousel–having been carefully itemized and properly packed, left Down Place destined for London. Sometime later I learned that not a single item had ever arrived. One might be tempted to question whether some bandit en route had actually liberated this rich loot, much as acquisitions officer Captain Maurice Bourque had done in the first place to assemble it all.

CHAPTER 4

Going Home

I got my marching orders in the second week of February 1946. Unfortunately, though I had no wish to leave my dog Flicka in England, there were rules about junior ranks taking pets aboard troop ships.

"Give her to me," said my cousin Budge Bell-Irving, who was a very senior officer by then. We were both scheduled to board the Queen Elizabeth I two weeks hence. "I'm told there are some posh kennels on the sun deck," said he. "With my rank I can take her home as mine. I'll just give you a note that will get her aboard, and you turn her over to the butcher."

"Thanks a whole lot," I said.

"Not to worry," said Budge. "It's the butcher's job to feed the legal pets–that is, those belonging to senior officers–as well as any illegal animals that turn up in other ranks' kit bags."

"I'll see your dog is well looked after, sir," I said flippantly. Very soon my beautiful mini-Alsatian and I went off to get her a tetanus shot and buy her a harness to which I attached an elaborate tag with information to cover every possible eventuality.

While I prepared to leave, Rai stayed on, hoping, he said, to leave Down Place in a month or so with the very last contingent of Army Show personnel. As for our relationship, for me it was as if a curtain had come down on a disturbing theatrical interlude which had no honest beginning nor satisfactory end. I knew, and I believed he knew, that we had no future together. Rai was keen to get back to his broadcasting business in Toronto, and though he had seldom mentioned them, I was aware he intended to rejoin his wife and family. We made no plans to keep in touch, and I honestly welcomed the freedom to contemplate a new phase in my life. I don't remember saying goodbye to him, though I doubt we simply shook hands on my last evening in the mess. He wasn't there next morning when I led a small platoon of homeward bound CWACs off the parade square to climb aboard a troop-carrier.

The QE1 awaited us in Portsmouth.

Once inside the dockyard and off the vehicle, we CWACs claimed our baggage. Slinging haversacks and balancing kit bags on our left shoulders, we formed platoon. Quite improperly, my right hand held Flicka's leash wrapped around it as many times as was necessary to keep her close to me. If the need had arisen, I couldn't have saluted. Luckily, the sergeant who met us had the good manners to remove his cap so he couldn't salute me and I, therefore, needn't return his. After listening to his instructions, I took my place in front of the women and gave the order: "Platoon . . .left . . .turn." I did my best to assume a military manner as I marched to the head of the file with Flicka on the wrong side of me. There I halted unsteadily and shouted, "By the left, left wheel, quick . . . march!" Out in front, my dog and I set the pace through several long, cold buildings at dock side. Although Flicka behaved nobly, only crossing in front of me twice to get to my left side as she'd been trained, it seemed to take forever. Like all the women following me, my kit bag carried everything I owned and I wished I had left a few things behind.

Eventually we arrived at the side of the ship which towered above us and we came to a halt. Resting our kit bags, we "stood-easy" to wait for an order to go on board. As on the outward trip, hundreds and hundreds of men had to board ahead of us CWACs and, because of her interest in all the soldiers around us, it was impossible to keep Flicka still. Being women in an army of men, we always attracted attention, and having a mascot definitely added to the men's interest. So, although we were the butt of jokes and facetious remarks for more than an hour, we were quite used to it and rather enjoyed being the centre of attraction. Trouble began when we tried to obey orders to climb the gangplank single file.

Halfway up, Flicka chose not to board after all and wrapped herself around my ankles. I turned a swift pirouette to unwind her, after which she changed her mind and galloped up the slatted ramp at full speed, dragging me at the end of her long leash–my haversack thumping and kit bag slipping–into the heart of the ship. With my left hand trying to control my kit bag, I could do nothing to shorten Flick's leash. Inside, hundreds of men milled about, and although posts with ropes kept them away from the doorway where we had entered and the companionways leading up and down, this was not enough to keep my pet from ducking into the crowd to visit the boys. Several times I stopped the whole parade when she entangled herself. Everyone but I laughed. I tried to, but embarrassment overwhelmed me. I began to sweat. Our destination was several decks below, and literally dragging Flicka to the head of the companionway, which was in fact a grand marble staircase, I slithered the poor creature down the stairs on her rump. At each level the crowd of men seemed more dense and Flicka more anxious to lose herself among them. I did my best not to seem like a poor sport, laughing too, but what I desperately needed was someone to carry my kit bag so that I could handle Flicka. All those men and not a single offer of help, except in jest.

"Ma'am, your dog's not with you, Ma'am."

"Enjoy your journey, Ma'am."

"Hey, Ma'am, what's your dog's name?"

"I'd sure like ta help ya. Honest I would, Ma'am. Ya gonna sleep with ya pooch?"

Having delivered my platoon to their quarters, located my own and dumped my kit, Flicka and I set out to find the butcher while he still had space for her in his posh kennels. Goodness knows how many illegal pets had surfaced from kit bags and haversacks to fill them, but we were still in luck. It was then I learned that, although the butcher would feed them, it was up to the owners to exercise them. Had it not been winter and the temperature sub-zero, this would not have concerned me. However, on the very first day out the ship was already weathering a rough sea and I felt less than well. An icy blast hit Flicka and me as we pushed open the heavy door onto A deck. Luckily I was wearing the prewar fur-lined boots and furry gloves I had bought as souvenirs in London. But poor little Flicka, pulling on her leash against the wind, looked as though she'd been put through a pencil sharpener. Flattened back along her head, her ears had quite disappeared. When she eventually stopped to pee, the wind whipped it against the rail where it froze. Once around the deck was all we wanted, thank you. I could only hope she would have the sense to do her big job inside the kennel.

Fortunately, Flicka's official owner invited me to his cabin, which was also on A deck, to which his batman brought a daily tray of delicacies including hot broth and lean, cold roast beef, especially for me. This service certainly beat descending six decks to the ship's mess hall. I stayed in my cousin's cabin taking life easy for most of the voyage, only returning to my bunk in the CWAC officers' cabin to sleep. One day a memo came to Budge's cabin for me. It was from CMHQ, London, telling me that my rank of captain had been confirmed. I wondered who had arranged that? Good to have a cousin in a high place! Or, could it have been the result of a memo from Rai?

One morning at dawn, as the QE I sidled in toward New York, I recognized the Statue of Liberty through a sea mist. My first glimpse of the great lady had been in 1936 from HMS Berengaria, now at rest at the bottom of the Atlantic, but on this day I had a deeper understanding of the statue's significance.

We disembarked at Staten Island and, after a cramping-cold ferry ride across New York harbour, found ourselves on solid dry land where a battered Canadian National troop train sat waiting to carry us lesser ranks home. Old and

44

tired, but at least warm, that train returned us to Canada and set us on our separate ways to our individual provinces.

Awkward as she made our various transfers, Flicka remained with me. For the major part of our western journeys we nursing sisters and CWAC officers were in the last coach next to the caboose. Whenever the train stopped, I exercised my pet, but she had to be very patient because some of the stops were long hours apart. At night she slept in the narrow corridor beside my lower bunk, and from here, although I wasn't aware at first, she guarded me with unblinking eyes, baring her teeth and nipping at the ankles of passers by on their way to the washroom. Because of this I lost some valuable friends, and as a result when, three days from home, a vicious flu bug put me flat on my back, I didn't get much sympathy. The nursing sisters smoking in the lounge next to the toilet looked the other way when, wishing my mother was there to hold my aching head, I was kept busy with diarrhoea and vomiting. After cleaning up my own mess, I crawled back to my unmade bunk, hoping to sleep off my misery. Some kind soul did offer to walk Flicka at the stations, but I guess she didn't give the pup time enough to properly evacuate. That night I tried to keep her on my bed but it was too hot, and high in the Rockies, sometime before daylight, Flicka found an open door between our car and the caboose and jumped out into deep snow at zero temperature.

Feeling a bit better next morning and suspecting that Flick had followed someone to the breakfast car, I dressed quickly and went forward through the train to find her. On my return to the last coach, my heart sank at the sight of the open door. Not until Jasper was I able to contact the RCMP, but the next afternoon when I called the police on arrival in Vancouver, they had no news of her. Saddened, I checked in at CWAC headquarters, received a pass for a month's leave and called a cab to take me home.

Well, not exactly home. My mother had rented a big house in Kerrisdale so that what remained of her family might gather after the war. She was waiting for me, ready for the big hug and the inevitable tears. Missing and still sorely missed were Dad, who had died in a military accident in 1940, my brother Malcolm, who had been lost at sea in 1935 and, for me, Norman. Already settled in the house were my 16-year-old brother Roger, now looking very like Malcolm at that age and ready for naval college, my sister Moira, newly demobbed from the WRCN, my brother Sedley's English wife, Diana (very pregnant) and their four-year-old, Nicola.

Mum showed me to my room which was actually the closed-in upstairs sun porch. In it was a huge bed made up with the softest new blankets turned back to show the snowy linen of Granny's embroidered sheets and cases. These antiques only surfaced on rare occasions to honour particular people. I was being royally welcomed, not only from the war but from having been away almost continually since the age of eleven when I had left home for England.

On my third day at home the RCMP called. "Expect a surprise in a crate at the CNR station," the constable said. "You can collect her from the baggage car when the train comes in tomorrow morning. No charge!" Later I learned that a line-man had come across Flicka's footprints where she had crossed and re-crossed the train tracks. It had taken him three days to coax her onto his little cart and get her to his home where his wife had given her a good meal. I was so glad I had harnessed and tagged her. When Roger and I picked her up, Flicka's crate was clean and dry. The poor little thing must have been bursting, but she still wanted to kiss me and tell me how glad she was to have found me. If dogs could cry, there would have been two of us.

After dinner that night with the family I suddenly wanted to be alone. That welcoming bed on the sleeping porch beckoned me. Still in uniform with Flick at my heel, I said my good nights and slipped away. When I had closed my door, I began to undress, removing my barathea tunic with its shining brass buttons and laying it over a big wicker chair. Then I unclipped my gold tie-pin, loosened my slim brown tie and unlaced my much polished Oxfords–British pebbled leather. They had been good to me. I placed my shoes neatly under the chair. My officer's cap and gloves were somewhere downstairs. So was my kit bag but I wasn't going down for them. Gently pulling the knot out of my tie, I drew it from under the stiff collar of my khaki shirt, straightened it and placed it on the shoulder of my tunic. Then I slipped out of my skirt, folded it inward from each side and placed it beside my tunic, opened my shirt slowly, button by button. Stockings, pants and bra came off quickly and were tucked beside the cushion on the chair. And there I stood: no longer a soldier. A whole new life awaited me.

Verity and Flicka

CHAPTER 5

Marriage

My sister Moira and I, reunited for the first time in eight years, now became great pals. Though very knowledgeable about theatre and music, she had chosen to sign up at the University of British Columbia, to become a social worker. However, through her membership in the Sir Ernest MacMillan Club, I was able to obtain funding from the Department of Veteran's Affairs to take expert dance training in New York. I contacted Maestro Vincenzo Celli who had been recommended to me by my role-models, Anton Dolin and Alicia Markova of the American Ballet Theatre. Though I had foregone their invitation to join that company following my audition with them in 1942; in 1943, when I joined the Canadian Army Show, Mr. Dolin had written to say there would surely be a place for me after the war. Now I must get back into shape. My plan was to attend Maestro Celli's class by July.

In the meantime, in Late April I read that a Vancouver businessman by the name of Sweeney (no relative), was planning to spend a lot of Tourist Bureau money on a project to celebrate Vancouver's 60th birthday with a show much like the one Rai and I had created overseas. Sweeney was advertising for a producer. It was, of course, the perfect job for Rai. I knew he was back in Toronto with his family, but I felt I should tell him. Maybe we could work together, I thought, though I had focussed on beginning a new life and had gone out of my way to describe my commanding officer as a gentleman and to let Mum know about his wife and children in Toronto. I sent a wire to Rai Purdy Productions. Although the job in Vancouver didn't materialize for him, I wasn't disappointed when, a few weeks later, Rai called and invited me to work with him on a project he'd been offered in Toronto - a huge show in Maple Leaf Gardens for the Red Feather Campaign. But his call was also to let me know his wife had sued him for divorce. My conscience reminded me that it was second rate to cooperate with any man who has deceived his wife. At the same time, it was delightful to feel very much wanted. I held my breath while my thoughts tumbled into understanding what Rai had just told me, then I mentioned my plan to study in New York. I told Mum that I wanted the job that Rai had offered and would be going to Toronto to attend an early conference. Rai borrowed a car so that he could meet me, not at the Toronto airport, but at a motel in Windsor. We kissed, and he held me in a long, meaningful embrace as though he knew everything would work out for the two of us. Even though I had invited the reunion, I wasn't positive. He didn't look so dashing in civvies. But still, the future could be good for two confident show people. We had worked well together.

From a large briefcase, Rai produced a bottle of rye and poured two drinks. "Cheers! Here's to us," he said. We ate frog's legs at a local restaurant and drank more rye while Rai described how in the early 1940s, when he had been riding high as a Toronto broadcaster, a deal had been a deal. If he told friends in the business that he had an agreement to do a show, no other showman would try to steal it. Discharged from the service and returned to broadcasting, he discovered things were no longer that way. He said he had been surprised and hurt to lose out to a one-time friend on his very first contract to provide entertainment for a festival in a town outside Toronto. He also told me how concerned he had been before speaking to his parents about his divorce, how he'd walked up and down outside their building

50

too scared to go in. They had surprised him by saying they had known for ages and wondered why it had taken him so long. Rai told me he had arranged to be the culprit in the divorce which was "the decent thing to do." I didn't ask him what he meant by "arranged" but said a quiet *thank you* that, although we had discussed marriage, I need not become involved in his divorce. However, he made it clear (more than once) that if we were to be together, children were not in his picture. I had to agree with him that show business was not much of a life for kids. I also reasoned that, though I was not born a night person, I had done it for so long it was probably "me" by now. "And," I said to myself, "there will be lots of time to swim, maybe sail and travel, should the two of us live in some glamorous penthouse."

The Red Feather show wasn't actually scheduled until November. Rai's idea for it was an adaptation of "Rhythm Rodeo," but this time it would be a combination Ice-and-stage show. Barbara Ann Scott had agreed to be the star, and the Granite Club would provide skaters. My job would be to choreograph the whole thing. But first I must get back in shape and the upcoming summer school with Maestro Celli in New York should do just that. Returning to Vancouver I felt full of optimism about my career, but not at all sure that I should have re-opened the affair with Rai. Still, with my enforced army savings in my hand, Moira and I shopped for new practice clothes and I packed a few summer dresses. Uncle Dick had already arranged through a business friend to borrow a flat for me in The Bronx. Life once again had a serious purpose. I would dance again, really dance.

Several times during my three months in New York with Maestro Celli, Rai came to visit and took me to Broadway shows. Once, when the city was impossibly hot, I went to Ontario to spend a week-end with him in a tiny cottage which he and John Collingwood-Reid had built on John's property in Unionville. They had put a sign, VERIPUR on the cottage door. Both men got drunk and I cooked a rabbit which John had hit with his jeep and dumped into wine–"Jugged hare," he called it.

When my New York summer school was over I went straight

to Toronto to work on the Gardens show. Then, in mid October, I flew home to tell Mum that Rai had asked me to marry him when his divorce was final. She was deeply upset. "Verity, how could you?" She managed to say before going to her room with a nose bleed. Confused and angry at her reaction, I flew back to Rai and the tiny apartment he had rented for me on Ste Claire Ave West.

My mother always was a conundrum: two such different people in one body-one body so different from day to day - one spirit hiding beneath another. My love for her was deep and real but, as I matured, her attitudes and behaviour often tested it. She really cared for everyone of her children - but only in amounts that reflected our importance in her life. Unfortunately, owing to her family background, male children were considered more worthy than females, and one of my brothers was extra special to her. My sister Moira and I took these standards for granted. Mother also implied to us, as she had been taught, that good breeding accounted for clean-cut features and good manners so that one should be very particular as to the type of friends one brought home. In other words, she was a perfect Victorian snob.

Yet this first generation Canadian, the eldest daughter of a Scottish pioneer, was in some ways as close to being a free spirit as I can imagine. Where she found the energy to accomplish all she did I could only guess. Early in her life she learned to sketch in water colours and gained a good enough understanding of the piano keyboard to accompany herself and others singing the old Hebridean songs. She also acted in amateur theatrics. She rode any kind of horse that was offered. As a girl, she had played all the boys' games, even in long skirts and petticoats. She was competent in boats. It seemed she'd always owned and paddled her own kayak and she swam, whenever possible, in the nude. (Every summer she managed to get an all over tan.) At the same time, this enigma, lithe and beautiful as a young woman had, when still in her early teens become responsible for running the family household. As a youngster she had helped her mother care for her nine other siblings, but when grandmother became too weary and unwell to cope, my mother

Verity's mother, Isobel Bell-Irving

took over as chatelaine of "The Strands", their Vancouver Home. She began travelling with Grandfather on his business trips (Selling canned Salmon), ultimately replacing her own mother at his side. She wore the beautiful gowns Grandfather bought for her when they were in London, Paris, or Rome, she waltzed with him on frozen lakes in Switzerland and played Hostess for him at the grand parties he gave at the family home. Today this type of patriarchal domination would have an ugly name, and I see this part of my mother's life in shadow.

However, in time, she grew bold enough to fall in love with, and become engaged to, an Englishman named Jerry Heath who, because he wanted to be an artist (which was *not* done you know), had been "sent to the Colonies" where my grandfather gave him a job in his cannery. When the first world war came, my mother became a VAD (Volunteer Auxiliary Division) nurse and followed Gerry and her six brothers (Army, Navy and Flying Corps) to England where she joined the staff of a hospital. In 1915 the man she loved was killed, and in 1918, just a few days before the end of hostilities, her brother Roderick also died in Battle. Meanwhile, in 1917 my mother had accepted an offer of marriage from my father, Ben Sweeny, whom she had known since childhood. I'm sure that he had always loved her, but Mother never quite stopped pining for Gerry, and though she thought the world of my dad, when I was in my twenties and Dad was dead, she admitted to me that, despite having born five children, she had never enjoyed the physical part of marriage.

When I was a child, though it had often made me feel like crying, I had loved the way Mum played and sang for us. Now I feel sure she played for her own saddened heart.

In 1947, after Rai and I had been working the Red Feather production for some weeks, he on booking talent and I on choreographing the skaters at the Granite Club, a Mrs. Fenkle, an influential woman on the R.F. board of directors, opened her mouth and put her foot in it. "Whoever heard of a stage and ice show?" she demanded. "And who is this Barbara Ann Scott any-way?"

Apparently no one else on the board had heard of Barbara

Ann Scott either: the fact that even then she was odds-on favourite to win Canada's first Gold Medal for skating in the 1948 Winter Olympics might have given them a clue. But on the advice of Mrs. Fenkle, preparations for the show came to a halt. I didn't go home to Vancouver. My life was in Toronto now. I soon met Rai's parents and was invited, from then on, to Sunday lunches at their apartment. I liked them both. Mrs Purdy seemed especially warm to me. But the old dear wasn't well, and one day when I was there, one of her 'Heart spells' took her away.

Meanwhile, Purdy Productions had managed to stay solvent while its namesake was soldiering. Rai's soap-opera, *Soldier's Wife*, his *Canadian Cavalcade* and several other shows had stayed on the air, supervised by his brother-in-law Ernie Edge, interim director Robert Simpson and his faithful secretary Vi Webb. When Rai returned, Ernie and Vi welcomed him home as producer in his own radio company and, once he had his office back, his brain whirled with ideas for expansion. As well as creating *The Steel Show of Canada*, featuring John Collingwood-Reid, and *Stars To Be* for radio, he envisaged himself at the head of a huge theatrical organization and planned to use everything he had learned in the Army Show.

First he contacted ex Army Show officers, Maurice Bourque and Dick Fonger and made them partners in the new Rai Purdy Productions. Next he arranged to move RPP to the big old Orange Hall on Queen Street East.

Renovations costing a small fortune transformed it into a multifaceted entertainment factory, with one of its two auditoriums fully equipped as a radio broadcast studio, including a stage and seating for over a hundred. The second became my ballet school, and it was there, with Rai's sister Bea as accompanist, that I opened the Anna Verite Studio with the blessing of the Royal Academy of Dancing (RAD) in England. When the Academy's representative, Mara MacBirney, came to Toronto, I invited her to use my classroom for the RAD exams. This brought many keen students and teachers to our doorstep, and Rai was amazed how quickly my classes grew, bringing a profit to RPP.

Maurice Bourque took on the tasks of procurement and sales and set up a department to provide shop-window displays. He also signed a fat contract with the Canadian National Exhibition (CNE)–back in action for the first time since the war began–to design and build sales booths. Dick Fonger headed the music and costume departments which were so essential to show production. Rai continued in the radio field but branched as well into small town "Old Home Weeks" and the production of nightclub floor shows. As my ballet school thrived, he encouraged me to develop a line of girls who could perform in nightclubs and at conventions. This idea didn't thrill me, but I obliged by teaching primarily top-notch classical dance and working in the other styles on the side.

Rai was incredibly busy but it worried me how much he drank and it seemed to me there were far too many projects happening around RPP with not one good business brain amongst us. Bourque thought he was safe signing contracts with time limits, never dreaming he might face delays representing thousands of dollars a week, and Rai had no idea that conventions held in his broadcast studio could get noisy and ugly. One catered dinner-party booked into my studio left the floor stained and foul-smelling. Still, there was money to be made.

Rai, meanwhile, never forgot he was a showman. Even in his private office he would strike a pose. Lounging back in a tall, black, swivel chair, he would neatly place his right foot above his left knee. Though he never bothered to shine them, his shoes were always a little unusual–desert boots or loafers with buckles. He scoffed at brogues. To the end of his days, while writing or talking, he would move his right hand through his hair and across his face, habitually stopping his hand just long enough beneath his nose to chew a knuckle or inhale the nicotine residue on his fingers. He did odd things with his eyes, too, like opening them wide and fixing a stare into the distance as though he expected to be photographed. In the middle of a conversation, he sometimes used a neat trick to baffle people: while looking straight at the person he was talking to, he would close one eyelid without

56

scrunching the other or even wrinkling his forehead, still carrying on the conversation as if nothing had happened. Although on the surface his manners were reserved and gentlemanly, like his father Lionel, Rai loved to tease. In fact, he teased unmercifully, especially if he had been drinking, often embarrassing his unsuspecting prey–innocent admirers, production assistants or musicians' wives. Rai also had a penchant for gruesome detail, and he routinely wound up woozy late-night parties delivering such clever and terrifying ghost stories that I forbade him to tell them within my hearing. By this time I understood why his radio dramas on *Out of the Night* had been such a great success.

In the midst of all this activity, Rai's decree nisi came through and he bought me a minimal engagement ring. Then in late September 1947 my mother and sister arrived in Toronto, Moira from a WRCN reunion in Halifax and Mum from Vancouver, ostensibly to meet Rai's father and siblings. It's just possible that things might have worked out quite differently had Mum not demanded, "Why not get married while we are both here, dear?" Although she may have been concerned about the disparity in our ages and backgrounds and feared for our happiness, I believed at the time (with no little resentment) that she felt our marriage in Vancouver might embarrass the family. But since I was wearing Rai's ring and could offer no reasonable excuse not to get married while they were there, I agreed.

Mum was very obviously opposed to my wearing a virginally white wedding gown so she and Moira took me shopping. We chose a simple (and inexpensive) blue-grey tweed suit, a little flat hat with a short veil and a cape in aqua wool. My brown, high-heeled, sling-back shoes would do for the "something old." As a surprise, the two of them ordered a small old-fashioned bouquet of Stephanotis, and Mum bought a bottle of champagne for toasts. This automatically placed her and Rai's dad, who disapproved of alcohol, at odds.

On October 8 Rai and I were married in the almost empty chapel at Bloor Street United Church, which in those days was one of the few denominations that would marry a divorced person. Doctor Andrew Sneddon altered the wedding vows to read: "Those whom God hath joined together, NO MAN CAN put asunder," meaning, I supposed, that God hadn't blessed Rai's first marriage. I wanted to believe that the Victorian backgrounds and ethics Rai and I shared were enough to guarantee a happy relationship but, except for the way we spoke, both with English accents–mine acquired in England in my early teens, his, courtesy of Auntie Maude–our backgrounds were not really similar. True, we were both in show business and indeed knew little else, but Rai was considerably older than I, and while my head was still full of dreams, he moved in a hard-hitting, realistic world. I loved to rise early, enjoy bird song and sunrises. Whenever possible, he preferred to sleep the morning away. Neither of us had completed secondary schooling, but while I had pursued a rigorous classical dance training, he had scrambled up through the ranks of amateur theatre, acting and producing, learning on the job, to become one of Toronto's top broadcasters.

There is no picture record of our marriage; Bob Simpson took a roll of film but he failed to remove the lens-cover. In addition to my Mother and sister, however, I did have two cousins there to vouch for the truth of it. Budge Bell-Irving, who had established himself in Montreal on retirement from active service, came to Toronto to take my late father's place and give me away, and another cousin, Gordon Bell-Irving, (RCAF posted to Toronto) whom Rai had already met, also attended. During the tense reception held at the home of Rai's sister Kay Edge–a teetotal affair except for Mum's champagne because their father attended–Budge, while complaining of a toothache, managed to imbibe much of the bottle of scotch he'd discovered beneath the Edge's kitchen sink. Then in his toast to the bride he blabbed about having met Rai at Down Place and seeing the two of us together in London.

Afterward, on the lawn as my new husband and I stood slightly apart from our families and friends, Rai grinned at me and said: "Take my hand and we'll fly!" I thought of Peter Pan high above the rooftops and saw small, questioning Wendy, reaching up and hanging on for dear life. When he hugged

58

my hesitant mother, saying, "I'll do everything I can to make Verity happy," I thought I saw her melt a little and suddenly I felt weepy. When we were ready to depart for our honeymoon in Rai's new "veterans-loan" Studebaker, I asked Gordon to take my flowers to his wife. At first I felt happy for Mary, then jealous. She had just given birth to their son at Toronto General, and I wished I hadn't agreed with Rai that we would not have children. Now I wonder how I could have believed that not getting pregnant was entirely my responsibility.

Late as it was when we arrived at Clearwater Hunting Lodge, about 50 miles west of Toronto, Rai behaved with extra chivalry. Foregoing his usual tipple of rye, he phoned for glasses and opened the bottle of champagne he'd brought. He seemed in no hurry to whisk me into bed. After several bubbly refills, I slipped into a silky gown and approached our nuptial couch with renewed hope. No longer "the other woman," I could enjoy my release from guilt. All was well until, forgetting his promise not to tease, he blew noisily into the nape of my neck. So much for romance. Never in my life have I felt so deeply depressed as during those few days of our honeymoon. The trees were bare and October hung grey and cold when we walked beside the silent lake. I could think of nothing encouraging and dwelt upon my guilt about having sold both of Norman's rings, at Rai's suggestion, to pay for this extravagance.

For the last two months of 1947 we lived in a sparse share-the-bathroom flat on Nina Avenue, but since the business outlook seemed brighter for the new year, after Christmas we moved into a decent apartment on Davenport Road. We bought furniture–by then I'd learned about credit cards–I made draperies, and together we refurbished the kitchen.

In January 1948 Rai brought Monte Hall from a radio station in Winnipeg where he was making $25 a week, and paid him $100 to host Ogilvie's *Find Your Fortune*. This game show set up Monte's broadcast career and greatly improved Purdy Productions' financial position. Rai rejoined the Variety Club and we both attended the opening of the trendy Club

Norman. I bought an elegant dress for the first night of Camelot, starring Bob Goulet, when the O'Keefe Theatre opened.

Although I had often felt awkward when meeting and visiting Rai's many friends before we were married, as Mrs. Purdy I began to feel at ease. It was pleasant going to stock-market-wise Sam Wacker's house, largely because his wife Wynn didn't drink and no one over-imbibed at their place. Sam was a big guy with a mop of grizzly grey hair, a beak of a nose, full lips and a husky voice. He also smoked cigars. According to Rai's brother-in-law, Ernie Edge, who was a statistician, Sam had questionable methods of making money on the stock market. However, whatever he made he spent generously. He backed Rai's project to sell a peacetime version of Rhythm Rodeo to the company which owned Earl's Court Stadium in London. It didn't fly, but the presentation piece, a magnificent golden book covered with horseshoes and stars, ended up in the museum in Aldershot where it tells the story of "RR" to this day. Twice the Wackers took us to their cottage on Stoney Lake.

Wynn Wacker was small and quietly spoken even when Sam was, in my view, rude to her. She coped with this situation by closeting herself for several hours a day to study the works of Mary Baker Eddie. She told me Sam gave her the astronomical-to-me figure of $300 weekly for housekeeping. Their physical surroundings certainly were comfortable. But she embarrassed me one evening when we went there to visit because, as she hung up my coat, she remarked candidly: "You two smell of smoke. It's in your clothes and in your hair." Having lost my sense of smell in my riding accident, I hadn't even thought about it. Everybody in the broadcast business smoked. Though I had never smoked more than a few cigarettes a day, Rai finished at least two packs.

The Wackers were the only people we knew who had a television set. It picked up a signal from the States, but while the pictures were fairly clear, only some parts of the settings had enough light to be properly visible. On Sam's monitor, anything that moved across the set changed from short to tall to short again and had a definite list to starboard. It really wasn't very good.

However, the Americans had beaten us to the television starting gate, and Rai decided he wanted to be in the race. Thus, when things began to fall apart in post-war Toronto entertainment, he began to dream about producing *Out of The Night* as a TV show out of New York, and he sent recordings of several of his dramas to ad agencies in that city. The only reply he received complained that his *Out of The Night* scripts were far too frightening.

Within a year after our marriage, the only jobs bringing in decent money for Rai Purdy Productions were Rai's own radio shows and the convention contracts that included food and drink. Every day I felt more depressed, sadder and sadder over the decline of RPP and less and less happy with my teaching. By this time I'd had all I could stomach of cleaning my studio after it had been rented out and apologising to my students for its condition. In any case, I knew the partners needed more space for catering, so I sent all my promising students plus my dance library to Betty Oliphant, one of the founding members of the National Ballet and head of its now famous school. Then I set out to find somewhere else to teach. It had to be cheap. I don't even want to think about the dingy quarters in which I struggled on with a handful of young dancers plus a few "Health and Beauty" classes for women, and with dear Bea doing her very best to accompany my remaining pupils on a piano that wouldn't stay in tune.

I hated going to meet Rai and his announcer at the end of a long day of teaching just to watch them and a few agency people down 40 ounces of straight rye out of paper cups before heading for the Bay Bloor Pub. There we would all stay till the place closed. I was concerned about Rai's drinking, not only for him but for myself; most of his friends drank heavily, and I knew that several of the wives were being treated rottenly. Often I was so tired that my knees shook and my throat hurt, and after awhile I didn't even try to stay cheery or be a good sport.

With the company in disarray, the production partnership was dissolved at the end of 1948, but having already decided to head south and break into television, Rai couldn't possibly consider going bankrupt since those proceedings would deny him entry into the US. He resolved this difficulty by buying out Maurice and Dick and assuming company debts amounting to $30,000–a huge sum in those days.

We had been married fifteen months and Rai and I were in Hamilton where he was directing a military tattoo when I sensed, with both joy and fear, that I was pregnant. I didn't tell him until it was a certainty and even then hesitated because I dreaded the thought of having an abortion. When I finally had the courage to confess–it was not my fault but the rhythm cycle's–and pleaded with him to let me keep the baby, he scowled at me. "You don't think I'm that kind of an SOB, do you?" I guess I must have done. My gloom quickly disappeared but returned within weeks when I suffered an early miscarriage. Then, after I'd plucked up courage to ask if we might try again and Rai agreed, the truth hit me: we could be normal people and have a family. I hugged him with a new kind of gratefulness. My wish came true in June. Suddenly and blissfully happy, I floated through the next few months day-dreaming a lot, as well as teaching some final classes. Then I arranged to sell our furniture and packed our suitcases. No question, there was considerable tension between us when on November19, 1949, (Rai's 39th birthday) he set forth to make his fortune in New York, and I, now 26, took my rounding body home to West Vancouver. Mother had agreed to care for me in her comfortable home. I took it for granted she would pay my maternity expenses.

Back in 1946 when my eldest brother, Sedley, having transferred from the British to the Canadian Army, had brought his family home to British Columbia, my mother had put a down payment on a little house in West Vancouver for them. Though she knew they were accustomed to the protocol of a British permanent-force officer's mess, she had been disappointed when both Sedley and Diana complained of the hapless, humdrum nature of military life in Canada. "The women are so gauche! They don't know how to dress!" moaned my sister-in-law. "Nor do they understand 'the form' ", said my brother. When they subsequently returned to England, my mother, then in her sixties, took over the rest of the house payments and moved herself and my sister into what she soon called "Sleepy Hollow" because of the nocturnal comings and goings of my younger brother Roger and his naval cadet friends.

This house, built around 1928, stood on a quarter acre below Marine Drive near the village of Dundarave where the land runs down quite steeply to the sea. In 1914 the Pacific Great Eastern Railway (PGE) had laid rails along the West Vancouver waterfront between the sea and Mum's house, but the cut through the rocks along this stretch of the line was deep enough to hide the trains from sight of her windows. In any case, the line was not in use when she bought the place. My mother loved her privacy, and the garden at Sleepy Hollow, though basically wild, contained small, hidden resting places where she took advantage of the sun or had tea with a friend. To the east and north, the trees had grown tall enough to screen the house but to the south and west, the property provided a sweeping view of outer Vancouver Harbour and the distant mountains of Vancouver Island. I can vouch that the sunsets beyond the blink of Point Atkinson's comforting lighthouse could never be fully appreciated unless seen from aloft in the substantial tree-house my brother Roger built for her. It was perched about twenty feet up and was accessible only by ladder, but she regularly used it for watching sunsets, saying prayers and ushering in the New Year.

The deciduous trees were leafless that November day in1949 when Mum welcomed me home for the umpteenth time since 1933 when I first departed for England. Now I arrived harbouring the guilty feeling that I was on probation with Rai, having pressed him, even though he was jobless, to agree to my completing the pregnancy. Real winter came in January with lots of snow on the mountains, and a good six inches of it in West Van. Mum held my arm as we took walks. How beautiful everything was then, and how well I felt! Responding to my positively glowing letters, Rai managed to write with brave optimism until spring when, after almost three months pounding New York's streets without reward, loneliness and discouragement had overcome him.

"I need you," he wrote. "At a time like this, isn't a wife's place at her husband's side?"

With less than eight weeks before the baby was due, his question struck me as thoughtless. "I believe I should remain in this peaceful situation for the sake of the baby," I responded. Of course, this made me feel doubly guilty and his answering letter confirmed he was not only disappointed but thoroughly peeved with me. However, I chose to stay where I was.

Our baby was born in the Salvation Army's Grace Hospital which sits solid and serene upon the northern brow of Little Mountain and commands an unobstructed view of Vancouver Harbour, Stanley Park and the still snowy mountains of the north shore. As the sun rose that morning I was watching the changes in colour of this magical scene through a curve of eight bowed windows when a nurse entered the room carrying our first born. Opening my gown she tucked the little girl into the curve of my left arm. Here she was at last! Peeking in through the east window, a sunbeam played along the coxcomb of her red hair. Someone had brushed it over a finger. My child was looking at me! And thank heavens her Delft-blue, wide-open eyes had clearly visible lashes and brows–not like my invisible ones.

For the first few weeks after the baby's birth, I sopped up Mum's care and attention, enjoying my infant and the fuss being made over us by an endless parade of relatives. Even though I instinctively knew that, had I asked him, Rai would not have approved (he once told me he didn't believe children were born in sin) I had our child christened at St. Francis-in-the-Woods in Caulfeild and called her Heather Moira; Heather being one of the few names Rai and I both liked and Moira to honour my sister who had agreed to be godmother. A few days after the christening, my uncle Dick Bell-Irving helped me, along with my baby who was on demand feed, to cope with the lengthy procedure of obtaining an American "resident-alien" visa. It was then the truth really hit me: Heather and I would soon be joining Rai in his sparsely furnished bachelor suite in the New York suburb of Hastings-on-Hudson. We would have to manage on a very tight budget, and there would be no more comforts. The closer Heather's and my departure drew, the more I dreaded leaving our cocoon.

In order to survive in New York until he found work, Rai had contracted to record a series of half-hour radio shows for the Department of Health in Ottawa. Once a month he spent a few days with his sister Kay in Toronto while he produced four or five episodes. That June of 1950 he was working in Toronto when he came to meet us at the airport. I was toting our angelic child in a carry-cot, eager to show Rai his daughter. He didn't even look at her, and he could not hide his displeasure–or perhaps it was jealousy. Later, at Kay and Ernie's house he found it so uncomfortable to watch me breast feed our child–an intimate experience I'd looked forward to sharing with him–that he simply left the room. Two days later, still uncomfortably tense, the three of us flew to New York where we took up residence in a sub-let close to the Simpsons, the same Bob Simpson who had guided Purdy Productions while its president served overseas. Day after day, while I occupied myself with the baby, Rai scoured the papers and then, travelling by crowded bus and the noisy El, continued without success to knock on doors of theatrical offices and ad agencies. Though Bob Simpson was an American, I had met him and his new Canadian wife, Eve, in Toronto shortly before our own marriage there in 1947. In the spring of 1950, with the elegant Eve and their year-old son Jeffrey, Bob had returned to his native land where he had already taken a position at CBS-TV as an associate director. Though both Purdys and Simpsons were on tight budgets, we constantly visited each other; the men talked television over rye and coke while Eve and I discussed our children and the merits of window-shopping. Over the next few years our youngsters, one blonde and one red-headed, magically matched in temperament, played without ever squabbling and grew up almost as brother and sister. But back in those early days it was a wonder to me how Rai, still without a job, retained his optimism over endless months of disappointment until, on that magical evening in 1950 when everything changed.

Purdy Productions' chorus line
choreography by Verity

Rai and Verity before marriage, Windsor Ontario

Anna Verite corrects Lois Halsey's position

CHAPTER 6

Fancy Dancing Reprise

In my case "Fancy Dancing" was the result of having had to accept being far from home for most of my growing-up years and losing close touch with parents and siblings. At the age of 11, I had been sent from Vancouver to be enrolled as a full-time student of classical dance in London, England. There I'd lived and studied dance for the next five years.

Except for the arts, I was given virtually no formal education. By the age of 13, I knew something important was missing, especially when visiting my Scottish cousins who took it for granted that I was properly schooled and socially equipped. When I declined my cousin Eva's invitation to play in a tennis tournament, saying, "I don't play," she responded, "Don't be ridiculous! Of course you play tennis. You're Canadian." As the years went on, embarrassed that I knew nothing about world affairs, sports, literature, math, history or economics, I learned to use my wits to dodge awkward issues. Though my confidence was still easily shattered, I hid my shame with bravado, and despite serious feelings of inferiority, I put on a good show.

Performing this kind of fancy dance is not easy. In order to survive, fancy dancers must be quick on their feet and fly by the seat of their pants when out of their depth, laugh when questions become too probing, out-manoeuvre and bluff with little white lies and, when caught out, have a bag of tricks ready to cover their embarrassment. When their hopes are dashed, most fancy dancers make-believe, tell themselves lies to appease the pain, but they know better than to feel sorry for themselves for long. If they can't win one way, they'll win another, for win they must or leave the game. And if–as in my case–show business is the only thing they're good at least they know which mask to wear and when, and they're not afraid to act the clown if the need arises.

Of course, we're a brave lot, but we are invariably hiding from reality. We pretend not to notice when criticised by others, but our own internal judge is privy to our weaknesses. And though we often try too hard and whistle too loud in the dark, we always rise to the occasion. I can vouch for that. Seeing the rainbow's treasure before us, some of us borrow courage, or settle for goods that are cheap but effective, or fall for the ersatz. The thing is–it works! Without a doubt, some of the world's most successful people started out as fancy dancers, some even got to the Big Time without being found out, but God, it's a scary road to travel.

As Luck Would Have It,[1] I had married another fancy dancer, and together we fancy-danced all the 43 years of our marriage, trying never to expose our own or each other's ignorance. But my heart ached as, time and again, sure that his next bright idea would fly higher, he would pull himself up from near defeat and start again. And in the end, he did succeed by the world's standard, though I'm not sure he–or I–ever quite believed that this was so.

No one seeing my husband, Rai Purdy, wearing his fashionable business suit with its Provanne label and his snap-brimmed hat, stride across the lobby of Columbia Broadcasting's building at 485 Madison Avenue, New York, one October day in 1950 would ever have guessed that this apparently self-assured Canadian broadcaster felt anything less than secure. The truth was that his suit (the only one he owned) had been off the rack and on sale back in 1946 when he'd left the Canadian army.

I knew and he knew that the fact he was there at all that day was due to the presence in New York of my Vancouver friend from

---

1   Vanwell Publishing 2003

childhood, Pamela Stumer. The daughter of frightfully British, outspoken and socially prominent Rita Rolston, Pam had been in second form at Crofton House School when I was in first. She was tall, immaculately tidy and always right, but I worshipped her, probably because she let me play with her beautifully real baby dolls. Pam's dad and mine (both well-educated) had been career engineer army officers before and during World War I, but neither had succeeded as businessmen thereafter, and both had suffered inferiority complexes as a result.

Pam's and my paths had crossed again as teenagers in London where her ambitious mother had taken her to acquire some polish and to learn several languages; we met again in 1938 following her first marriage in Vancouver. In 1950, happy to be reunited after so many years, we met for lunch, and while we gabbed about our lives, our travels and our husbands, I learned that her newest husband, Louis Stumer, was an executive with the Music Corporation of America. Pam assured me Louis knew everyone my husband needed to meet in order to break into American television. A few days later, she invited us to their home in Pound Ridge where she had arranged a cocktail party. As soon as Pam introduced Rai to Louis, the two men engaged in enthusiastic conversation about their mutual interest–broadcasting. Within minutes–perhaps Pamela had primed him–Louis introduce Rai to his friend Bill Paley (William S. Paley, that is, president of the Columbia Broadcasting System) who seemed delighted to discuss Rai's television aspirations. Soon their conversation touched on contracts with CBS, and Rai realized to his astonishment that Paley–totally unaware that his own director of television programs had only the week before turned down Rai's application–was offering him a job. Without hesitation, in the middle of a party, with but a simple shake of hands, Bill Paley hired Rai Purdy to produce and direct live television shows for CBS-TV. That's why, on that October day in 1950 when Rai crossed the CBS lobby and rode the elevator to the seventh floor, he looked so confident. He was on his way to an appointment with the comptroller, Henry

On the set over Grand Central Station

Rai, Robert Lewis, Frank Satenstein

White, to sign a seven-year contract as a director/producer.

In 1950 most of the Columbia Broadcasting System television studios were in the building over Grand Central Station. There were no editing facilities. All shows (as well as commercials) were "live-to-air." And CBS had no school. "Observe from the control-room and take notes for three weeks," was the only TV experience that executive producer Harry Ommerly could offer.

Rai's first "live" broadcast–five minutes, using two cameras to show various angles of a black pianist at the keyboard–long shots, close ups, dissolves etc.–came off without a mistake. Immediately following the show, breathlessly excited, he called me from a phone- booth: "Sweetie, I did it! I did it! Not bad for a 39-year-old! My head felt as though it was going in and out! It's still pounding, but I did it!" I wondered if the life he'd chosen wasn't more stressful than a man of his age should attempt. Too late now. I pushed aside my concern.

For three months Rai and I with our infant daughter, Heather, had been living in a sublet on Long Island which Rai's Toronto friend Bob Simpson had helped us find. Bob had recently returned to the States and a job at CBS-TV, bringing with him his wife, Eve, and their 18-months-old son, Jeffrey, as well as Eve's widowed mother, Mrs. Matheson. We had enjoyed having them nearby but, since we had no car, transportation to and from Long Island had been a headache for Rai. However, once he got the job at CBS, Pam Stumer invited us to sublet her dark and minuscule, two-flights-up Manhattan apartment on 83rd Street. Tough as I found it with a small baby in that confined space, it was a godsend for our new breadwinner. Pam kept in touch by telephone, drove all three of us to their home for weekends and several times took Heather and me to the beach at Coney Island.

One of the earliest and most rewarding series Rai produced during 1951, called *All Around The Town*, was CBS-TV's first major "remote" (a show broadcast from a location outside the studio). It was a "live" documentary about the city of New York, directed by Frank Satenstein with host Mike Wallace– already a great commentator–and his then wife, Buff Cobb.

In the course of production we got to know Mike and Buff quite well, and we had a wonderful time with them before Christmas, sharing our recipe for making realistic snow to decorate their tree. It went: "Put one cup of Tide in three inches of water in a bucket. Froth with an electric mixer. Scoop up the thick foam with your hand and throw it at the branches the way the wind would, all in one direction. It's so stiff, once it dries, it doesn't fall off." But after getting snow all over their carpet, we added a post script to the recipe: "Be sure to spread a big drop-sheet under the tree."

Rai's crew for the show included 16 technicians who used three cameras. One of the early episodes recorded the building of the new airport at La Guardia Field. To get a true perspective of one enormous hangar, Rai and his #1 cameraman had to climb to roof-level on a steel ladder flat against an inside wall of the as-yet-roofless building. Using a crane to place one of the cameras–they were huge things in those days–on a platform at roof level, they were able to capture an extraordinary, sweeping view. On another occasion they set out to televise the construction of a TV tower being added to the already sky-scraping Empire State Building. This required Rai and some of his crew to scramble along loose catwalks on scaffolding attached outside the top floor ("I didn't dare look down," he told me) in order to decide where to set up the very first television camera to take pictures from that vantage point. Though not good at heights himself, Rai never asked his cameramen to go anywhere he would not go, and this kind of daring got cameras installed in damned-near-impossible locations. No one complained. The pictures were breathtaking.

All Around The Town also broadcast the first TV pictures from the Statue of Liberty. Another show came from Play Land at Coney Island where, as Mike Wallace described the parachute ride, a cameraman–focussing his camera–dropped, as would a tourist, from the top of the parachute tower. Another episode came from the Sailor's Snug Harbour, still another from the bell tower at Independence Hall. Extremely moving scenes were caught within a famous New York orphanage.

That New Year's Eve around 11 pm, while Mrs. Matheson baby-sat both children, Bob and Eve Simpson and Rai and I joined the swelling crowd in traffic-free Times Square, the heart of New York's entertainment industry. The Simpsons had described to us the American tradition of counting down the last sixty seconds of the old year while watching a ball of light creep up the face of the clock-tower, reaching the top precisely at midnight. With everyone walking down Fifth Avenue, we caught the excitement long before reaching 42nd Street where people were emerging into the square from all directions. We had plenty of time to navigate between bodies to find a perfect view of the clock-tower and to note the particularly friendly mood of the very visible police. Everyone seemed free to make conversation with people near them, some openly offering a swig of whatever they were drinking, others engaging those around them in song. The crowd packed in tighter and tighter, though everyone took care not to upset the good feeling. Around us, coloured lights flashed from top to bottom on every building, advertising everything from Broadway shows to money-lending. Just being there was a wonderment to me, but to Rai, fired up by the breadth of television's possibilities, this adventure represented the one giant television spectacular he couldn't wait to get his hands on.

The hour slipped magically away until any minute now "The Light" would begin its journey. The crowd became quiet as anticipation settled in, then suddenly a bulb like a full moon flashed on just above the heads of the crowd, and they roared: "THERE SHE GOES!" As it began its climb, everyone counted along with a broadcast voice . . . fifty-eight, fifty-seven, fifty-six . . . fifty-three, fifty-two, fifty-one . . . as the moon rose steadily. Whistles and shouts added to the counting and "Auld Lang Syne" began in several places. . . . Thirty-nine, thirty-eight, thirty-seven. . . . Almost halfway. The volume rose as the counting closed on the last seconds. . . ten, nine, eight, seven, six . . . then fairly pounded out . . . FIVE, FOUR, THREE, TWO, ONE ! The crowd roared again as a rocket, splashing light everywhere, burst open the sky to welcome in 1951. The voices of the people and every kind of horn and siren hollered "HELLO!" to the New Year. The singing went on and the drinking too, but everyone felt quite safe, though in the years to come it was never quite the same. The New York celebration took on a cynicism. Police had to confront ruffians. And within the next two or three years it was considered unsafe to gather in Times Square on New Year's Eve.

Within twelve months, having taken television to his heart, Rai assumed responsibility for several shows a week, producing and/or directing many more firsts for CBS-TV. I couldn't have been more proud; my guy was really flying and he loved every minute of it. On the other hand, he was so busy I hardly saw him, and I began to wish I had some activity of my own.

When the Purdy family graduated to a neat old apartment-with-doorman on 72nd Street near Third Avenue, I began to dream about my own side-tracked career in dance. At the age of twenty-nine I already wanted to escape from home and its responsibilities. Therefore, once we were settled in Manhattan and Rai's career was assured, I broached the subject of my own. He wasn't opposed to my taking lessons so long as it didn't interfere with his schedule and provided that two-year-old Heather was in good hands. It wasn't too hard to get household help on a part-time basis in those days, and Harriet, the Brooklyn woman who turned up, assured me she could manage my child several hours a week. I contacted Maestro Vincenzo Celli, the ballet master I had studied with following my discharge from the Canadian Army back in 1946 and, full of nervous excitement, returned to his school. During the first lesson my muscles, though weak, were obedient and I managed a respectable barre, but by the end of class my whole body had turned to jelly. For several weeks, though I went through agonies of stiffness, Rai never heard me complain.

After only a few lessons Celli suggested that a stint with the ballet at Radio City would speed my return to professional strength. He advised me to audition. Neither Rai nor I knew anything about Radio City Music Hall nor did I expect to be taken on, but Rai seemed delighted to let me have a try. Although my house-and-child helper complained about working the peculiar extra hours I asked of her, she hadn't failed me yet, so one March morning in 1952, carefully made up and my red hair slicked into a high pony-tail, I set off for my audition.

"Dreary day," said the doorman as he held open the glass door of our apartment building. I headed briskly down the awning-covered walk to 72nd Street carrying a small zipper-bag filled with my practice clothes. I felt quite exhilarated as the usual New York wind caught me as I turned toward the Third Avenue elevated railway. Not until I had climbed the stairs, entered the coach, sat on a bench and put my bag between my feet did I recognize the pressure of guilt on my shoulders. This day I was taking my first serious step toward recapturing my career.

It was raining as I left the "El" at 49th Street and hurried to Fifth Avenue. Looking up the avenue, I saw what I was seeking: a marquee advertising the Radio City Music Hall on a hulk of a building facing onto Fifth Avenue and occupying the entire block between 50th and 51st streets. My step quickened. Approaching a ticket wicket, I asked through the hole in the glass, "Where do I go to audition?" I must have looked pretty wet and bedraggled.

Sorry, lady. I haven't a clue," said the woman inside. I had turned away when she called, "Say, yoo-hoo, are you a dancer?"

"Yes," I said. "I have an appointment."

"I guess you'll find them on the fourth floor. The elevators are on 50th and 51st. Take your pick."

I thanked her, and since I was facing that way, walked on toward 51st Street. Turning right at the corner, I saw a group of women standing under cover of a roof over a doorway halfway up the block and hurried toward them. Although they wore wraps or raincoats, they all stood in high-heeled silver sandals. Then my eyes opened wide as I saw their flashy make-up. Feeling totally inadequate, I enquired, "Is this the entrance for dancers?" They all turned to focus on me.

"Sure is," said one of them." Take the elevator. The dressing rooms are on three." I passed them and let myself into a gloomy hall. The elevator, just arriving, emptied more show-girls into the lobby as the operator snapped, "Going up!"

"Three please," I said weakly. "There is an audition today, isn't there? I have an appointment."

"I guess you'll find them on the fourth. Ya wanna be a Rockette?" She said it more like "Raakit."

"What's a Rockette?"

"A line-girl. What kinda dancer are you?"

"Ballet." We had stopped at three. She opened the gate. "I'm a ballet dancer," I said, but she hadn't heard me. The elevator emptied and refilled with girls in every sort of dance outfit.

"Going up!" We all poured out on four, and I followed the girls into a room the size of a gymnasium. Oozing along a wall, we joined a waiting crowd of auditioners. Someone was banging out a jazzy rhythm on a piano while six or so candidates rattled their tap-shoes doing time-steps on a wooden floor. This must be the wrong place, I thought, and thanked goodness that I hadn't followed my urge to get off and change into my ballet clothes on three. Still clutching my bag, I slipped out of the room and hurried to press the down button. Once back on the street I flew in the rain to Fifth Avenue, turned left and ran to 50th Street, then went left again and through a doorway where I now realized there must be an elevator to a ballet dancers' dressing room on the third floor and a ballet audition hall on the fourth. In fact, I discovered later that there was just a wall separating back-to-back elevators leading to the separate dressing rooms and rehearsal halls for each group.

It has never been generally known that, quite apart from the Rockettes, there was an equally large, classically trained corps de ballet. At times, for special effects, the 36-member ballet corps plus the 36 Rockettes wore identical costumes and were combined in the same production. This did nothing to soften the traditional rivalry that existed between the Ballet and the Rockettes, and though the Rockettes were world-famous, the members of the Ballet looked down their noses at these "cheap show-girls." That the ballet dancers were as good in their way as were the Rockettes in theirs didn't alter the fact that they never spoke to each other.

Dressed in my black tights, leotard and soft shoes, I entered the hall carrying my blocked shoes, but I very soon sat down to change footwear. The girls who were being auditioned were working en pointe and the rest were already in pointe-shoes. As it had been only a few weeks since my retraining had begun, when my turn came, I prayed my pointe-work would look strong enough and that I could perform clean pirouettes and hold a high arabesque. Fortunately, although most of these girls were younger and fitter than I, my years of experience must have shown. I was accepted and told to show up at the next rehearsal.

In the weeks that followed, I shared the terrible conditions under which these performers had to work. To my despair, almost everything the ballet did on stage was en pointe in pink satin shoes, and it entailed endless bouree-ing in complex patterns at high speed over a concrete floor that was anything but smooth. Not only did the dancers have to avoid the brass railway tracks encircling the stage without upsetting the precision of the patterns. There were also dozens of brass-ringed holes for installing set pieces and more holes along the back of one stage for the jets of a water curtain. My biggest fear was of falling off the stage! Between the front curtain and the last backdrop, the Radio City stage is divided into three sections. The two rear sections, stages two and three, which were often separated from the fore-stage by heavy black curtains, could be lowered hydraulically about 30 feet to the basement for set changing or raised 10 to 20 feet above the fore-stage, making possible fantastic city and mountain effects. If, when working on the fore-stage, a draught of air caught the black curtains behind us, we dancers could look down into an enormous gaping hole ready for us to fall into should we put a foot wrong.

In the1950s the Music Hall drew as many as 1,500 people from all over the world for performances 365 days a year. Each production ran for three weeks, with five performances between noon and ten pm on weekdays. On weekends and holidays a sixth performance was added, finishing at midnight. Each presentation consisted of a five-star movie plus an elaborate, 40-minute stage show featuring music hall acts, a huge vocal ensemble, a corps de ballet and a line of 36 Rockettes. These famous chorus girls

79

in their high heels and exotic costumes performed flawless kick routines on a stage which, including an apron on either side that curved out around the audience, must have been 150 feet wide.

Studio rehearsals for the upcoming show began at seven every morning and ran concurrently with the public performances as did costume fittings. There were, of course, many more singers, dancers and chorus than one ever saw at one time, since 25 percent of the permanent cast was always on leave. Singers and dancers worked three full weeks followed by one week off. Days off were scheduled so that a dancer could leave partway through a run and return in time for the final week of the next show's rehearsal. The mechanics of organizing all this must have been horrendous in those days before computers.

For me the pay at Radio City was less than the cost of my nanny/housekeeper, the work was exhausting and there was little job satisfaction. I found it difficult to adjust to being only a number (#3 since I was one of the shortest) in a mob of dancers. My soft heels had blistered on the first day and never had a chance to mend. At home, when there was time, I sat on our kitchen counter with both feet in a sink full of bran mash. Except that I am stubborn, I don't know why I stayed. More than once I lost my household help, and Rai had to take our two-year-old to stay with Court and Grace Benson, old friends from his acting days in Toronto, who fortunately lived close by. Surprisingly, Rai didn't become angry. When he came home to find the apartment empty, he would phone Grace and go there to collect Heather. Meanwhile, between shows and in full makeup, I would dash up to the employment agency to hire a new girl. Once I was sent to the wrong line-up because they thought I wanted a job. Still, Rai supported me, giving me the opportunity to put on that heavy makeup and perform in a big show.

The enormity of the Music Hall theatre and stages affected every move the dancers made, some of which took courage, such as leaping into a dark hole–getting lost it was called–should your body be one too many for a final pose. Some of the things required of us were bizarre, like the times several girls had to sit down and slide backwards on their rear ends to fit perfectly into a circle of sylphs in their final pose. One strange sensation I noticed was the total lack of communication between performers and audience. Because of the distance between us, when we took our bows after a production number, applause from out-front sounded like the faintest rustle of tissue paper–deflating, I suspect, for artists of low self-esteem. However, there were a few dancers for whom that separation covered a multitude of sins and allowed for many a laugh. The perennially popular "Water Ballet," for instance, opened in blue-green lighting with the stage covered entirely by a layer of undulating silk. Beneath that surface, to create the effect of waves, dancers bodies rose and fell as they moved here and there in loose formation–looser, I soon discovered, than had been intended. During the run of this production number, a few of the old-timers knew they could enjoy a beer or two at lunch and get away with considerable giggling "under water" without being found out.

The next production, designed to celebrate the Fourth of July, was a very complicated bit of show business which allowed absolutely no room for mistakes. Without mentioning sloppy behaviour under the sea, our distinguished choreographer, Florence Rogie, laid a threat of dismissal on anyone who talked or put a foot wrong, and it was lucky that she did. As might be expected, this presentation had flags and soldiers, gunpowder and flaming buildings as well as red, white and blue sequins on everything. The extra size of the sets called for the joined forces of Ballet and Rockettes dressed alike except for footwear. Smiling as though we liked each other, enemies had to cross paths time and again. Everything went well at the opening performance until the final scene when the Ballet section, entering at stage left in pink satin pointe shoes, was faced with an unanticipated challenge. As the final heroic tableau appeared out of a puff of smoke at centre stage, gold curtains opened upon the tall statue of a soldier on a snow white horse. The fore and hind hoofs of this horse were close together on a small circular base and the soldier, sword aloft, was standing in his stirrups. But this was no statue!

This was a real man on a real horse! And we knew this to be true because the horse had left steaming droppings for us to dance through! We might have made light of it and let the audience in on the humour but not after that warning from Rogie. We had to do some mighty tricky footwork, but not one of us soiled our shoes.

That July 4th show was particularly painful for me. As the last dancer in the line, it had been my lot, (nearing the end of a previous Chopin production) while travelling at full speed, to spin around, sit down hard and slide backward the last three feet to stop in a graceful position with my back to the centre of a perfect stage-centre circle. I did this, show after show, until at last the blow as I hit the concrete floor splintered my coccyx. Weeks later, my 4th of July costume, adorned with 20 pounds of red, white and blue sequins, weighed heavily enough on my shoulders to compress the injury and send me howling into the wings as the final curtain closed. It was, in fact, my last professional performance.

There is nothing a doctor can do for a fractured coccyx. It has to heal itself, and even after several weeks of sick leave the pain persisted. Finally, with no hope of rescuing my career, I had to put my pointe shoes away. Anyway, the struggle to keep help had been exhausting and my guilt about leaving Heather and Rai had deepened daily.

In 1953 producer/director Yul Brynner left CBS to star on Broadway in The King and I, and Rai took over from him as producer and director of a CBS television remote show called The Stork Club. Located in a Manhattan nightclub for the rich and famous, this half-hour weekly dazzler featured restaurant owner Sherman Billingsley with his illustrious guests dining in the Cub Room, an inner sanctuary of "The Stork" where mirrors covered the walls. It was common gossip that here "the rich come to stare at the stars who stare at themselves in the mirrors and everyone is lost in admiration."

Through his columns and his highly popular radio show with its signature opening–"Good evening, Mister and Misses America. Let's go to press!" Newspaper columnist Walter Winchell had promoted his buddy Billingsley's insignificant

Stork Club restaurant into a famous nightclub, describing it as a posh eatery on Fifth Avenue at 47th near "Rockerfella" Centre. Its stork-delivering-baby emblem inferred that it catered exclusively to white Anglo-Saxon Protestants–WASPs–and was thus a safe place for young socialites to dine among the theatrical luminaries while they enjoyed New York's nightlife. Its exclusive clientele was guaranteed by the large liveried doorman who stood outside the club's small but gilt-framed doorway off "The Avenue" and carefully surveyed each mink-draped and camel-coated customer before unhooking a heavy gold chain to let them in. But if this gentleman doubted their ancestry or credit rating even slightly, he would turn them away, saying the club was full, at the same time summoning an even larger, darkly clad official who threatened by his very presence.

It was routine for the Stork's clientele to sit at the bar–drinking, of course–for anywhere up to an hour before a table became available. Then, depending on their importance, they were either moved to the main dining room with its orchestra and dance floor or escorted to the elite Cub Room. Music, which was fed to the Cub Room on speakers, followed the drinking pace. As long as corks popped and plenty of alcohol flowed, the pace was easy and the melodies sweet. But as soon as bar tabs reflected a slow-down, the lights brightened imperceptibly as did the tempo and volume of the orchestra. These tricks never failed to speed up demands on the bar.

During the club's successful years Winchell never missed an opportunity to mention something in his column about Mr. Billingsley and his glamorous clientele at the Stork. He described Billingsley as a connoisseur of fine wines and perfumes and emphasized the culinary expertise of the Stork's chef and the suave elegance of Red, who had the reputation of being the maitre d' to end all maitres d's. In fact, it was only through his connection with Winchell that Billingsley had gained exclusive New York rights to Dom Perrignon champagne and the highly sophisticated Sortilege perfume as well as a line of lipsticks. In the club's foyer the atmosphere was heavy with Sortilege as were the powder room and elevator. And if, after visiting a table, Billingsley was impressed with the quality of his guests, he might send each of the ladies a package containing a large Sortilege cologne, a small perfume, a lipstick or all three.

In reality however, Billingsley was an illiterate product of the Great Depression and a one-time bootlegger. Though certainly a large and quite impressive man, he still feared old enemies from his days of making big money illegally, and it was quite obvious that strapped to his body under his expensive suit coat was a revolver. It was also said that he wore a bullet-proof vest. In spite of all this, from the first day they met Rai and Billingsley had a good rapport, and when Rai took over The Stork Club show, the two men became close friends. Well before the fashionable dinner hour, CBS broadcast the weekly Stork show "Live" from a studio mock-up of the Cub Room that had been constructed on a floor above the restaurant. Here the evening's special guests (usually theatrical names) gathered around Billingsleys' table to be interviewed by him for the cameras. As producer for the show, Rai was responsible for its content. He and his scriptwriter prepared the stars as well as their interviewer and gave them all cue-cards on the cameras. But Billingsley needed more help than that and wrote on the tablecloth such brilliant conversational bon mots as: "HI! MAR-IL-IN (or GLOR-EE-A or TA-LOO-LA), HOW ARE YOU?" Cameramen were careful never to shoot the tablecloth.

Billingsley often invited Rai to the club on evenings other than broadcast nights, and according to his whim I was sometimes expected to be there, sometimes not. Never knowing until the last minute, I always had to be prepared for an evening at the Stork. For these events I wore my bright red, curly hair piled on the top of my head in a chignon to set off one of the mostly black, décolleté Stork Club outfits that Rai had chosen for me. Fine hose and high heels emphasized what he called my "racy legs." Vetted before leaving the apartment, I obediently accompanied Rai to the Cub Room. Sometimes Billingsley came to our table and we were served a sumptuous meal with expensive champagne–which I liked but Rai didn't–and quite

Rai and Verity at the Stork Club

Rai and Sherman Billingsley

often I received gifts. At other times a phone would be brought to the table for Rai to receive a call bidding him to Billingsley's office alone. The two men would then be closeted hour upon hour to discuss upcoming shows while I sat alone in the Cub Room. Why didn't I object? I didn't know I had a right to.

At other times when Billingsley visited our table, I, being a chatty show-biz person, entered the conversation whenever I could, and he seemed to enjoy that. However, on one of these occasions I mentioned something I thought was wrong with the show and blamed a technician whose name I didn't know. Billingsley thought I was talking about Harry Junkin, a Canadian friend of Rai's who was the show's writer. Much later, although Rai didn't admonish me, I learned to my horror that Junkin had been fired because of me.

Although it didn't seem to matter how poorly Billingsley hosted the show, the appeal of his snobbish establishment got CBS a good rating. But as time went by, Rai coached him considerably so that he was able to talk more confidently with the stars when they were on camera, and over time it even became possible to add substance and humour to the interviews. The show became even more interesting and took on some class when Rai added a popular musician or the odd slick nightclub act, and as long as he was the producer, the show's ratings continued to improve. By way of thanks, one Christmas Billingsley sent Rai six magnums of Dom Perrignon. We bought some holly to jam into the ice that we had packed around the huge bottles in our apartment bath tub. Then Rai called Mike and Buff Wallace, the Bensons, the Simpsons, Romney Brent and Sylvia Sydney, the Stumers and CBS executives such as Harry Ommerlie, Henry White and Ed Saxe and their wives–most of whom came–plus quite a few writers and production assistants. I had bought nuts and celery and some crackers and cheese, but unfortunately it wasn't the kind of food that could sop up champagne. As the apartment filled with cigarette smoke, I caught sight of our pyjama-clad daughter peeking between the railings which separated the entrance hall from the sunken living room. She grinned at me and

I put my finger to my lips while our noisy guests, getting higher and noisier, slithered laughing to cushions on the floor. Not until the sixth magnum was empty did the last guest stumble home. This aspiring hostess had much to learn about entertaining but, awkward as I felt in this milieu, and often embarrassed, Rai didn't seem to notice. He was ecstatic to be hobnobbing with the elite. He had come such a long way from his roots.

CHAPTER 7

Rai at CBS

By the end of 1952 Rai was well established with CBS and I, having put my dance career on the shelf, had become a reasonably proper wife. We had made many American friends, though the people we saw most often were Canadian expatriots. Little Heather loved actors Court and Grace Benson who had so kindly cared for her during my stint at Radio City, and she was always happy to see Rai's sister Beatrice and husband Linton Cole whenever they came down from Toronto. She adored Pam Stumer who took us to Coney Island beach. It was about this time that Rai bought an ancient Hudson.

Harry Raskey was an especially wonderful and funny Canadian who came into our lives when he became a writer on one of Rai's shows. I met him on a summer day in Central Park where Rai had arranged that he join us for a picnic lunch. I remember how like a kid he seemed as he took off his shoes and sat on the grass, how smart he was, how he and Rai played with words and kept us all laughing. Harry had recently written The Seven Year Itch and was looking for backing for a Broadway production. We didn't grow very big wings, but we did buy a share or two and thought of ourselves as angels. Since the Broadway run starring Tom Ewell and Vanessa Brown was long and successful, we expected to get a little benefit, but not a penny ever materialized, not even after Marilyn Monroe played the lead in the movie. Oh, well! Harry didn't forget us. He later looked us up in other parts of the world.

For someone working at CBS, our apartment on 72nd Street was the perfect place to live. I enjoyed the shopping and found a good hairdresser there. Even more wonderful, after Harriette (my Brooklyn home-help) left, I found a well-trained nurse-maid, Madame Nellie Calame-Biset, who cared for Heather with much affection, and I was delighted that our child's vocabulary soon became partly French. Nellie also helped me to remember my own French and added songs that all three of us sang together. Rai and I were able to catch most of the Broadway shows. (My Mum visited and was shocked by Guys and Dolls.)

The Christmas before her fourth birthday, Nellie had left us by then and I was once more a full-time mother–Santa Claus brought our little girl a red wagon. After that, nearly every day Heather and I made the journey along 72nd Street, crossing Fourth, then Madison, then Fifth to get to Central Park. I say "journey" because of the many side trips Heather enjoyed. After parking her vehicle, she would climb, holding onto the iron railings, up one side and down the other of every staircase on the south side of 72nd Street. As a result, though she may have left our apartment looking tidy and clean, when we entered the park, my precious, bright-eyed daughter looked like an urchin beside the pristine children we met at the sand box next to the slides and swings. The uniformed nannies who sat on benches there, some of them rocking expensive English-style perambulators, looked at us askance, nodded, and returned to their conversation, breaking it now and then to caution to a child on a swing, "That's high enough, Angelene," or "Don't sit down in the sand, Rebecca.". But it was difficult to keep clean in New York City. No matter how swank one's apartment, a layer of soot landed daily on the white painted window sills.

Rai and I took a vacation in Bermuda where he introduced me to Canadian radio man Gerry Wilmott who now ran the Bermuda radio station. Gerry explained that the brown

90

patches we had seen on our approach to the island by air were the result of illegal importation of some plant life responsible for the catastrophic disease that had recently destroyed all Bermuda's cedar trees. He told us that quantities of lady bugs, which could have killed the parasites, had been let loose on the island but they had been blown out to sea by a hurricane. Though the dead trees were a sad sight, nothing could spoil the magical quality of one particular Bermuda night. After dinner in the deep dusk before the moon had risen, Rai and I wandered away from the music and chatter of our hotel down a winding path we knew led to the water. Leaning on a balustrade overlooking a little dock, we watched the approach of a sail. This was all we could see of the silent craft which, piloted by a man whose colour was as dark as the night, turned into the wind and, with a slack sail, slipped alongside. Though I could see no one, I waved and called softly, "Hello, down there!"

"Lovely evenin', ma'am," answered a deep voice. "Wouldja care to sail?"

Rai took charge. "We sure would ... be right down." He took my arm as we felt our way down stone steps in darkness and then out onto the dock. I could see our pilot now. He stood and reached for my hand to help me aboard.

"My name's Jim," he said. "Beautiful night for a sail, sir. Moon's comin' up shortly."

"I'm Rai," said my husband, "and this is my wife, Verity. What a delight that you should arrive just at this moment." Rai climbed into the cockpit and Jim asked us to sit opposite him so as to balance the boat, then he pushed it gently away from the dock. The wind caught our sail and a little way out we could look back into the curve of a bay and see the lights of the hotel and other lights along the shore. There was enough wind to move us along, and the rhythmic swoosh of waves was like music. Out and out we went on an easy tack. For the longest time, no one spoke. We didn't need to. And then the moon came up. Talk about a perfect setting for a holiday.

Very soon after Bermuda, Rai and I decided to quit the cigarette habit. With the help of a book called How to stop Smoking, we set a date and ceremoniously smoked our last. Although we both suffered withdrawal symptoms, I worse than Rai, we never did go back on our agreement. Sometime later when Rai looked into the possibility of building a show based on the book and its successful solution to the problem, he discovered that the rights had been bought up by a tobacco company.

First house, Davenport Neck, New Rochelle

CHAPTER 8

Producer/Director Purdy

Under the CBS system, the dual responsibilities of production and direction were given to one man. The first involved format, contracts, budget and the hiring of talent; the second meant he was responsible for direction, stage movement and lighting plus directing the cameras. In this producer/director role, Rai rated the help of a technical director, a production assistant, a musical director, a set designer, script writers, a lighting engineer, a floor manager and other helpers on every show. Although it was a heavy responsibility, he thrived on the technical challenges. He particularly enjoyed making live commercials because, within the two-minute sequence allotted for each one, there could be dozens of shots, each one rehearsed and pre-timed. He quickly became an expert in this area, and fortunately for us, fees for these live commercials were paid to the director separately through the ad agency and were in addition to his CBS salary.

CBS's management had early recognized Rai's natural aptitude for camera work as well as his ability to handle television's complicated lighting problems, so when colour-tv became imminent and the company began experimenting with it, they chose Rai to create a technically complicated, closed-circuit pilot broadcast using colour cameras. It is now history that as a result of this test CBS was able to demonstrate the superiority of its colour system–designed by Doctor Peter Goldmark with whom Rai had collaborated–over all other companies' systems for broadcasting in colour. The CBS system ultimately became the universal formula for colour-tv cameras.

On the strength of this success, Barrie and Enright Productions asked Rai to direct their new children's show on CBS using a technique called key-insertion–two camera images widely different in proportion within one frame. Thus a person, greatly reduced in size, could walk among fish that were in reality occupying just a small tank. The next gimmick Barry and Enright came up with was a show called Winky Dink and You. For this series, young viewers could send for a kit to use on their TV monitors at home and actually take part in the show. The kit included a sheet of clear green plastic which could be cut to size and pressed onto the TV screen, also a box of coloured chalks and an eraser. Instructions were given to draw a picture–perhaps mountains and a lake–by following the dots that appeared on the screen like flashing lights. "Now draw a bridge from one mountain to the other," host Jack Barrie would say. The fun was to watch animals and even children walk over that mountain or climb up the ladder the children had just drawn or see a fish jump out of the lake. Though Heather's favourite show remained The Lone Ranger, which she always called "Hi Ho Silver," she adored Winkie Dink and You and couldn't wait for her producer dad to bring home a kit.

At the end of 1953 Rai handled a sizable chunk of CBS's network New Year's Eve coverage. The pre-midnight antics in Times Square made a natural background for the broadcast, which used cameras in a dozen locations to tell the world about New York's unique people celebrating the year-end in their favourite night spots. Top commentators wearing head phones manned microphones on hotel and theatre marquees. I watched the show from home and felt enormously proud of my husband. Later reports held nothing but praise. As the years came and went, however, rowdyism changed the once peaceful atmosphere in

94

Times Square as it did in Central Park. Also changed were the expressions on the faces of New York's famous constabulary– from friendly and trusting to distant and businesslike.

During the next several years while Rai worked for CBS, though we both enjoyed his successes and the steady growth in his income, his frustrations were steadily growing. Until he came to New York, his lack of worldly knowledge–he never read a newspaper–and his ignorance about American talent never caused him concern, but now there were times when his limitations showed, and these incidents were invariably painful. One such embarrassment occurred in 1954 when CBS brought singer Robert Q. Lewis in for a series of music and variety shows and assigned Rai to the job of producer/director. These were expensive productions with a big orchestra, and Robert Q came with lots of ideas and a list of the guests he'd like to have join him. At the beginning he and Rai got along well since Rai's directing was imaginative and his timing excellent. Connected from the control booth to all three cameramen, he directed their movement with what seemed to me effortless dexterity–considering the camera's ponderous size and the monstrous appendages of cables attached to them–to get the shots he wanted. The crew included an extra man for each camera just to handle the cables that sometimes had to be lifted high enough to let another camera and its cables pass underneath, all this being done at great speed and without making any noise. I was terribly impressed.

After being introduced to me, Robert Q invited me to watch the rehearsals, and one day shortly pre-broadcast, while the show was still new, I took Heather to visit the set. Robert was enchanted with our four-year-old and asked if he might hold her hand as he knelt to sing "When you are among the very young at heart." My daughter still remembers how the spotlight suddenly shone on them and how strange it felt not to be able to see anything. Not a show-biz child, she wore a natural look of wonderment.

The Robert Q Lewis Show got good ratings but, as the weeks went on, the star began to run out of materials and guests and looked to his producer for fresh ideas. Although Rai had a good production assistant, he himself was totally unfamiliar with American talent and currently popular music. This led to awkward instances of Robert being snide about Rai's weaknesses. However, Rai's technical work was so good and the show did so well that the working arrangements remained until the end of the run and the two men parted good friends. His parting gifts to Rai–a leather briefcase and a chafing-dish–were thoughtful and in good taste.

While Rai's quick wit made him popular and his pay cheque steadily increased, he remained naive regarding some aspects of the show-business and big business worlds of which he was now a part. This had begun to trouble him, and he sometimes spoke of "knives in his back" and once admitted to me that there were times in executive meetings at CBS when he didn't understand what was being discussed. He said that, though he could joke his way through most sticky situations, occasionally a trip to the washroom was the only answer. Once I suggested that life might be more comfortable for him if he reverted to the position of technical director, but that conversation came to an abrupt end with a comparison of the salaries offered, never mind the loss of excitement that came from directing live shows.

Rai and I enjoyed the technicians and executives and their families whom we met, but New York's social life was expensive, and a chunk of the Toronto debt still remained. By that time he was earning enough to make healthy payments on it, but since his creditors had agreed to accept fifty cents on the dollar, he wanted them paid off as soon as possible. It bugged him, however, that the people he worked with had suburban houses with gardens and dogs and that their children went to private schools. So, when our Heather was nearly ready for pre-school in the autumn of 1954–though not at all sure where the money might come from but encouraged by an eager female salesman– we talked ourselves into buying a house in Westchester.

Timing and events came together dramatically on the September day we three Purdys went looking for our first home. The realtor had picked us up at the New Rochelle train station and driven us through tree-lined streets of pretty houses to a bluff where she stopped for us to see Long Island Sound. There appeared to be an island between us and the wide open water, but what we hadn't seen was the spit of land which joins that "island" to the mainland. The realtor then drove to the left down a steep road which turned right at the base of the bluff. There the road crossed the spit of land before curving right again up through trees onto a ridge at the top of the peninsula named Davenport Neck. Continuing along the crest, she drove us past some old houses on big properties but soon turned right into one of the lesser streets where smaller lots had newer homes. Almost immediately we came to a halt in front of an attractive Tudor-ish house. With dark beams over stucco, leaded panes and tiled roof, it sat back from the road on a carpet of lawn which was surrounded by climbable trees. Whoopee! But it was the vista looking down "our" street (back toward the mainland) which really captured our attention. Protected by a seawall that made a little pool beside the spit, several large-as-life swans glided about in their inimitable fashion. Then, right beside us, came a new surprise. "Who cued the pheasants?" exclaimed my husband as a female pheasant with brood in tow came out of nowhere and trickled across the trim grass. Our agent asked if we wanted to look at the house. Of course we did! What more could we possibly ask? And this was the house we bought, plus a tiny Austin convertible so that I could drive Rai to New Rochelle railway station and get around the countryside by myself. Almost as soon as Heather was in school, the Purdys became friends with the parents of her friends. Luck was really with us since they were bright, active and intelligent people who knew each other well and visited and sailed together.

We were barely settled into our new abode when Rai was assigned a five-a week morning show in which CBS would introduce their smart new talent, Dick Van Dyke. This contract certainly helped Rai to breathe more easily money-wise, but it meant that he had to catch the 4:30 am milk-train (not his favourite time of day) to Grand Central, Monday through Friday. One positive thing the new show did was to put me back into Rai's activities because he had to come up with at least ten new settings each week, depending on the lyrics Dick was to sing. I happened to have a good imagination and could assist with hair-brained ideas like, "Couldn't he be up a hydro pole fixing wires for 'Oh! What a Beautiful Morning'? All you'll need is a waist-shot of Dick in a safety sling at the top of a pole, with some sky and a tree behind him." (Well, maybe it was not quite as simple as that, but I did help him.)

The Dick Van Dyke show was well worth getting up early for. Rai was happy, and I didn't miss Manhattan at all. We had time in the afternoons to give our house a face-lift. Rai turned the garage into a workshop and I gardened madly. Heather had lots of friends and because the house had four bedrooms, friends came to visit. We went to parties and gave parties, all of them boozy but pretty much fun, on most Fridays and Saturdays. I remember this as one of our best times.

It had been years since I had seen my cousin Pemberthy, generally known as Penny, the daughter of my mother's youngest brother, when she came to stay with us in New Rochelle. As a fiery five-year-old, she had been one of the children I'd taught to dance the year I turned seventeen. She had really got the feeling when I suggested the children pretend to be seagulls running along the beach trying to fly with a broken wing. After that, every time she came to my class, Penny wanted to be "the poor birdie." It was difficult to recognize that this mature adult, who now dressed like a country cowgirl and sounded like a real horse-woman, was once that child, was once that "poor birdie."

Penny quickly got into conversation with our four-and-a-half-year-old who watched The Lone Ranger on TV and insisted on wearing a cowboy hat and boots. For her fourth Christmas we had given her a moulded yellow horse on springs. This "Silver" had reins and foot-rests like stirrups and would bounce her as high as she could push him down, and Heather demonstrated for Penny how he dipped forward, sideways and backward.

"Have you ever been on a real pony?" Penny asked Heather.

"No." Our cowgirl wrinkled her brow.

Brenda Purdy - 1955

The Purdy family grows

"Would you like to go for a ride today?" I can still see the child's wide eyes looking at my cousin. Since Rai wasn't due home for several hours, I could consider the idea. Penny telephoned around and found a riding stable in a slight river valley a couple of miles away. We piled into my little car with its top down and, with help from the local gas station attendant, found our way.

Penny went inside the stable to make arrangements to rent one of the small shaggy fellows we could see tied to a fence across the paddock. They wore bridles–with the bits out–as well as halters. Heather pulled me toward the one she had already chosen. A woman appeared with a western saddle that looked three times too big for the horse, but he didn't flinch when she dropped it over his withers, slid it down, pulled the girth under his tummy and buckled it. Heather's face was close to the pony's nose and her hands held his head gently.

"Just you aim us at a trail, okay?" Penny told the woman. "We'll be back in about an hour."

During the entire adventure, I hardly spoke a word, but from the time Penny boosted Heather into the saddle, adjusted the leather stirrups, released the halter and fit the bit, she hardly paused in her quiet instructions. "You must never," she said firmly, "grab onto the pommel, this blob right in front of you. It's not meant for hands. I'll give you an ice-cream if you manage not to. Hold the reins lightly but don't pull on them. Keep your back up straight but stay soft. Let your legs hang down loosely and look forward between the pony's ears." Heather grinned and obeyed. Walking at the pony's head, Penny led her charge across the paddock and through an open gate. I followed a little distance behind them on a path that led between trees and down a steepish hill. "No, dear, don't lean back," I heard Penny correct my daughter, then she explained, "To take the weight off the pony's hocks and give him better purchase, you must lean forward when going down a hill. Let him have his head." The lesson went on and on with kindly repetitions as we walked along a river's edge. I guessed Pemberthy knew her business and was delighted for Heather to learn the basics correctly. Despite

100

the fact–Heather remembers to this day–that Penny forgot the promised ice-cream, I suspect that by then my daughter was as hooked on horses as I had been in my teens, but unfortunately there would be no more real ponies for several years.

Heather was barely five when I became pregnant again. Although I was still caught up in thinking I needed my husband's permission to carry a baby, this time I knew I had it. In fact, Rai had become enchanted with his cheery little daughter and willingly agreed she should have a playmate. This had eased the stress for me of counting days and worrying how Rai might react should I inadvertently disappoint him again. A bona fide housewife and mother now, sex, for me at least, had taken on more honest and fulfilling proportions when it included the distinct possibility of creating life. And since Rai's salary continued to increase and we could afford to keep up with the activities of our friends and neighbours, having this new child promised be a wonderful experience for both of us. He even agreed to go through the delivery with me. I had read Dr. Spock from cover to cover before Heather's birth and was already doing the breathing exercises.

So busy and happy was I that at first I failed to recognize a serious change in Rai's attitude toward his work. But as he began to tell me more of the problems he'd faced from the beginning of his contract, some of the mean things people had said about his lack of education, every production assistant, it would appear, had a bachelor's degree at least–I suddenly awoke with a thud of understanding. I began to recognize his vulnerability, to feel some of his hurts and fears. At long last we were talking about real emotions. I remembered clearly the night he had come home looking particularly glum and told me about having been snubbed in the elevator by his close friend Henry White. "Turned his back on me–wouldn't speak to me," my subdued husband complained. "I can only guess he's found out I'm making more money than he is." I had laughed at the time but, from another confession he'd let slip months before, the picture came back to me of a CBS girl on the subway escalator barraging him with questions he couldn't answer about actors and musicians. "They're such smart-asses, so self-assured," had been his petulant comment at that time.

Now I became angry for him all over again as I remembered other instances. At about the time Heather was two-and-a-bit, I had taken her with me to spend the summer in British Columbia, and as a surprise Rai had come west to join us for a whole week. Since he was producing three commercial shows every week, the only way he had been able to arrange the time off was to make a deal with another director who also wanted a vacation. While the other director was away, Rai had handled both of their shows, taking care to maintain the other man's productions exactly as they were, handing them back in perfect order along with his own three shows. Then weary but happy, Rai had come to Vancouver, hired a water taxi and joined us at my family's retreat on Pasley Island. But while he was away, the other director not only made changes in Rai's shows–complaining to management that Rai didn't know what he was doing–but he actually stole one of Rai's shows including the commercials. This added up to a loss of $600 income per week. Although he had tried from the beginning to ignore the knives, by then Rai was questioning the benefits of his CBS contract.

A book about positive thinking that my neighbour Dorothy Collinson had lent me early in my pregnancy came to our aid at almost the same time that Rai began talking seriously about needing to be in a place where he was really wanted. By this time I had begun to understand what made New York a tough place for him to work, while at the same time I was longing for an environment where we could bring up our children that was less money-conscious and competitive. Our discussions grew lively when, at almost the same time, we both asked, "Where is it we want to be?"

"We really don't belong here, do we?" I said. "We should go somewhere gentler." He agreed. We needed a place with an easier climate. Somewhere less commercial where the people wanted what we had to offer; a country where people spoke as we did.

"Canada? England? Australia?" I tossed into the air. Whoever listens must have heard us. One day in June 1954 Rai, tired and depressed, ran into Vic George, our ex-commanding officer, who was visiting New York from Montreal. Talk soon turned to Rai's disenchantment with the American scene.

"Have you heard what Roy Thomson is doing?" Vic asked. "You know Roy, don't you?"

"Well, yes, I know who he is. From Timmins, isn't he? A newspaper man? What's he up to?"

"He moved to London and he's bargaining for the independent television licence in Scotland. He's already bought The Scotsman so he's very confident about getting it. If you've had it with New York, why not write and tell him you're available?"

"What a hell of an idea! Do you know where I can reach him?"

"Just write care of The Scotsman in Edinburgh. That will get him."

Full of excitement, Rai told me this news when I picked him up in New Rochelle. "Vic's having a dinner party with some other Canadians tomorrow," he told me. "Wish you could come." I wished I could, too, but I was two weeks overdue with the new baby, and my doctor's appointment the day before had set tomorrow for inducement of labour. Next morning, Rai drove alone to catch the 4:30 milk-train to Grand Central. Later that day I asked our neighbour, Dorothy, to take Heather home along with her daughter Dickie after kindergarten, and I called a cab for my doctor's appointment.

"Go home," said my doctor. "You're not nearly ready yet."

"Not even to be induced ? You said . . . ."

"I know. I thought you'd be ready, but . . . ."

"Can I go into Manhattan then? There's a dinner party of Canadians I'd hate to miss."

"Go ahead. Have a good time. See you."

Home again, I called Dorothy and begged, "Could you keep Heather overnight? Please?"

"Sure. What's up?"

"The doc says I'm not nearly ready yet. Rai's staying in town to meet with Vic George. I know what they will be talking about and I want to be there."

"Sure thing. The kids get along swell. Have fun!"

I called Rai, getting him out of rehearsal.

"Okay, get the first train you can," he said. "Call me when you know and I'll meet you." I rummaged through the pile of maternity clothes lent by friends, picking the outfit least worn–a brown velvet skirt with the front cut out and a rather gorgeous white lace top with an exaggerated ruffle to cover the bulge. I had safe white shoes, and as it was summer I didn't need a coat. I left a message for Rai at the CBS switchboard, then called another cab and caught the 5:30 train. On a long down escalator in Manhattan I got the giggles when I noticed the surprised expressions on the faces of people riding up as they passed me. It was obvious they'd had a weird view of the bulge under the ruffle!

Rai met me as planned and took me to the party which was already in progress. We were received with enthusiasm. It was good to see Vic George and my old friend Louise Spencer from Vancouver as well as others I didn't know. Conversation flowed easily and Rai, in comic mode, caught everything anyone said, twisting it to make us all laugh. I laughed probably more than the jokes deserved. Rai and Vic discussed Roy Thomson's newest venture, and I know Vic encouraged Rai once again to write to him about the job in Scotland, but it didn't seem important to me anymore. I was having a great party. Suddenly Rai looked at his watch and excused us. "We must hurry to get our New Rochelle train because there isn't another for an hour. Thanks for a wonderful evening, Vic. Good bye, everyone." And off we went.

It was difficult to hurry but I knew we must. With Rai's arm for support, we made it into Grand Central's marble rotunda with just five minutes to catch the train. Halfway across this great open space, however, I felt my water break and begin to trickle. "Where's the ladies' room? I have to go there now!" And so we switched course, taking an elevator to a lower floor. There Rai aimed me down a passage saying, "I'll wait here!" What else could he do?

When I gave the large, black attendant in the ladies' room my news, she opened her mouth very wide and her grey hair stood on end. Speaking a kind of gibberish, she began to flutter. When she finally handed me the napkin I'd asked for, I disappeared

104

into a cubicle. By this time I could hardly stop laughing, but I heard her dial a number on the telephone. "S'that the po-lice? Yeah, I got a lady heah needs a ride ta hospita'." As I emerged, I saw her grab a sign that said CLOSED and rush with it to the outer end of the corridor. When she returned, Rai was with her.

"Hi, sweetie. You all right?"

"Of course I'm all right. It's terribly funny, don't you think?"

"Can I use the phone?" Rai dug in his pockets–no dimes. "Can I borrow a dime?" he asked the large lady. "I want to call my wife's doctor. I've got to get her home."

"No! No sah!" she almost cried. "Y'all cain't do that. Ah's a'ready caw'ed the po-leece. He be heah right away. They's all mid-wives, din' cha know?"

"But we must get home."

"Sakes!" squeaked our lady. "That'ud mess up the ho'e thang. Once they's caw'ed, they gotta take her ta hospita'." Just then the cop showed up.

"Can you lend me a dime?" asked Rai. "I need to make a call."

"No problem, sir. Here!" Rai put the dime in and asked for information. Alas, the dime tinkled into the box. He couldn't even get the operator. The cop produced another dime and this time Rai got through. By then we'd missed the train we'd planned to catch.

"Get her onto the first train you can," my doctor ordered Rai. "Do not, repeat not, let the police take Mrs. Purdy anywhere. If they ever put her into that institution on the west side, we'll never get her out. It's where they take all the drunks and derelicts. Just tell her to walk slowly and get on the train. They can cope on the train if necessary. Go straight to New Rochelle Hospital. I'll be there."

It was a long inch-by-inch totter to the next Westchester train. We clambered aboard and nothing disastrous happened. Rai, having promised to be with me through the whole thing, stayed at the hospital for several hours but finally took the advice of a nurse who said, "There are far too many deliveries ahead of Mrs. Purdy. We'll have to put her to sleep for awhile. Why not go home and get some rest? We'll call you

105

in plenty of time." But they didn't. The message he got when they did phone was, "You have a son. All's well." This was a sadness to us both because we had planned to be together.

About two months before the birth of our son, Rai had received a Toronto call from Brenda, his 16-year-old adopted daughter. Unhappy at home with her mother and brother Brian, she put the situation rather bluntly. "You may not like it, Daddy, but I'm coming to live with you." Looking back, it was extraordinary how quickly and positively we both responded. We had the accommodation, we would make her welcome and, most of all, we made a pledge not to bug her. The poor girl needed acceptance and affection which she appeared not to be getting at home. We must prepare her room with generosity and give her the freedom she deserved.

Heather was five and the baby six weeks old when Brenda arrived. Knowing nothing about handling teenagers, my heart was open to receive her unconditionally. Brenda must have thought she'd landed in heaven with all the doors wide open, but I was in for some surprises. Within 24 hours I had to call the police to report her disappearance. They found her a few blocks away, chatting with a workman in his truck. But a pledge was a pledge: no criticism, no reprimands. When we registered her at the high school in September, we were told she must take grade ten again. Many an evening when the small children were asleep and Rai wasn't yet home from work, I sat with Brenda, usually on the floor in the kitchen, working on her assignments. I felt hurt that she could dump her belongings in the front hall after school and leave again without saying where she was going or when she would be home. I was chagrined when she invaded my bathroom and helped herself to my lipsticks, and I couldn't believe how dishevelled she left her beautiful bedroom. Had I been wiser about teenagers, I would have known that these annoyances were only minor infringements of rules that should have been in place. Subtler and longer-lived upsets that I was unaware of then, came out of Brenda's unfriendly treatment of Heather whom I allowed to be pushed out of her prime position in our family. I believe now that Brenda must have been jealous that "lucky little Heather had always had a dad and a mum." Still subtler and more threatening to me, was Brenda's determination to take over our new baby. "Give him to me. I'll change him," or "I'll take him for a walk," or "You go with Dad, I can look after Roger." She later told me the only thing she knew about her birth mother was that she had been a nurse. I tried to be generous, but I must admit the first few years with Brenda were difficult for me, though probably no more so than for most parents of teenagers. (It's a very different scene today. Bren and I are fast friends.)

Verity and Roger

CHAPTER 9

Thomson and Coltart.

In the 1950s it was common knowledge to many Canadians that Roy Thomson, the son of a Toronto barber, was a self-made man. Born in 1894, he had worked his way through business college by the time World War I began. When he attempted to enlist in the army, he was rejected because of poor eyesight (he had worn thick glasses since grade school). He then tried farming in Manitoba, but by 1919 he had returned to Toronto where he acquired the northern Ontario agency for De Forest Crosley Radios. However, it was tough selling radios where there were no radio stations, and as a result he decided to establish one himself. His first station, CFCH North Bay, went on the air in March 1930, followed by CKJB Timmins in 1932 and CJKL Kirkland Lake in 1933. It was downstairs in the building that housed CKJB that Thomson lucked into the piece of equipment that would start his newspaper empire–a printing press from the town's recently defunct paper. Within a year he was publishing his own newspaper, "The Press," and from this beginning he made a mighty fortune during the Depression years by buying poorly managed and struggling newspapers for minimum cash, cutting the deadwood, placing ads on the front page and instructing the editor to print the politically popular view.

*Rai, Roy Thomson, Lady Stephens, Verity,
and Sir Edward Stephens*

Director of Programmes, Scottish Television

Whenever possible, if a small town had two papers, he bought them both and closed one down. But he didn't abandon radio. In fact, toward the end of the 1930s he entered into partnership with newspaperman Rupert Davies to put two more stations on the air–CHEX Peterborough in1942 and CKWS Kingston in 1943. Both stations were granted television licences in 1954.

In 1952 Thomson took a run at politics as the Conservative candidate for York Centre but was soundly defeated. This setback in his search for more clout in Canada as well as the death of his wife from cancer the previous year left him, at age 59, very much alone and very frustrated in his upward climb. Then, having learned that a majority share in The Scotsman newspaper empire was for sale, he decided to leave Canada and make a new life for himself in Britain. He was persuaded to return to Canada in 1953 to take one more run at a seat in Parliament but was again defeated. Leaving Canada behind for good, he opened an office in Edinburgh where he had previously bought the upper half of an old house in which he planned to live for part of each year. A man with amazing initiative and determined single mindedness, Roy Thomson now avoided all pleasurable activity while he built his British newspaper empire. He loved to boast about his business successes; his greatest pleasure, he told everyone, came from reading balance sheets, even though he had to squint at them through his huge, thick lenses.

After the New York dinner party with Vic George where Rai and I learned all this about Thomson, Rai took Vic's advice and mailed off the job application we had worked out together. "Wouldn't it be great to live in Edinburgh?" I enthused. "Such a beautiful city!" I was familiar with it from my early teen years when I had been sent for dance training in London then off to Scotland for my holidays.

Thomson's letter, almost by return mail, invited Rai to accept the position of director of programmes for Scotland's first privately owned television station. "I expect to have the licence momentarily," he wrote. At the same time he offered Rai the challenging job of turning his newest acquisition, the Theatre Royal in Glasgow, into an   ultra-modern television facility. He also said that if Rai were interested, they could meet right away in New York. It certainly seemed as though positive thinking had worked. Our spirits soared.

Together Rai and I met Roy Thomson for the first time over lunch at the fashionable Harwin Club where Thomson "sort of" introduced us to an elderly Scottish couple, Sir Edward and Lady Stevenson, two of his Scottish trustees, investors in his bid for the Scottish television licence. I knew the Stevensons must be rich and/or very influential (I'd heard that Sir Edward was the Queen's Purse Bearer) but to me they seemed to be just dear, bumbly people who had accompanied Thomson to see what commercial television was like in the US. Although essentially mannerless, Thomson was perfectly comfortable in this snooty club. Back then I had no clue how rich he was and how much clout he had, and I didn't realize until much later that he and the Stevensons had flown all the way from Edinburgh just for this meeting. Rotund and open-faced, Thomson grinned while he searched our faces through his honest-to-goodness coke-bottle-bottomed spectacles. After he happily answered Rai's queries about the position of programme director, I heard Rai ask him what he wanted from his new television.

"Fun!" he said. "I have all the money I need. All I want out of this venture is to build the best station and produce the best shows possible." Cheerful and palsy-walsy, Thomson used first names right from that New York beginning, and he seemed almost childlike in his excitement about the strong possibility of winning the Scottish television licence–there were no other contenders– and having Rai as his programme director. That day around the table, he and Rai discussed the future we would all share in Scotland, and he welcomed Rai's ideas with great enthusiasm. He said that he and Rai would always work closely together and assured him, "You will always have direct communication with me. There will be no one looking over your shoulder."

But that was not quite so. Thomson Enterprises had recently acquired a managing director whom Thomson had failed to mention. Disguised as a genial Scot, Jim Coltart was the next

112

Thomson representative to visit Rai in New York, and we were astonished that he came to our house in New Rochelle rather than expecting us to go to the city as we had been required to do for Thomson a few weeks earlier. Rai drove to the train station to collect Coltart, while I tidied the living room and laid out afternoon tea on a silver tray. The two men came into our house chatting cheerily, and my first impression was of a small man, dark-haired and bespectacled with pale skin and sharp features. A starched white collar framed his little face. To me he looked like a mortician.

As soon as we had settled down to tea, however, Coltart waxed charmingly enthusiastic about Rai's accomplishments, the lucky coincidence of his availability and keenness to move (once his CBS contract ended) to Scotland. We were quite taken with him. The timing, Coltart said, was perfect since Thomson's plan couldn't proceed for at least a year. Then he explained that all things were coming together as planned and were part of the world's great movement toward Moral Rearmament which he explained was a new name for the Oxford Group. Coltart followed this by saying that "he had been sent" to tell Rai that he was "one of the chosen." This probably frightened Rai, but for me it rang bells I hadn't heard since 1932.

During the Great Depression, many normally emotionally secure people, including my parents and my uncle Dick–caught in the uncertainty of the times–had joined the Oxford Movement, a vigorous modern Christian revivalist program founded in 1922 by Frank Buchan. After winning influential converts at Oxford University, the movement had become centred there, hence the name. Members "lived by faith guided by God's will and moral absolutes." And though it did not appeal exclusively to the influential and wealthy, it is a fact that few converts came from the working classes. But it was also, as I recalled it, a way of teaching about God's greatness that made sinners out of the most upright citizens and reduced to pulp those spoiled rotten folk like my parents who actually had food on their tables. In 1931 after my Dad, an unemployed former WW I army engineering officer, had settled us in a primitive cabin at

Gibsons Landing while he hunted for work in Vancouver, Mum had taken my brother Malcolm and me (ages 9 and 11) to Oxford Group lectures held in a cold hall full of hungry people. Soon my brother and I took to asking the Almighty for guidance and made note of our purified thoughts in our little black books. I remained haunted by the dour atmosphere of those Gibson's Landing years. The movement lost followers during the war because of the alleged Nazi sympathizers in its ranks but gained ground again after the war when these allegations were more or less disproved and its name changed to Moral Rearmament.

All this seemed a world away for Rai and me until Coltart, discussing the early group activities in Vancouver, used my uncle's name. Suddenly I was listening to this intense and creepy character with no little regurgitation of guilt. Might there be some positive value in this moral rearmament idea? When Coltart turned his attention back to Rai, he announced that the new television station was part of the world's great movement toward Moral Rearmament. Rai listened politely and then, under pressure from Coltart, even tentatively agreed to attend a Moral Rearmament conference at Trois-Rivieres the following year. It was only after returning Coltart to the railway station that Rai expressed the anxiety and fear he was feeling. He was deeply concerned at the prospect of working with Coltart and he wasn't pleased that Coltart had swayed me. However, as it became obvious during the ensuing months that by some curse or spell Jim Coltart held Roy Thomson enthralled, Rai agreed that it would be worth humouring him to assure the job in Scotland.

What Rai and I didn't know was that the job was anything but secure at that point. In the summer of 1955 an independent network (ITV) in the UK was just in its final planning stages, and over the next two years all the companies that were launched in England to give television coverage to London, the Midlands and the North took a financial beating. Thus, when Roy Thomson tried to enlist investors in his bid for a licence to open an independent station in Scotland, he was turned down; nobody wanted to put money into another loser. Fortunately, in the end this situation worked to his advantage because no one else wanted the Scottish licence–for exactly the same reason.

Meanwhile, to complete the final year of his CBS contract Rai produced *The Celebrity Show* and directed a number of commercial series.

By the time Coltart made contact again in August 1956, our Westchester house had been sold along with most of its contents, I had packed the bare necessities to keep Rai comfortable for the next six months in a Manhattan apartment, and taken the children to the west coast. I was at Mum's house in West Vancouver when I received a letter from him, pages and pages of it filled with frustration and fury as he described a weekend journey by chartered plane from Harvard University to Trois-Rivieres, Quebec, at Coltart's behest. With a promise that the same plane would return him to New York in time to keep his next television commitment, Rai had attended the conference there on Moral Rearmament. He wrote that the setting was beautiful, that he'd been given a tour of impressive buildings made from lumber donated from local forests and "labour given for love," sort of thing but he was upset to see young women in drab clothing without makeup stand up in meetings to admit their faults and ask to be "changed." The conference organizers, Rai wrote, had treated him as a special guest until he refused without apology to testify to gathered crowds how he had "seen the light and been changed." Then, when he most needed it, the promised plane was no longer available. With great difficulty, at high cost, and aware that he must already be in Coltart's black book, in the nick of time Rai found someone who would fly him out.

I knew that Rai had negative feelings about religion in any guise, and I also knew he had been willing to attend the conference only to humour Coltart, but I hadn't dreamed the encounter would be so compromising. In another letter Rai told of his disappointment that Thomson expected us to live in Glasgow, not in Edinburgh as we had hoped.

Nor was the atmosphere happy in Mum's small house. I should never have expected her to put up with us for six months. All

115

three children had problems. Brenda, who was simply being a thoughtless teenager, was trying without much luck to finish grade eleven in a new school, and Heather was being taken by her classmates as a smarty from New York. Roger, a year and a half, was in the middle between Mum who believed he should be picked up and held whenever the noisy Pacific Great Eastern train went by and me who insisted he would soon get over crying if she'd leave him in his play-pen. By the time Rai arrived on December 27, 1957, to spend a few peaceful days at Mum's house before flying to Scotland, every joint in me ached and I had taken to my bed in Mum's basement suite. Then on the day Canadian Pacific confirmed our seats on one of its earliest flights over the Pole to Amsterdam, we learned the airline wouldn't confirm the last part of our journey to Scotland (the bit between Amsterdam and Prestwick International) because that was the beginning of a New York flight. To add to the tension, that was the day I dared criticize Rai's new, glaringly red waistcoat, which he chose to wear over his yellow sweater!

The polar flight was horrendous. All three kids were sick but Heather and Roger managed to up-chuck all over me. Thanks to the stewardess, who lent me her shirt while she washed mine, we arrived sweet-smelling in Greenland where the plane had to put down because of a very low ceiling. Amsterdam was another horror. For the entire four hours of the stopover I followed Roger at the run, attached to him by his harness, in, around and out of every shop and restaurant in the airport. The girls stayed with their father from whom I had grabbed the wad of free drink tickets provided by the airline; no way was he going to escape into a bar! When at last we boarded a Royal Dutch aircraft at 10 pm, we flew that lap in luxury. Their first class seats became beds, and Roger fell asleep face down on my stomach for the hour or so before landing in deep fog at Prestwick on January 4, 1958.

There we were met by a Thomson representative, Jack Hardy, a small, dark, bespectacled chap with a broad and friendly Scots accent. It was a relief to learn that Roy Thomson was in Toronto and wouldn't be back for several weeks. This,

Hardy assured us, would leave "gude time ferr me tae find y' a hoose." The night was cold and the foggy air almost too thick to breathe. Regaling us mostly with the Suez crisis, with which we were unfamiliar, he drove us 20 or 30 miles through the foggy night–I don't know how he navigated with Roger now wide awake and screaming hysterically–to the Belhaven, a decrepit residential hotel on Glasgow's Great Western Road.

Hardy helped us carry our luggage into a dimly lit foyer and introduced us to the management, who then introduced us to Avril Byrne, a nursery nurse my Aunt Bea Abercrombie had arranged to have waiting for us. My mother's youngest sister, Beatrice, quite recently reunited with her Scottish husband John, now lived in Inellen, a village near Dunoon.

Having promised to see us in the morning, Hardy wished us a comfortable sleep and departed. Avril held her arms out to carry Roger who didn't, thank heaven, resist as we followed a maid up a stairway to our two rooms on the second floor. She explained that the bedroom where she and Roger were to sleep was another flight up and that she had already put shillings into the gas metres and lighted the fires to warm our rooms, then she came in to show us how to operate the metres. I quickly located the bag of immediate baby needs and followed Avril up to see the room they would inhabit, minuscule quarters with the barest furnishings including a crib and a cot. I felt sorry for them both but was too tired to even think of complaining. Avril had spread a towel on her cot for changing the baby and said she could "manage the wee boy just finely, Mrs. Purdy. Jest you huv a gude rest the noo." Her voice had the burr but was soft and lovely. Too late at night to thank dear Aunt Bea for finding Avril. I reminded myself to make the call next morning.

The Bellhaven Hotel looks south across tram tracks on that part of the Great Western Road which passes on its way to the heart of Glasgow through the nose-in-air district of Kelvinside. Grand as all this may sound, in spite of its name in large gold letters across the front of four identical entrances, the ancient Bellhaven was no different from any other row-housing in the city where each of the eight or ten houses jammed together in a block has a separate entrance, lobby and staircases. The only differences between the Bellhaven Hotel and the adjacent private houses were that in the hotel each landing ran the full width of the four houses which comprised it and that gas fireplaces had replaced coal fireplaces. Looking at it from Great Western Road, the whole street seemed symmetrically even and black–coal-smoke black.

Next morning, after a few hours of groggy tossing, I left our bed before Rai stirred. The shilling's worth of gas long gone, both chill and fog greeted me within the room. No dressing gown visible, I pulled on my camel-hair coat, tiptoed out of the room and climbed the stairs to Avril's quarters. To my delight, she and Roger were snuggled in her bed giggling over some game they were playing. "Mum-ee," he squeaked but he didn't cry and Avril, wisely I thought, stayed where she was. "We're jest fyne, Mrs. Purdy, M'um. Don't ye be wurryin' aboot the likes uv us," she said quietly, "but would ye mind hangin' the nappies t'dry on yer fire screen?" I made my exit, taking with me the stack of diapers already washed and neatly folded, happy that Avril was obviously in charge.

Fog was everywhere. Even though I had not opened our bedroom windows, fog in its greyness had seeped through the ill-fitting frames. Rai awoke when my metre-shilling dropped, the gas came on and the fog turned pink. "Morning, sweetie," he said cheerily. "How's everyone?" Holding my wet laundry aside, I leant to kiss him. "Hi, love. I haven't looked in on the girls yet, but this nanny, Avril, we've acquired is a blessing. She has Roger charmed, she's been up and washed his diapers, and they've both been downstairs to breakfast already!" Although we could no longer see the gas flame in our room, the overly large, metal-framed fire-screen made a fine clothes line, and steam soon rose to join the fog. I threw off my coat and crawled back into bed, tucking soft old woollen blankets around the two of us.

"We don't have to get up just yet, do we?" Rai asked. "What day is it, anyway?"

During the next few days (I did remember to thank Bea for

118

finding Avril for us) the fog, quite customary in Glasgow in January, was as heavy in the daytime as at night. Sometimes it was so thick that it made a film between the door and the coal fire burning at the far side of the sitting room. There was no point in going outside to look around, so while Rai sorted out stacks of television material he had brought for Thomson, the rest of us investigated the various public rooms of the antiquated hotel. We joined Rai for meals in the dreary dining room where we sat among the old folk who were obviously permanent residents. Rai said he couldn't abide these "biddies" who "washed their food down with tea and farted with total abandon."

From the beginning, Jack Hardy was a real friend. Cheerful, patient and a hundred percent honest, he took us on as his charges. When on the third morning the fog was somewhat less dense, our whole family was dressed and breakfasted by the time he arrived to take us to see a particular property that he'd said was too good to miss. The place had been built by a wealthy baker who had attended the last International Edinburgh Exposition before WW II. While there, he had bought enough16-inch boards of western Canadian cedar to panel his main hall. During the war the Royal Navy had commandeered his home and still owned it but, no longer requiring it for an officers' mess, had put it up for rent. As Hardy drove us westward along the River Clyde toward the town of Helensburgh, he described this home he had found for us as an unusual abode built of sandstone blocks which supported a real thatched roof and boasted a spectacular view of Faslane, the naval dockyard on the Gare Loch. We were fascinated to learn that in this short, salt-water inlet running inland from the Clyde estuary and superbly hidden by hills, there lay one of His Majesty's battleships aboard which Roosevelt, Chamberlain and Stalin had met.

Just past Helensburgh the fog lifted. We turned north and saw, immediately on our left, that the loch had widened and appeared like a child's pond full of gigantic toys; in reality they were a mothballed fleet of warships and included the magnificent King George V. I found this an extraordinary sight but difficult to bring into proportion with the insignificant looking trees and shrubs on the loch side. To me, it seemed very sad. These ships that had saved the nation had been left here to rust away.

On our right, uncut hay lay flattened in fields surrounding what appeared to be a pale castle with small turrets and tall windows. To reach it, Hardy left the shore-road and circled up a long driveway, passed under a stone archway beside the house and turned into a courtyard where he parked. Roger had been very good sitting quietly on Avril's knee, and once we alighted, Avril steered her charge toward some overgrown shrubbery and the sound of chickens further up the hill. They were soon lost to sight. With Heather and Brenda on our heels, Rai and I followed Hardy toward a heavy, round-topped, metal-studded door set in curves of sandstone. To unlock it, he produced an enormous key. As it opened, he stood back for us to enjoy the two-storeyed, cedar-panelled entrance hall he'd told us about. With much gasping and chattering Brenda and Heather pushed past us to make their discoveries. Stepping inside, I saw a copper-hooded corner fireplace with a wide sandstone chimney rising to the ceiling. Sandstone archways opened into reception rooms. The whole place was flooded with light from windows in the upper part of the turret which surrounded the circular staircase. Our voices echoed in the empty rooms and our feet clattered as we crossed a shining wood floor and passed under an archway. Another huge fireplace, this time sandstone, took up most of the north wall of what I assumed was the living room. But under a row of large, lead-paned windows looking east were two enormous hot-water radiators. Across the room to the west, two wide steps took us down to the dining room which also had radiators under its windows. "Do you mean this place is centrally heated?" I asked Hardy. "Is there a basement?"

"No' exactly. A gas heater'll be oot there 'neath the road." He pointed beyond the building. What, I wondered, did he mean? Rai and I kept exchanging glances and muttering, "What a view! How could we be so lucky? Can we afford it? Where's the kitchen? What's upstairs? Only two bedrooms? But there's

120

that nook off the staircase. Only one bathroom? But where is the kitchen?" Now came the shock. *Servant's quarters* no less! And behind the green baize door we'd seen in the entrance hall, we found another all-but-empty chamber containing two horse-troughs with taps and a great black gas-range. A board, rather like a picture-rail with many hooks on it, ran along two inside walls. A second room, a pantry I supposed, had a door leading back into the dining room. How could anyone build such a place in this day and age? Still, we both loved it and decided on the spot to become the new tenants.

Fortunately, our moving and temporary dwelling expenses were being paid for by Thomson since we couldn't occupy the castle right away. The ship carrying Rai's 1946 Packard and the crate holding other belongings such as linens and a dining table we had recently acquired in New York hadn't arrived at the Glasgow dockyard. Having lived in Vancouver for six months after packing the stuff away, I couldn't remember exactly what else should be in the crate other than clothing and kitchenware. When our belongings did arrive, we discovered that our linens, all but one pink pillow slip, had been filched, but we had gained a dead-beat sofa and a perambulator which were not ours. All four new white-wall tires that Rai had put on the Packard before shipping it had been replaced with duds, but it took several scary blow-outs to bring that theft to our attention!

However, when we did move in, the generous bedroom close to the bathroom with its sunken tub proved to be made for Rai and me. Roger 's crib fit nicely into the girl's room and Avril managed cheerfully in the nook off the staircase. Despite a hectic move and a great lack of furnishings–no chairs at all and only basic kitchen china–during the second week at Faslane I put on a formal paper-cup, stand-up, finger-food lunch party so as to meet the women who lived on the farms around us. Jack Hardy had made a list of neighbours for me to contact as soon as we had a telephone. Their voices sounded reserved and "terribly proper," but they all turned up, most of them wearing gloves. Having decided to behave with western nonchalance, I

121

memorised all their names, first as well as last, and introduced them to each other saying "I'm Verity Purdy, this is Mrs. McCallum who's name is Irene. Do you know Mrs.Graham? Her name is Janet." The trick worked and everyone used first names, even calling me Verity, sat on the stairs as though they did it every day, enjoyed my well-spiked punch in kitchen glasses, ate hungrily and laughed at or with me. I didn't care which. When it came time to leave, they trooped upstairs to fetch their winter coats and, returning gloves in hand, said, almost to a woman, "Thank you so much, Mrs. Purdy. I had such a nice time."

We Purdys were, of course, oddities for that neighbourhood, different from the local folk in so many ways. I'd say Rai had, if anything, an eastern Canadian accent, and it hadn't changed much in seven New York years. Brenda's was the same. I had lost a bit of my Brit affectation since my dance training days in London. Heather, however, spoke almost pure Yank, but she was at a flexible age with an obviously musical ear, and within a month after she began attending the Gare Loch Head School, I couldn't understand a word she said. Because of the local pronunciation of vowels she found spelling frustrating and got poor marks, and "Hi Ho, Silver" didn't mean a thing to the Scottish children. I didn't realize then how unhappy she was at school.

Meanwhile, I was anxious to get Brenda into a high school so that she might make friends with the local girls. The only trouble was that we couldn't find one where her average scholastic achievements were acceptable. That was all right with Bren since she would rather go to nursing school. But there again it was difficult because she was already eighteen and Scottish nursing students began training at sixteen. Before very long, however, Rai found a friend who helped him solve Bren's difficulty.

We felt blessed to have landed in such a romantic and friendly spot. But much as we loved our castle at Faslane, there were problems. The central heating worked well once we found out where and how to light it–drop through a trap door in the kitchen, navigate an underground passageway with flashlight, pull out a huge arm from a furnace located under the driveway,

122

turn on and light the twenty-odd gas jets and return the arm. The resulting boom was only the gas going on full. We relished the heat until it began to draw moisture out of the sandstone. Then the hearth became a puddle and the carved sandstone above the windows dripped buckets for weeks. By the time the place was dried out we had a gas bill of forty pounds for January alone. By February we knew we couldn't afford to continue in this way and tried lighting fires. We might have burned the place down if a local person, seeing smoke from our chimneys, hadn't told us that the fireplaces were only for show. Indeed, we climbed into the attic and saw that the unfinished chimney flues passed beside blackened roof beams, charred by the efforts of other tenants trying to do the same thing. We bundled up well and hoped for an early spring. But to add to our discomfort, there were mice. One of them got into the sunken bath and couldn't get back up its slippery slope. Bren, always kind to animals, said, "You don't need a trap. I'll get him and put him outside." The thankless beast bit her. How long had the place been empty, we wondered?

Accustomed as he had become to commuting to and from work in the US, Rai was nonplussed when he discovered how few trains ran from Helensburgh, the nearest village, to Glasgow. Their schedule was of no use to him, and with fuel rationing still in effect, the aging Packard Rai had shipped from New York couldn't go very far. At Hardy's suggestion, Rai bought an old Riley which provided a second ration card. He could now drive into Glasgow when he wished. If the sky was clear and he chose to use the Packard, he enjoyed the disbelief of the passers by who would stop to watch him manoeuvre, thanks to American power steering, into what seemed to them a ridiculously small parking space. But winter driving wasn't too pleasant. Depressingly often, fog took the fun out of speeding in the old Riley.

We became used to dark skies over Glasgow and to the surrounding countryside being full of wetness. Although heavy rain was rare, the grass never dried and soot-filled drops hung from every branch and hydro wire. In no time, my camel-hair coat became unwearable. I quickly learned why tweeds, seen on close inspection to be woven in an unbelievable mixture of colours, can be worn in all weather and don't show the dirt. (All three primary colours mixed together make black!) As a going-away present, Mum had paid to have a suit made for me by Island Weavers who had an outlet in West Vancouver at that time. The tweed was a fine navy-blue-and-white hounds-tooth and the fitted jacket had a velvet collar, navy-blue, of course. I thought it was very smart and wore it now in Scotland whenever I wanted to look well dressed. As the result, it soon needed to be cleaned. On the advice of my neighbour, I visited a low stone building on a grassy field along the way to Helensburgh. Inside the ever-open door, a small sign said "Laundering and Dry Cleaning" There I left my suit. A week later, when I returned to pick it up, the lady displayed it on a hanger. It looked to me as though it had been hung out-of-doors in a rain storm. She took it off the hanger and proceeded to fold and wrap it in brown paper. My mouth hung open as I watched her tie the bundle tightly with string. Perhaps Harris tweed can take that sort of treatment, but I felt sure mine couldn't. I swore to myself I wouldn't go there again. However, glancing through an open door at the back of the shop, (wind whistled right through) I spied something mighty interesting. Row upon row of glass jars, about eighteen inches in height and as broad as beer barrels, sat in deep grass. Instantly I was reminded of a lamp I had seen in an elegant home in Canada. When I asked if I might take a closer look, the woman explained that these bottles had once held bleach for the laundry. Most were clear glass, a few were golden, others pale green, but the one that had caught my eye was dark green and stood taller than the rest with a slender neck. I asked if I could buy one.

"Weel," she said, "I'll be havin' tae ask t'mon in charge."

"Would you, please, and ask how much it might be?"

"Yus Mum," she said, "A'll dae tha fur ye."

"I'd really like to have that tall green one," I said, pointing to it as I walked away with my bundled-up suit. The following day Rai and I went into Glasgow and, when we returned home, there beside our door sat the bleach jar with straw packed around it in an elegant metal basket. Next time we passed by the cleaner's shop, I popped in to ask what we owed for the jar. "Ut's a wee gift," said the lady. Not long after, a reliable friend pointed out to us that this particularly handsome gift of glass had air bubbles, obvious signs of having been hand blown, and that its colour and shape suggested it had likely existed for around two hundred years. To our delight, this exciting bit of historic data was later confirmed by the owner of an antique shop. I almost forgave the lady in the cleaner's shop for the hand-me-down appearance of my suit.

Theatre Royale

CHAPTER 10

Refurbishing the Theatre Royal

The Theatre Royal on Hope Street in Glasgow had been the venue for grand opera since its opening in the early1880s, but by the1950s both the theatre and a sizeable piece of land beside it had been put up for sale. When in 1957 Roy Thomson began pursuing the Scottish Television (STV) licence to broadcast, he purchased both properties to house his television station, promising to maintain the theatre's original appearance on the outside and change the inside as little as possible.

Other than updating the plumbing and exchanging the whole mezzanine floor for generous control booths, the interior structure did not need much change, but getting the place clean was a major task. Several generations of soot had to be removed from the ornate proscenium arch and the sculpted gold trim on the private boxes. The fine ceiling paintings, in keeping in their day with the rich oriental carpeting in the foyer, along corridors and on stairs (so filthy now as to render the pattern invisible), needed a lot of scrubbing.

Though it suited Thomson's frugal side to keep the antiquated seating, additions such as a new lighting grid and camera-ramps couldn't be avoided. Because he had told Rai he wanted to be informed about the most modern lighting systems and camera hook-ups available, he was very pleased that Rai had already procured for him a copy of plans for a New York studio which CBS-TV had not yet built. Thomson gave the plans to the London building contractor he had already hired and made Rai responsible for choosing the sound and lighting equipment.

Construction began right away. Once the wheels began turning, no transformation could have moved more swiftly. In less than eight months the old theatre, though still looking the same from the outside, became a modern broadcast facility. Everything beyond the public view was other-world-ish. While I only had the vaguest notion about this part of the transformation, I knew that administrative offices took up most of what had been "the gods" gallery and that excavation two floors deep beneath the entire building had made space for *telecine* and a labyrinth of broadcast apparatus and offices.

Rai took me along on many of his early visits to the Theatre Royal while it was under renovation. His mandate to create the entire programming for this new station was his dream realized, and I was amazed to learn how completely at home he was with the mechanics of it all. He knew how many cameras he needed on the kinds of shows that would get an audience. He knew how to budget a show and how to schedule rehearsals. He could train the lighting men and sound operators, he could search out the talent, dream up the shows and slot them at appropriate hours. It was an extraordinarily complicated assignment for one man, but I never saw him more invigorated.

Roy Thomson was often at the theatre in those early days and I gradually got the feel of his presence, rather like that of a jolly giant. He treated me as a show person and Rai's equal, and I thought of him as Rai did, a good friend. Rai asked me, "Do you recall what he said in New York when I asked him, "What do you really want?" And he answered, "I want FUN and the best programming in Britain."' To Rai, this challenge was the most fun he could possibly imagine.

But "fun" for Rai and "fun" for Thomson were two different things. In fact, the most prominent thing about Roy Thomson

128

(apart from his generous waistline) was his embarrassing honesty about his plans to make a lot of money out of Scottish Television. He also spoke about his aspirations to sit in the House of Lords; a mere baronetcy would not satisfy him, he said, perhaps because Beaverbrook (his friendly Canadian competitor on Fleet Street) already had one. I remember hearing Roy speak of his close relationship with the royal family (due, I was later told, to the magnitude of his investment in North Sea oil), and I recall him giggling as he explained just how *bottom-pinchingly* familiar he was with Princess Margaret. So it did rather surprise me that although he bragged about the people he knew and the money he had made, he always wore the same shiny-with-age shabby suit. Ultimately it became clear that he wore it deliberately, used the underground to go and come from his London office, and was driven about by his "man" Gunter in an ancient Daimler with a roof that leaked (not on Thomson but on Gunter) in order to teach his Scotsman staff frugality. At the time I didn't recognize these pinch-penny tactics as part of his power trip, but while I continued to think that he appreciated Rai's talents, as time went on my respect for him dwindled. Perhaps it had something to do with having spent so many of my youthful years among people who, rich or poor, never ever talked about money. It simply wasn't done.

Meanwhile, free to employ his own office staff and choose his own writers and announcers, Rai felt sure he had Thomson's full attention and support and believed they were on the same track. Scottish Jack Webster, recently returned to his native land from Canada (where as a radio personality he had become known as the "Oatmeal Savage"), came in as head of news, John Grierson, the Scottish creator of the National Film Board of Canada, was hired as head of documentaries, and the Scottish author John Watson became head of writing. Then one evening Rai came home full of excitement to tell me about a character who had appeared in his office to ask for a position as a writer. This man had come with lots of material for Rai to read, but his great line of chatter and his wonderfully zany face were so appealing

129

Rai had offered him a job on the spot as host on a five-a-week noontime comedy show to be called *The One O'clock Gang*. Larry Marshall, with his delicious Scottish burr, beak of a nose and riveting brown eyes–one of which looked elsewhere–was to become a personal overnight hit and gain a huge following.

But Rai did have difficulty with Thomson's attitude about payroll. All salaries, Thomson insisted, must be minimal, so while fully trained union cameramen were available in London, he refused to pay union technician salaries. His employees were expected to learn the business as they went along, and Russell Galbraith (The Scotsman, September 8, 2001), quoted him as saying, "Anyone who is underemployed in one job [would assist] his mate in another. . . . Press photographers learned to work the big cameras, radio mechanics handled cables, repertory actors announced news." But not for long. Ultimately the union got its way, though not before Rai had wasted a lot of time teaching television technique and jargon to a collection of still photographers. The unions also forced Thomson to hire more staff, causing him to rage, "It can't take three Britons to do the work of one American!" However, in spite of his tight-fistedness, everything moved ahead so well that, before summer arrived, he decided to begin construction of a second studio on the property next to the Theatre Royal. A modern structure built from scratch, it was designed according to the plans Rai had acquired at CBS.

Ironically, although Thompson had begun to pursue a TV license during 1955, it was not until September 15, 1958, almost five months after Rai began working for STV–that Thomson actually received his licence to operate a television station in Scotland. He had never been worried about not receiving it as in the end no one else had wanted it. By this time every other station in the Independent Television Network was on the financial ropes, and the same fate was expected for STV. Thomson, on receiving word that he had been awarded the contract, told newsmen that he had no studio, no artists, no announcers, no producers, no technicians, no musicians, and no programmes. What he did have, he said gleefully, was

130

Roy Thomson

a "contract." This was, of course, all patently untrue, but it wouldn't have been good business to let it be known that he had progressed so far without a mandate to broadcast. Now, however, he could have so much more fun studying his balance sheets.

While all this proceeded, I enjoyed a summer on the Gare Loch. Having a nanny gave me time to look around for furniture and to visit the site of STV. It was on one of these visits while Thomson was still personally involved that Rai brought up the subject of putting dancers on staff. Thomson liked the idea and agreed that the big old greenroom, up several flights backstage, would make a good studio where I could teach dance (without pay, of course) and bring along a well-matched line of girls for musical shows. I wouldn't be the only choreographer but my theatrical experience could be of value.

Thus, I was with Rai one day when he auditioned a group of Scottish lads and lassies who, accompanied by a single piper, performed for us on the big theatre stage. The men, who wore kilts, had the laces of their dancing slippers crisscrossed up their tartan knee-socks to tie just under the knee, and they tip-toed about self-consciously. The women wore ill-fitting white dresses which were uneven in length as were their tartan sashes. Once they had all walked slowly into place on the stage, the piper blew air into his pig-skin bag so that it droned and squawked until he was ready to play the single long note that was the signal for the gentlemen's solemn bows to the ladies, who then curtseyed to the men. All this was done without a single smile. The performance which followed was orderly but serious and slow. Under his breath Rai said, "If this is the best the Royal Scottish Dance Society can produce, you can teach our own dancers the steps and get some excitement into it. For starters, the men will wear brogues, and who needs all that bowing and scraping?" Of course, I was delighted that this challenge fell into my lap as I knew Rai planned to feature Scottish reels in the opening show.

Documentaries and remotes were already in his plan, and one of the first people he interviewed about a documentary was the matron at Glasgow's Hospital for Sick Children. This kindly woman was delighted to consider making the hospital and the children available for the production of a show sometime in the coming months. As they talked, it dawned on Rai that this new connection might also solve a problem that worried us, that is, what to do for Brenda. He must have charmed the dear lady because she agreed to accept Brenda for training in spite of her age, and within weeks our girl was in residence at the hospital. Almost at the same time, I lost Avril, our nanny, whose mother had become ill, and for a short while I really enjoyed having the children to myself, though I knew I'd have to have help once I started teaching.

Our problems concerning Heather's schooling were resolved after we came to know author Patrick Fitzgerald O'Connor. He had made his living as a freelance newspaper columnist, mostly for the Scotsman, before Roy Thomson had bought that paper, and it was Thomson who introduced him to Rai, hoping he would take him on as head writer. Rai, however, had already hired John Watson for that job, but he found O'Connor's flamboyant carriage and personality so intriguing that, having given me a quick call to get my okay, he invited the man, his wife and child, to visit us at Faslane. The meeting of our families was one of those rare occasions when everyone seemed to have known each other forever. Lightly built but wiry, his crisp grey hair theatrically cut, Patrick O'Connor wore his camel-hair coat like a cloak, never putting his arms into the sleeves. His lovely wife was Janet, a woman of my age who had experienced the most extreme exigencies of life without losing any of her softness and charm. Their only child, Fiona, and our Heather, although opposite in character, liked each other at once and, after Janet asked our daughter where she went to school, all three O'Connors immediately decided that a place for Heather must soon be found at Westbourne School for Girls in Glasgow where Fiona was enrolled as a weekly boarder.

Perhaps Janet O'Connor had money, though it soon became obvious that her husband had none. By this time "Sharko," Patrick O'Connor's wildly successful book about his own

Purdy family in Scotland

Rai, Heather, Roger, Brenda and Verity

and Janet's shark-hunting adventures from the bleak Isle of Coll in the North Sea (until shipwrecked mere weeks before Fiona's birth), no longer brought in pots of money. He had lately become better known for vivid storytelling while consuming other peoples' whisky. His appointment to Scottish Television would come later, for although he didn't write show material, he was a man of many talents whose understanding of promotion and publicity would make him invaluable.

After we had known the O'Connors for a very short time, Fiona invited Heather to spend a weekend in their castle at Strath 'Laughlin. Since Patrick would collect his daughter from Westbourne School on Friday, he said we should drop Heather off there so that she could go home with them. The following Sunday, Rai and I with three-year-old Roger found our way as far as Strachur where we asked directions to Castle 'Laughlin to collect our daughter, and it was here the Purdys fell in love with Scottish country life. The O'Connors did, indeed, live in a castle, but only in part of it. The MacLaughlin family still owned magnificent Castle 'Laughlin (as well as the picturesque ruin of an even older castle on a vast property known as Strath 'Laughlin), but they lived in a few dark rooms on the ground floor at the back of the edifice. On its western face a great staircase led to the main entrance and to a suite of rooms on the first floor which the O'Connors rented for next-to-nothing, according to Patrick. From their windows we looked out that Sunday over grazing land and across Loch Fyne to rolling hills. Never mind that the castle leaked and the wind came in around the window frames, the drawing room fireplace blazed with huge logs and each bedroom, they told us, had a coal fireplace. While Fiona and Heather went for a climb in the old ruin, Janet adopted Roger so that Patrick could drive Rai and me in his rattling sports car about a mile further down the loch to show us the possible weekend retreat he'd been talking to Rai about. I loved it at first glance. Without even peeking inside, I knew the cottage was perfect, though I doubted Rai would want such an obviously rundown and shabby property. When he, too, showed real interest, I dared to hope. We returned to Janet's high tea (a jolly good meal with boiled eggs and hot scones) at Castle 'Laughlin where she invited us to spend the night. Rai, however, said we should get back because he had an early start in the morning, but as we retraced our route to Glasgow, we were full of excitement. We had posed two important questions to Patrick: one, would he ask the owner of the two-acre shepherd's croft down the way what he wanted for it, and two, would he follow up on the suggestion there might be a place for Heather at Westbourne School for Girls? Within a few weeks, thanks to Patrick and Janet, the Purdys owned Garrien Cottage and Heather had been accepted as a day student at Westbourne School.

Patrick took it upon himself to oversee our sprucing up of Garrien Cottage and recommended a second-hand shop in Oban. He also found a local mason who knew about pointing and waterproofing the stone walls and replacing roof tiles. Before the work began, Rai and I had hacked away at the overgrown path to the shore, the children had discovered a tumbling bourne (a small stream) that totally enchanted them, and I began to reclaim the front garden. Together, Patrick and Rai ripped out the interior termite-infested plywood lining from the whole cottage then replaced it in the central room only–a plenty big job even with two of them working at it. Rai paid the bills, except to Patrick who would not take money. Scotch whisky? Yes. And that's the way it was.

Our nearest neighbours, Sue and Mary Manton, lived in a small house called Barnacarrie surrounded by vegetable patches on a property that ran far back from the road and up onto the heath. Each time we drove by on our way to Garrien, we would see chickens running free beyond the fenced garden. Then one day after we had bought three second-hand cots and a big bed, some soft old blankets of pure wool, boots and rain gear, pots, pans, a flashlight and matches and had actually moved in, the Misses Manton came to pay us a call. Patrick had prepared us for trouble because, according to the ladies, we New Yorkers had no business buying the croft which had long been rented out to the local postmaster and his family. However, their dour expressions changed to cheeriness as soon as we opened our Canadian mouths to speak and Rai produced a bottle of sherry. It turned out that, long ago, a third Miss Manton had visited British Columbia where she'd worked for a summer on a hop farm in Chilliwack. Stranger still, the hop farm had belonged to my distant cousins. The following weekend Mary and Sue arrived at Garrien with raspberries and a freshly plucked chicken. They even offered to take us fishing. We could not have felt more warmly welcomed. So began an enduring friendship.

At the time we fell into Scottish country life, the tempo of life in Argyllshire was slower than it had been a hundred or so years earlier when clans were fighting and battlements fell. No doubt we stirred things up a bit, arriving in our big, though ancient, American car, but we were forgiven, partly, I think, because we so obviously loved the place. No matter how foul the weather, we set out for Loch Fyne most Friday evenings. If their dad was late home to Faslane from Scottish Television, the children would already be wearing pyjamas and warm dressing gowns, ready to climb into the beds we made for them in the car, Heather's on the back seat of the Packard and Roger's on the shelf behind it where the convertible top folded down on sunny days. The children would sleep on the journey and stay in their nests until Rai and I got the fires going at Garrien and warmed the blankets. Then we'd carry them, often still asleep, into the cottage and up the steep, narrow stairs to their real beds. On Saturdays they awoke in their most favourite place in the world!

Rai really liked the look of Jaguars and, when the Packard finally let him down, he bought a used Jaguar for a very reasonable amount. However, he should have invited me to sit in it before he bought it because the driver's seat was so low I could barely see out of the windshield. As a result, I managed to put a long scrape on its silvery door while trying to navigate a narrow stone-walled bridge. Meanwhile, the Packard waited for Roote's Motors to bring in a part for the automatic transmission. When Rai got fed up with their letter-writing to and from London, he telephoned the mechanic at our old gas station in New Rochelle, who put the part on a plane next day. Roote's representative, duly impressed, suggested a face-lift for the aging Packard and we fell for it. The new paint colour was Cadillac yellow (very pale) and the new top jet black—not exactly in tune with Glasgow fashion, but stunning! After that we didn't drive it to the croft any more. It just didn't belong there. In fact, when a friend suggested, "I'll bet you could get a mint for it if you advertised it in London," Rai sold it for 4,000 pounds—a fortune in those days.

In a round-robin letter to friends we hoped might visit us at Garrien, I wrote:

It doesn't take long to leave the bleakness behind if you drive due north from the west end of Glasgow toward Loch Lomond. If the day is clear, you'll very soon see Ben Lomond across the loch as you navigate the narrow and winding road to Tarbet; perhaps 40 minutes if you don't stop to gape at the view. It's glorious! From there, head west toward Arrochar on route 83 for about an hour past the head of Loch Long and over rolling Argyllshire hills known as 'The Rest And Be Thankfuls.' But do take care because you can't see a thing beyond the blind curve you are on or over the hill you are climbing. In these parts, flocks of sheep and herds of Highland cattle are free to roam and often choose to sleep on the warm tarmac. If you aren't shocked by the speed with which a chap on a motor bike can catch up to you and pass you on the brow, you will be when six more of them do the same thing, waving as they go by. There are no speed limits. Fortunately, these travellers are pretty good drivers and one does get used to them. Otherwise, the countryside is peaceful and beautiful and yours may be the only vehicle on the road for miles. When you reach the village of Cairndow, you must leave the main road and turn south on A815 (or else find yourself in Inveraray). Follow this one-track road with very few "passing places" for 20 or so miles down the east side of Loch Fyne. This is a sea loch, very deep out in the middle and very cold. Once you pass Strachur and enter Strath 'Laughlin, you will pass the castle on your right. Then there are no buildings on the Loch-side until you reach an ancient shepherd's croft on which there is a small stone structure with two chimneys and a tile roof. You have arrived at Garrien Cottage. Do come in and get warm.

138

You may ask how long have we owned Garrien? Only a few months 'Twas Patrick Fitzgerald O'Connor found it for us. Luck o' the Irish, is it? And isn't Purdy an Irish name, then?

Growing on the hillside above the road, an evergreen forest keeps the croft in shade until mid-morning. Before then, however, by wading up one of the nearby bournes, navigating a lovely waterfall and clambering on through shoulder-high heather, you may come upon a moor aglow in the early sun, and feel the warm wind which lays the tops of tall grasses almost flat. Looking down upon the loch, or back across the heath, north to mountains or south to more of them, vistas to cherish encircle one. Our particular delight (daughter Heather tried it first) is to fall onto the purple heath and roll down from the hill's crest over its deep, springy mattress. I adored the wild tumbling. Picture Roger shrieking with delight as, wrapped tight in his father's arms, the two of them roll over and over and over down the hill. Talk about freedom!

Garrien, the two-and-a-half acre fenced croft we called ours for three incredible years, sits on a promontory below the road looking almost due west over Loch Fyne. The only window on the weather side of its 20-inch-thick stone walls presents the wide view as though framed in a shadow box, vast and dramatic but extraordinarily peaceful. As one looks, the colouring changes with the swift and perpetual movement of clouds across the sky and the bloom and fade of opalescent mists. When the tide goes out, rivulets falling on either side of the property from mountain Corres reflect the sky as they cross paths on the wide, rock-strewn foreshore. Having oozed through peat bogs before tumbling seaward, their fresh water is the colour of fine whiskey.

On sunny days with the tide far out, the creatures between and under the rocks held endless entertainment for our children. As the sea came in, they used their blow-up mattress to travel upon rivers and visit tiny islands. One evening, when the tide was fully in, we four were watching a sunset from the cottage when suddenly a big fish jumped above the loch close to shore.

139

Rai quickly donned his hip waders, grabbed a rod and hurried down the path. Moments later we watched his silhouette cast a line and reel in a salmon. How heavenly can things get?

Though Rai didn't know much about boats, had never enjoyed bare feet and still didn't swim, Patrick told us where to find a 14-foot dinghy and oars and life jackets for sale. He then instructed us that, to cope with the loch's extended foreshore, the boat would need to be moored to a buoy anchored well beyond the lowest tide on a "never-ending" rope. So long as it didn't twist or kink, the spliced loop of rope would run smoothly through one pulley attached to the buoy and another attached to a tree ashore. Wherever the tide happened to be when we came home from a boating experience, we need only clip the boat painter onto the rope and pull in on the opposite side of the loop until the boat reached the buoy out in deep water. Patrick suggested Rai should order 300 feet of one-inch hemp, which he did. This large coil of rope was subsequently delivered and dumped outside our gate.

The following Saturday afternoon, having "lifted a couple," Patrick decided to show Rai and me (Janet stayed ashore with the children) how to untwist the new rope by towing it for some distance behind the dinghy. This, he explained, would get the kinks out of it. At about half tide, Patrick carried the huge coil, heavier than Rai could lift, down the steep path to a rough piece of grass where our new little boat lay overturned, hiding our two-cylinder Seagull engine and a can of gas. While I carried the oars and a second gas can, the two men lifted and dragged the boat down the rocky beach to the water's edge. Then Rai fetched the outboard motor and together they bolted it onto the boat. Patrick made a trip back for the rope which he dumped amidships then tied one end of it to the centre thwart. We all had a hand in the launching (I had thrown my shoes into the boat but Rai chose to get his wet) and the two of us scrambled aboard. With me perched in the bow and Rai sitting on top of the rope, Patrick pushed off, hopped in and started the outboard. He headed westward out into the middle of the loch. By that time, the sun was long gone and a stiff breeze had already begun to chop the water.

Roger and Heather

Stretching the rope

Well away from shore, Patrick slowed the motor and turned north toward the head of the loch, shouting at Rai to pay out the rope slowly over the transom, keeping it well above the engine. This meant he had to stand up. Since it was getting rough, Rai spread his feet as he stood, and I descended to sit on the floorboards. Patrick steered and we moved along fairly briskly with the south wind behind us. As more and more rope dragged astern, however, he had to rev the motor increasingly to keep us moving. It seemed like hours before the rope was all paid out. Crouching in the bow, I could feel Rai's relief as he sat down. Then, with the throttle wide open, Patrick steered a tortuously slow, wide circle starting toward the east so as to avoid later collision with our tow. Still pushing the motor at full speed, he then steered north and west again inching toward the far shore as wind and waves hit us from the port side. With every wave I felt sure we'd roll far enough to take on water until finally Patrick headed the boat south into the wind. As spray splashed over the bow drenching us, the rope, now in a full circle behind us, felt as if it would pull the boat backward. I was really scared but knew there was nothing anyone could do—just hope the engine would keep going. As darkness closed around us, I could hardly make out the land on either side of Loch Fyne, but at last I could feel that we were turning again and must soon be on the homeward stretch. Please, please keep us moving, I prayed to myself in the darkening night, but I was also thinking, *shouldn't this job have been tackled in daylight? What sort of idiot is this O'Connor person?* Then I saw the light in Garrien's window. Janet must have put it there. Good old Janet. Silly old Patrick.

Of course, the man was used to this sort of thing, and he had known that the tide would be in again by the time we got back. As we neared the shore, I could see that Janet had found our flashlight and was coming down the path. What had I been worrying about? We all helped drag in the wet rope and stash it on the grassy knoll. Tomorrow would be time enough to "stretch it to dry around the fence posts," Patrick said. Stretch it to dry? How would we ever get it up the hill? But with help from his neighbour down the loch, the men did it the next day, stretching it from post to post. By the following weekend, again with help, the three fellows had successfully rigged the "never-ending" rope and buoy and it worked without a hitch.

Fruich Island, ten minutes away by outboard, provided a world of wonders. On the Purdy's first solo visit, we circled it slowly to see where we might land and were surprised how much bigger the island was than it had appeared from the croft. Puttering around the southern tip we came upon a shallow lagoon, just the right size for mooring our small boat, with low rocks to climb out onto. Only a few feet of water covered the shale bottom, which under the clear green water looked like a white carpet decorated with sea urchins, star fish and sea cucumbers. I knew it would be lovely to walk on with bare feet at a lower tide. Next time we came, the water was shallow enough to pull the boat up onto this snowy shale.

Having investigated the nooks and crannies at sea level, my natural impulse was to climb to the highest point of the island (in bare feet, of course.) In only a minute or two I'd reached the summit where I discovered a crater-like depression filled with grass and shrubs–sure enough, a safe nesting place for seagulls! Heather wasn't far behind me. "Look what I found!" I shouted, "Come and see! These must be old nests. I don't see any eggs." Before we understood that we really shouldn't have been there, Heather and I had walked among the nests, sometimes only inches apart, on guano, so soft and springy our feet sank with every step. Bluebells and other wild flowers thrived on the rich droppings and grew unusually large. On later visits I swam with the girls in and out around the rocks, peering down at colourful sea life through clear cool waters. Even though the water wasn't warm enough for him to float about in a life jacket, three-year-old Roger loved to come with us to Fruich. Rai would hang onto him on the rocks or row him in the boat around to the far side of the island where they plucked clusters of giant black mussels from the sheer rock face. In August when school was out, Rai left the children and me at Garrien

143

during the week, and then Janet and Fiona became like family. Janet taught me about cooking shellfish. "A touch of vinegar in the water," she said, "and a bent pin for extracting mussels.

Before the end of our first summer at Garrien Cottage, Rai decided we should give up our rented "castle" at Faslane and buy a house in Glasgow so as to be close to Scottish Television. This appealed to me because of my interest in teaching dance in the new studio, but the private houses belonging to people we had met in Glasgow were all very much alike–brick or sandstone row-houses or narrow, deep houses several storeys high with dark wood panelling inside and a strip of so-called garden behind. There being so little light, few things grew in these gardens other than evergreen shrubs made bleak by soot and fog. Most of the kitchens in the houses I was shown were below street level and reached by concrete steps down to an "area" in which coal might be stored. But we were once again lucky. Number One Redlands Terrace on the west side of a block of six houses on a rise above the Great Western Road was available. Much wider than most row houses, those in Redlands Terrace had no basements but enjoyed comparatively large walled gardens. These two-storey-plus-attic dwellings were said to be the last grand houses built in Glasgow during the shipping boom on the Clyde. They even boasted electric central heating and built-in wardrobes.

Number One, panelled in teak with thick red carpet in the hall and on the stairs, had a cloakroom (with toilet) at the beginning of the entrance hall, then a huge living room as well as a library next to it at the front of the house, plus a wide staircase-with-landing which led up to the bedrooms. On the ground floor beyond the front hall, a dark passage led to servants' quarters and a pantry. After that, a bright kitchen ran the full width of the building with light coming in from both west and north. Beyond the kitchen came the scullery from which the solid back door opened onto a large lawn and rose garden. This was made completely private by a high stone wall. The grass looked green though there was a tell-tale blackness to the soil around the roses. Upstairs, three large bedrooms and two bathrooms were more
144

than enough for us, and I made use of the large finished attic space to lay out fabrics which I found at Sanderson's (wholesale through Scottish Television) for our draperies. I only made a few mistakes with the furnishings. For the sake of its warmth and cheeriness, I should have kept the red hall and stair carpet, but I am not a red person. Blues, greens and yellows suit my red-headedness best, so I replaced the richness of red for the coolness of blue and regretted it. I also nearly got Rai's head chopped off by Coltart, who was now the managing director of Thomson's London office, for buying a certain French velvet for pelmets and a fire-stool without asking the price. Most of the rich and beautiful fabrics were mere shillings a yard but the velvet cost in the tens of pounds! Fortunately, Rai just laughed. I didn't even try to change the vast kitchen in which a refrigerator was the only modern convenience! We didn't buy new furniture but found that buying old and re-upholstering it was a cheap and satisfactory solution. Second-hand Indian carpets, inexpensive and in quite light colours, were fine for covering large areas of hardwood floor.

As we grew to know the city of Glasgow, Rai and I haunted the auction rooms on Sauchihall Street. Had we known the rules of Canada Customs and been able to look ahead, there was no end of treasure we could have gathered. As it was, we did very well on such things as furniture and cutlery, and we did pick up some interesting copper pieces. Before long, we were ready to entertain Rai's production staff and our new friends–Jack Hardy and his wife Joan and the O'Connors.

Business acquaintances of Roy Thomson and supporters of STV, Iain and Jean Stewart and the McQueen family invited Rai and me to their fine old country homes. We connected most warmly with the Stewarts who, like us, had two children. Both their boys attended Loretto School as boarders and, as one of the school's directors, Iain suggested we "put Roger down" for Loretto for the time when he'd be old enough to attend. This amused Rai but seriously interested me; several uncles and cousins of mine had been educated there. The O'Connors, the Cummings (Don was a Canadian sports commentator and his wife Pam was Scottish), and John Watson (Rai's head writer) and his wife Helen, had quickly become part of our daily lives. Rai was especially close to his head of news, Scottish Jack Webster, and to John Grierson, well-known creator of the National Film Board of Canada, who was his head of documentaries. Larry Marshall was Rai's favourite comedian and Arthur Mumford, Lorne Freed and James Sutherland were his top directors. We had also enjoyed meeting Harbourne and Erica Stephens and their daughters, Layle and Virginia. Harbourne held a senior position with the Glasgow Daily Express, and we had met him and Erica when Thomson, along with Coltart, had entertained an important group of Scottish newspapermen with a tour of Scottish Television. Thomson had no problem convincing these local competitors that his plan for commercial television advertising, far from adversely affecting their sales, would actually increase the sale of newspapers. The Stephens lived quite near us in Glasgow and their girls also attended Westbourne School.

Needing to find a new nursery nurse, I asked Erica if she could recommend a replacement. I hired the woman she sent us but I found her far too strict, in fact, cruelly so. I first suspected trouble when I entered the kitchen at the children's breakfast time one morning, saw Roger sitting in his high chair and heard Ingrid (not her true name) shouting at him. Abruptly she changed to hugging and kissing him. When I later faced her with complaints from Heather that, among other things, she regularly turfed the child out of bed in the morning and made her stand naked while washing her down with cold water, Ingrid simply shrugged. "It is good discipline," she announced. After I had queried her at some length about her own childhood, she finally admitted that her father, who had been in the Hitler Youth Movement, had shown no lenience with his children. Did she not understand, I asked, that the unfortunate treatment she had received from her father gave her no right to bully my children? Her reply was unbending, and I faced an extremely angry woman when I refused to add a recommendation to the written notice I gave her. Erica told me that, when Ingrid had served as nanny to their children, she had never seen this side of the woman. It made me ask myself what I had done to invite such spitefulness. However, I simply had to have help with the children because of my involvement in the dance school at STV, so in trepidation I contacted an agency for nursery nurses. The lass who came for an interview took away all my doubts and filled me with confidence. Isobel from the Isle of Skye had music in her voice and laughter in her dark eyes. We all fell in love with her. Grizzo, as Heather and Roger called her, was to be with us for years.

The old greenroom did make a great studio, especially after the installation of barres and mirrors, the acquisition of a good piano and a particularly fine accompanist. The wooden floor, however, though in good shape was coal-black filthy. I needn't have worried. As soon as reconstruction was completed in any area of the theatre, char ladies with buckets of soapsuds, mops and brushes set about scrubbing and polishing. Often on their knees, they worked in pairs, keeping up an animated conversation in a language that was at first beyond my grasp. For weeks the smell of ancient grime being loosened with wet scrub-brushes permeated the building, but day by day the polished wood shone again and colours returned in the carpets. Then eight or ten of these garrulous personalities, having finished cleaning the theatre offices and corridors, showed up to scrub my studio floor. I didn't ask for them. They just arrived and arranged themselves facing each other, on all fours, on either side of the room with brushes and buckets at the ready. It was as if the music (fully orchestrated with guttural Glaswegian conversation) started, and the dance began. Shouting at first as they started to slosh and scrub toward their opposite partners, the ladies moved ahead as though choreographed. Then, passing side-by-side, they carried on to the other wall, muttering, mopping and squeezing, drying up the mess. In all, it took about ten minutes! Their performance deserved an ovation. The once black floor had turned to gold.

It took but one advertisement to gather more than a dozen strong young dancers who, with the hope of employment with

Scottish Television, wanted to take my ballet classes. I was aiming for professional speed and precision in preparing them for STV's first show that Rai had decided must include several dance sequences. My dancers showed up regularly and came early enough to be thoroughly warmed up by the time I arrived, and they rewarded me with their keen interest and energy. This enthusiasm was heart-warming and helped me to rise to the challenge, pushing them and myself to polish our techniques. Rehearsals began after my dance class. As Rai designed the production numbers, I choreographed the dance sequences with the help of an expert for the Scottish jigs and reels. It was hardly surprising under the circumstances that I felt like a valuable member of Scottish Television. As time went by, without any awareness of possibly negative reaction from management, I sort of adopted the "royal we" when talking about "our" (Rai's and my) plans for STV programming. However, Coltart, up from London, heard my chatter and reported me to Thomson who sent a message to Rai that I was out of line and should be reminded of my position. The rebuff hurt. Still, Rai and I had long worked as a team, and I understood more than any of them how concerned he was to represent the Scottish people honestly, but with extra professional flair, especially for the grand opening.

Garriene Cottage

CHAPTER 11

A Royal Performance

Eight and a half months after Roy Thomson received the studio plans which Rai had brought from New York, and just three and a half months after Roy was awarded his "contract," Scottish Television was ready to go on the air. To celebrate the occasion, Her Majesty Queen Elizabeth II, accompanied by a large entourage, honoured Mr. Thomson with her presence at the Theatre Royal in Glasgow for the eight o'clock launch on September 15, 1958, of his private television station. Other than Thomson, his managing director and sponsors, few members of the staff were allowed close enough to even have a peek at the royal party. There weren't supposed to have been any hidden cameras, but one bouquet on the staircase must have hidden one.

Russell Galbraith, writing in the Scotsman on September 8, 2001, remembered the drama and excitement of that long ago evening–the clock ticking off the seconds to air time, Rai Purdy "settled in front of a small bank of black and white monitors," his production assistant performing the countdown, Rai saying calmly, "Keep it steady everyone!" And then they were on the air. Galbraith's article continued, "Purdy, relishing the moment, leaned forward in his chair and began issuing rapid instructions. The quiet-mannered Canadian had been lured from New York, fired by the challenge of opening a brand new television. "Very few people," he later recalled, "have the opportunity of opening a brand new television station from scratch, and I do mean scratch!" To the audience's great delight and the production team's considerable relief, the opening show started on cue and on time.

STV's opening broadcast, "This Is Scotland," which was received all over Britain, synthesized the wisdom and wit of the Scottish people, the grandeur of Scotland's scenery, the romance of her history, the strength of her industry and the richness of her music. Tailored to feed the people's pride with lots of modern theatrical effects, the broadcast was hosted by James Robertson Justice, not Rai's choice, but pressed upon him because of his fame as a movie star. A large man (six-foot-three) with a sizable opinion of himself (as well as a sizable appetite for scotch), JRJ refused to wear a kilt saying, "Only Sasanacs wear skirts." He managed, with a little guidance off-camera, to introduce the famous Scottish artists on the show. Some, like singer/comedian Jack Buchannan and tenor Kenneth McKeller were "live" on the theatre stage. Others were on film; these included actors David Niven and Deborah Kerr, ballerina Moira Shearer and Sir Isaac Shoenberg, who headed the research team at Electric and Musical Industries (EMI) and had launched the world's first public television service for the BBC in 1936. All these were celebrities with skills recognized over the decades in many parts of the world. There was plenty of comedy and poetry, combined on stage with lyric voices and highland dancing. But although the performers included the Clyde Valley Stompers and the Glasgow Police Pipe Band, kilts and pipes were carefully understated and, to balance the past with the present, the musical score was the work of London's Geraldo and his orchestra who were equally well known in Scotland. Accompanied by Mr. Justice's ever-so-slightly blurred "voice-over," there were clips of Scotland's great rivers and herds of cattle and sheep, sights of industrial wonders and close-ups of famous cathedrals and castles.

Of course, there had to be a party after the opening and, of course, our house was the natural place for it. Everyone on the staff of STV came, including Thomson and Coltart, though they didn't offer to pay our expenses. Neither did they stay long, having dignitaries to celebrate with elsewhere. But James Robertson Justice made himself at home. Descending the stairs from having had a look around, he stopped a step or two up and, smiling as he leaned over the bannister, said to me, "You know, when you look up at me like that, I can see right up your nose!" I began to understand why he had such a miserable reputation as a human being.

STV's opening show was followed by a full daytime programme schedule which included news and sports, The One O'clock Gang featuring Larry Marshall, This Wonderful World with John Grierson, Jig Time (full of Scottish music and dancing), and a talent show, Stars of Tomorrow. Rai directed many of these studio productions himself, and the station proved itself quickly. An astonishingly large audience of Scots, who had resented the BBC's condescending attitude toward them, moved over to STV and remained loyal.

When opportunities arose to insert remote sections, Rai's experience in New York paid off. His very first remote for STV was from Glasgow Children's Hospital, and it was a telling expression of the patience and care shown to the very young by a warm and sensitive staff. The Watchnight Service on Christmas Eve at Saint Giles Cathedral in Edinburgh was another great remote, and I watched from home with no small thrill, aware that, although Rai himself did not attend any church, he had shown proper respect for the solemnity of the festival. He also added creative and beautiful touches for the viewing audience that the congregation could not have enjoyed, such as close-ups of the choir boys in their stalls and, at the exact moment of midnight, the senior choir entering the cathedral from the darkness outside.

I can't put my hand on it after all these years but more than once I have re-read the letter which Rai received from the moderator of the Church of Scotland praising him for capturing the very essence of the service and presenting it faithfully. He said he had never before really seen the cathedral until, by dramatic lighting, Rai had drawn his attention to the beauty of it.

Rai expected a pat on the back from Thomson for all this work, but instead Coltart came up from London to tell Rai he was spending too much money. In fact, he quoted as excess the number of cameras and microphones Rai was using, particularly on *The One O'clock Gang*. This really riled my husband, and he promised himself Thomson would hear about it.

Smart enough to utilize the brains of people who knew more than he did, Rai had hired erudite department heads, each artist well-known in his or her individual field. Though these men and women respected Rai's showmanship and gave him their best, he was sometimes out of his intellectual depth with them. He knew this and so did they, especially John Grierson, who once while they were discussing *This Wonderful World*, the weekly documentary they had dreamed up together, suddenly saw through Rai's defences and announced, "Purdy, you are illiterate!" Later, Rai told me what Grierson had said and admitted that the words hurt, adding, "And he wasn't kidding, either." I should have been supportive then, at least said I was sorry, had not Grierson's words rung true for both of us. I made no comment. However, Rai's ignorance of the wider world didn't stop any of those bright people, including Grierson himself, from becoming his fast friends. Indeed, they came and brought their families to visit us at Garrien Cottage where the simple life offered refreshment from the driving routine at Scottish Television.

One weekend at the croft, we Purdys drove from Garrien down Loch Fyneside to Dunoon, near the mouth of the River Clyde. Here the Abercrombies–my Aunt Beatrice and her husband John–ran a white heather farm. During the visit, Rai and I left the children with them and set off on foot toward the next village. Walking hand in hand along an old lane between crumbling stone walls under a high, leafy ceiling of autumnal elms, we enjoyed the peacefulness which invariably attended our visits to that part of Argyllshire. In my usual way I directed Rai's attention to every little delight of nature, glimpses through the trees of the Clyde estuary, the shadowy blue of Michaelmas daisies or blotches of sunlight on the path. Lifting my head, I gasped at the brilliant pattern of leaves high above us saying, "Oh honey, isn't it beautiful? Doesn't it thrill you? Look at it!" "I can't," he said. "I've tried. It hurts." His voice was unsteady. "Even when I was a wee boy I couldn't look up through the trees. It's too beautiful." I remember being touched and saddened at the time, but I can still feel my disappointment hearing the questions in my head: What's wrong with this man? Why isn't he interested in any of the delicate and treasured things of life? He keeps letting me down. What an opportunity I missed! Had I been even slightly more aware, I'd have shut up and held him, feeling his pain. I, too, knew such pain from my own childhood. We might have cried for each other. Instead, I walked away from him that he might pull himself together.

On Sunday we returned with our children to Garrien where we tidied the place and packed the car for our crack-of-dawn return to Glasgow and the darkening shadow of Coltart. Although the STV employees were a hard working lot and a happy team, it was becoming clear to Rai that Jim Coltart and Roy Thomson were in some kind of conspiracy to keep him ignorant about the financial aims of the company. I wasn't too surprised when Rai informed me that the dancers were being let go; they would be "Hired peace-meal when called for in future," was Coltart's explanation. That decision naturally put an end to my teaching which, though great fun, had been tying me down. Now, while Rai sweated over the politics at STV, I could take the children to meet their cousins in Wales during Easter holiday when my elder brother Sedley's girls would be home from boarding school. Heather and Roger thought they were in heaven! First there was an overnight train ride with bunks in a sleeping compartment followed by a drive through the Welsh mountains with my sister-in-law Diana. Then the hill farm with real animals! Their cousins, Nicola, Terry and Robin, showed Heather and Roger sheep-dogs and cows and the sheep on the hill and Taffy, their Welsh hill-pony. My children's eyes registered bliss.

Sedley was understandably proud of their small acreage which produced just about everything his family needed

153

plus some for sale. Diana took us up on the hill and showed us how the collies worked for her. In the dairy, she made delicious cheeses among other healthful delicacies and kept the kind of charming farmhouse one sees in English Homes and Gardens, in this case the up-dating of a truly ancient stone building. Though no softy, Diana was a picture of gracefulness. Immaculately coiffed at all times, she wore a tweed skirt and lisle stockings with real brogues while walking the hillside.

But it was Taffy who stole the show. He was thirteen hands, an Anglo-Arab-Welsh cross, dappled grey (actually snow-white), short coupled and sound. Strong enough to carry my six-foot brother shepherding on the hillside, yet easily handled by young children. Taffy was Pony Club trained, enjoyed pulling a cart and knew about clearing a hillside of sheep. Many years later when Taffy came to his end at the age of thirty-two, he had guided three generations of children through every conceivable form of equitation. He had won trophies in the Prince Philip Games and carried high points for pony jumping, hunting etiquette and junior dressage. If ever an animal understood the human qualities of pride and *joie-de-vivre*, Taffy did. After a couple of days in his company, my children, especially Heather, knew exactly what they must have one day. It was wonderful for us then, in return for their treat, that we could offer the Sweenys a holiday at our croft on Loch Fyne. Rai and I thoroughly enjoyed our visitors.

No one outside ourselves ever entertained STV's staff or talent. Thomson never spent a dime on the people who worked for him. In addition to casual gatherings, Rai and I held the Christmas party in our house on Redlands, and everybody except Thomson and Coltart came. Each time we put on a party, we tried to make it different. Once we served Chinese food from a famous cook-house down on the Glasgow docks that someone had told Rai about. The joy for me was that I didn't have to arrange a thing about the ingredients or the serving of them. Four or five quiet people simply brought the utensils and at three pm moved into our house to cook a sumptuous variety of dishes which gave the place a pungent aroma. It was a pleasure

Rai with his four top producers, STV Glasgow

Commercial TV Scotland

to see the faces of our guests as they caught the first whiff of it.

In the fall of 1958, with all productions showing high ratings and the staff ready to tackle a really big remote, Rai began work on the Hogmanay (New Year's Eve) production. Having cut his "remote teeth" in Times Square, he knew just where to begin: the Glasgow constabulary. He was royally received there, and plans fell into place rapidly. The stage at the Theatre Royal became "Studio One" where a musical extravaganza entertained a full audience. In "Studio Two," the new building next door, the story of Hogmanay was dramatized seriously with music. Between the variety acts on stage, cameras situated at Glasgow Cross brought pictures of the celebrations there to a huge screen at Theatre Royal. But the highlight was the count-down at midnight. With police very much in evidence and all kinds of comedic side-shows to catch the final blow-off, a light a la New York climbed a church tower. To add glamour to the finale back at the theatre, show-girls perched in bird-cages descended from the flies while cameras cut to fireworks and other ongoing events. It all happened without a hitch, garnering rave notices from London where millions of people watched STV instead of the BBC!

Meanwhile, headquartering himself in Edinburgh, Roy Thomson had hung around in Scotland only long enough to be able to boast, "In the first year of operation, STV's commercial sales have paid for the purchase and re-construction of the Theatre Royal plus a million pounds." Then he added his now most famous remark: "STV is a licence to print money." With that goal achieved in the fall of 1958, he had turned his attention to new projects, handing over control of STV to Thomson Enterprises' managing director, Jim Coltart.

When Coltart left the London office to live in Glasgow, he moved into a grand old house in Bearsden, the most exclusive residential area, and took over Thomson's office in the theatre. Though Thomson still visited occasionally, Coltart made sure that he was no longer available to Rai for discussions about programming and staffing. From that time on, the big problem for Rai, as director of programmes, was that Coltart, who knew

156

nothing about television programming or talent or studio requirements–nothing in fact about show-business–was making decisions in these areas, cutting budgets, limiting the use of cameras and firing personnel. More serious for Rai's ability to function as a producer/director but less possible to pin down, Coltart saw himself as a world ambassador for Moral Rearmament which, from the beginning, Rai had refused to adopt. Coltart's attacks began innocently enough with a reception at his house. On the friendly pretence of getting to know us, he invited Rai and me along with the production staff and their husbands and wives to meet at his place early one evening. Coltart met us at the door and, having offered us a choice of juices, issued his captive audience into a long room he called his library. As bidden, we arranged ourselves on chairs that had been placed at an angle toward a small dais at the far end of the room. Here Coltart seated himself on a tall chair facing us. Without apology, he explained that his mission was to ensure that all who worked at Scottish Television understood the importance of good moral behaviour. He went on to outline the need for moral rearmament throughout the world and told us how he had been shown the light. Now, he said, he held the position of a world ambassador and was able to speak with and advise heads of state anywhere in the world. The lecture went on for over an hour. When it was through, he wished everyone good night.

It was of considerable concern to Rai that Thomson appeared not to know about this side of his managing director's character. Either that or he didn't think Moral Rearmament could do any harm. Or could it be that Coltart and Thomson were of one mind? Although Thomson never mentioned, let alone publicly condoned, Coltart's forceful application of Moral Rearmament on the staff of STV, he could have been using it indirectly. He and Coltart had come from similarly parochial backgrounds. Their families had been financially strapped, morally and religiously strict, hard-working and narrow-minded. Neither man had enjoyed a carefree childhood or experienced the indulgences of youthful affairs-of-the-heart. Each had married and had children

157

but, compelled by their desire for money, had one way or another virtually deserted their families for months on end. Each had eventually lost his wife to cancer. And since they had joined forces, these two hard-boiled, chauvinistic, self-righteous, single-minded money makers had one goal–to amass wealth and power.

That winter when Coltart brought Rai the first of a series of videotapes on the subject of Moral Rearmament and told him to "air it" the following Sunday afternoon, Rai refused to schedule the tape without an order from Thomson. But Thomson was not to be reached, and the show did not go on. Coltart's next interference was the firing of Rai's head writer, John Watson, on the premise that he was having an affair with one of the female staff. Whether or not this was true, in Rai's opinion, it was no business of Coltart's. Then one by one the production staff secretaries were replaced by devotees of Moral Rearmament–all of them severely dressed women with no makeup and absolutely no self-confidence. That Coltart appeared to be having an affair with his secretary who had a key to the building and let herself into his private office after hours seemed not to disturb the managing director's own conscience. When one day Rai saw a full-page ad for Moral Rearmament in the Scotsman, Thomson's own newspaper, he decided that something underhanded was definitely going on, that Coltart was using his connection with Thompson and his newspapers to advance his personal interests. It didn't take much sleuthing to learn that, as Coltart assisted Thomson in finding and buying newspapers in many parts of the world, he regularly ordered space in all of them for articles on Moral Rearmament. How could Thomson not have acquiesced to this? we asked ourselves. Under these uncomfortable circumstances Rai stood up to Coltart as well as he could without complaining and never lost sight of the challenge to create good shows.

Even though this was a stressful time, Rai came with me to London early in 1959 to see my youngest brother Roger, by then an officer in the Canadian Navy, who had come to England on a tactical anti-sub course. Neither Rai nor I had been in London since the war years. For me, it was nostalgic to take my baby brother to meet Peter Pan in Kensington Gardens and to watch grown men sailing model ships on the Round Pond. Rai and I returned to Glasgow in good spirits in time to enjoy a performance of Howard and Wyndham's *Five Past Eight*, a fast and meaty variety show featuring Scotland's finest comedians, Jimmy Logan and Stanley Baxter. This permanent company boasted world-class actors and dancers and proudly presented tenor Kenneth McKellar. It had come as a surprise to Rai to find an extremely high standard of theatrical production in such a dour and dark climate, and it pleased him that Thomson had made an early agreement with Howard and Wyndham to use members of this hugely successful company on his new television station.

Since we had wonderful Isobel to take care of the children, it was possible in the spring of 1959 for me to be with Rai when he finally took a much needed break from dealing with Coltart. We'd heard about cheap rates in Mallorca and that's where we headed. Rai was exhausted, and all he wanted to do was sleep in the luxurious American hotel. As was usual with me, I was geared up to see olive orchards and the non-touristy parts of the island. When finally Rai had slept enough, he wanted to sample the local rum, see a bullfight and visit Blood Alley. I hated the bullfight and would never attend another, but I'm glad now to know the difference between a picador and a matador and be able to experience the full drama of the opera Carmen.

Not long after Spain we decided to buy a smaller house. Since we had completely redecorated and furnished Redlands Terrace, Rai figured it made sense to pay for a splashy, typically American advertisement in "The Scotsman," putting a high price on the place and setting a date for occupancy six months ahead. It worked, but I felt quite ashamed of the draperies and those palest-pink sheers I'd used to cover the huge windows which, following several months of Glasgow's fog, had turned a horrible grey. Fortunately Heather and Roger were settled in fee-paying schools so that our next move didn't upset their routines. By then we had bought a ground-floor flat, # 9 Beaumont Gate in snobby Kelvinside, at a fraction of the price we'd received for Redlands and we proceeded to refurbish it. The rooms were spacious in these old Glasgow tenements and one could go wild with fabulous but cheap European fabrics. In those days I was disrespectful of moulded ceilings and works of wonder in plaster and tore them down. I painted deep colours over blackened panelling and put flamboyant wallpaper in the bathrooms. People loved what I did and also loved the heavy pots, pans and huge salad bowls I'd brought from New York. As a result, we were able to make a good deal when, much sooner than expected, we sold Beaumont Gate (again for the high price we asked) and included these American goodies.

CHAPTER 12

Deja Vu

In 1959, the position at STV in which Rai found himself was in many ways similar to the New York scene of three years earlier. Ever since STV's exciting first year, Thomson had been so preoccupied with new adventures, he'd forgotten his pledge to Rai that he would "always be available," and as Coltart continued to cut, cut, cut, the joy was fast leaving what had been a cooperative and happy company. Soon Rai was fed up with being told how to run his department and longed for a change. He had given Thomson his best, but although the station had gone from one commercial success to another, bringing much credit to Thomson, it had brought serious stress upon his director of programmes.

The situation suddenly improved for Rai in the fall of that year, when Thomson, recently returned from a trip to Toronto, came to Glasgow to talk to him about another project in which he was interested. A year earlier, the Canadian government had created the Board of Broadcast Governors (BBG) to be a watchdog over the radio and television industry, and on October 8, 1959, this board had announced that it would accept applications for a licence to set up and operate the first private television station in Toronto. Hearings would commence on March 17, 1960. Two of Thomson's close friends, the highly respected entrepreneur John

Bassett and the wealthy but unpretentious John David Eaton, who were already co-owners of the Toronto Telegram (along with Thomson, I later learned), were forming a new company called Baton (Bassett Eaton) Broadcasting and were about to apply for this licence. Thomson told Rai that he expected to invest in Baton and, recognizing the value of Rai's television expertise, invited him to assist in the preparation of Baton's presentation to the BBG.

Rai made a quick trip to Toronto where he enjoyed meeting the outspoken John Bassett. A tall, lean, lithe and physically fit man of 44, Bassett had entered the newspaper business as a reporter for the Toronto Globe and Mail, but when war came in 1939, he had enlisted and gone overseas with the Black Watch Regiment. Emerging from the war with the rank of major (Rai, as a full colonel, had out ranked him), Bassett had bought his father's newspaper, the Sherbrooke Daily Record, following that up in 1952 with his investment in the Toronto Telegram. In 1950, looking for new worlds to conquer, he had turned his sights on television.

Bassett introduced Rai to Eddie Goodman, his (and Baton's) legal advisor, a thoroughly open and likable fellow with whom Rai felt immediately at home. Having discussed Thomson's proposal at length with both of them, Rai agreed to become involved in the upcoming presentation.

Among the other companies vying for that first private licence was Aldred Rogers Broadcasting Ltd. It was fronted by Joel Aldred, the strikingly handsome, mellifluous-voiced and highest paid television advertising personality in Canada–a McLean's Magazine article dubbed him "the $100,000 voice." Though a Canadian, he spent much of his time in California where he appeared as the commercial announcer on the Dinah Shore television show and as the on-air advertising personality for General Motors. However, as a tobacco farmer himself, he was best known as the "Rothman's Man" in that company's advertisements.

Aldred's partner in the application was Toronto-based Ted Rogers Jr., son of the inventor of Roger's Batteryless Radio and the creator of radio station CFRB where Rai had begun his broadcasting career back in 1931. But Ted Junior, though scion of the Rogers family, was still a university law student at the time; as a result, while it was mostly his family's money that backed the application, it was Aldred who was the mouthpiece for the Aldred Rogers Broadcasting bid

Word soon got around that Thomson planned to invest in Baton, and just as quickly it became apparent that, because he already owned several broadcasting enterprises in Canada, his proposed investment would not be welcomed by the BBG. Consequently, he withdrew his offer to purchase shares in that company. When Aldred heard that Thomson had backed out, he jumped at the opportunity to improve his company's chance of winning the licence by joining forces with Baton. Bassett, who readily admitted that he knew nothing about broadcasting, was impressed with Aldred's elegant forty-ish rugged appearance and high profile and believed that he would make a perfect executive for the new station, giving it class and flair. In addition, since Aldred was already in the broadcast business, Bassett believed he would be able to recruit television producers and other personnel as well as influence media advertisers, so he was delighted to arrange the merger. The new company was called Baton Aldred Rogers Broadcasting.

Meanwhile, Rai had made a second trip to Toronto, this time with Thomson, which had given him the opportunity to broach the serious problems facing STV's production department due to Coltart's interference, in particular his pressure to air stories about Moral Rearmament. Rai told Thomson that, because Coltart had consistently blocked communication between the two of them, his position as director of programmes for STV had been reduced to a mere title. (It is history that Thomson ultimately told Coltart to choose between himself and Moral Rearmament, and that Coltart dropped Moral Rearmament like a hot potato in order to keep his lucrative position in the Thomson Empire. |But that is another story.) When Rai then asked Thomson to release him from Scottish Television and allow him to join Baton Aldred Rogers–should they need him–Thomson reluctantly agreed. However, as might have been expected from the man, he immediately reminded Rai he would have to sell his few STV shares (now worth a goodly sum) back to Thomson Enterprises at their original value. Never mind! Rai said to himself. If Baton Aldred Rogers wins the licence, I'll soon be director of programs for CFTO, Toronto.

Rai then began working closely with John Bassett who gave him a free hand to determine the broad picture for CFTO, and he put together a well-rounded program of mostly live TV with news and sports as well as movies and shows for children. But he strengthened it with educational and rich cultural programming, religious festival coverage, documentaries, art, music, opera and dance, all of which was readily available locally. So far as Bassett was concerned, Rai's formula was on track, but Rai knew that in order to win the licence the promised programming must appeal to all the BBG's members. Everything, therefore, would depend on their presentation.

According to Michael Nolan's book, CTV: The Network That Means Business, when Baton Aldred Rogers Broadcasting began work on their BBG presentation, lawyer Eddie Goodman "had to exercise considerable control over Aldred. . . ." Goodman told Nolan that "Joel Aldred, if he had his way, would have 'been' the presentation and we would have lost." In fact, it would be Rai's innovative presentation concept that ultimately won them the licence.

"The hearings themselves in the Oak Room of Union Station were something of a circus," reported Pierre Berton, at that time a columnist for the Toronto Star. He confided to his readers on March 28, 1960, that he had never seen so many "distinguished Canadians gathered together under one roof," all of them involved in the applications. They included, said Mr Berton, who obviously enjoyed the spectacle,

> Mr. Mavor Moore, giving one of the finest dramatic readings of his career, Mr. Johnny Wayne of the Ed Sullivan Show, the comedy team of Eugene Forsey and Emlyn Davies (who should

be on the Ed Sullivan Show), Mr Joel Aldred, that wealthy car salesman, Sir Ernest MacMillan, Foster Hewitt. . . Sir Robert Watson-Watt, the inventor of radar, John Fisher, the inventor of maple syrup, Dr. Reva Gerstein, beautiful girl psychologist, and beautiful Larry Henderson, beautiful boy newscaster. . . . In these hearings for a TV franchise, Virtue predominated. . . . Words like "public service," "community interests," "cultural fabric" and "educational responsibility" were studded like sequins through the briefs and submissions. One heard practically nothing about old movies, TV westerns, rock 'n' roll or Mighty Mouse. The accent was on Canadianism and the Arts. Buffalo [the New York State city that was at that time providing CBC-TV's only competition in southern Ontario] was a wicked villain, and everybody was trying to out-CBC the CBC.

When it came to Canadian content, all the contenders tried to outdo one another. Berton reported that

... a while back ... there was some whimpering and hair-rending by the private interests over the BBG's insistence that all programming be 55 percent Canadian in content. I'm happy to report that the carping has ended. Indeed, the applicants at the Oak Room were falling all over themselves to top this figure. It remained for Mr. [Jack Kent] Cooke to lead the field with 64.4 percent .... He is the sole owner of CKEY, a radio station that has devoted 58 percent of its time to popular records, more than 20 percent to commercials and less than one-half of one percent to public service, children's programs, drama, interviews and documentaries. Yet there was Mr. Cooke

165

promising to deliver great gobs of these on the screen. The only item missing was Great Hymns of All Time, but another applicant proudly unveiled that the following day. (P.S. He won the licence.)

Michael Nolan, in CTV, The Network That Means Business, described that following day's presentation by the licence winners:

Baton Aldred Rogers Broadcasting Ltd. (new name) emerged with the Toronto licence largely on the strength of its vibrant presentation before the board ... Rai Purdy's idea to provide a visual production on the company's capacity for innovative programming was highly effective ... "It was his suggestion that knocked everybody sideways," said Bassett, "that instead of getting up and speaking about the programming that we put it on tape, which was just brand new then, and we put little receivers for all the Board and big receivers in the audience .... Well, it was just spectacular ... I don't like to boast," Bassett recalled, "but I gotta tell you, our application was a knockout!"

Not mentioned in Nolan's book is that, a few minutes into Rai's personal part of the presentation to the BBG, the fuses blew, throwing the room into darkness. Rai, showman that he was, continued to talk in the darkness until the fuses were replaced—a good ten minutes later! Nolan gives Eddie Goodman credit for this—but I remember Rai telling me how it felt to "ad lib" for all that time in the darkness.

We could see the spring in his walk when he returned to Glasgow in late March 1960. He hugged each one of us before shouting at me, "You'd better start packing, Mum. We're all going home!" But not quite all of us left Scotland.

Even though we knew that Brenda had faced criticism from other, younger student nurses about favouritism, her marks were high. With one more year to complete, we felt it was crucial she graduate, so sadly we left Glasgow without her.

While in Canada for the BBG presentation, Rai had located a temporary rental for his family in Toronto's Rosedale district–a big, old, dark house (much like those in Glasgow) where the owner had locked away all her "good linen" before she let the house and went on holiday. I mended her "second" sheets and towels and cleaned the place so well that afterwards she was embarrassed and wrote to apologise. We remained friends for some time.

Fortunately, within weeks of our arrival Rai found us a charming place with almost half an acre of land on Arnold Avenue in Thornhill, not far from the CFTO development at Agincourt. Here we unpacked our Scottish stuff and counted our blessings. Full of light, this house was just the right size for Rai and me and Heather and Roger and dear Grizzo. It also provided a grand space for parties as it had been recently updated, and a huge living room with a white floor and wall-to-wall windows added. I soon regretted that we had sold most of the old pieces of furniture we had bought in Scotland, as it was friendlier and better made than anything we could afford in Toronto, and had brought with us nothing but pictures, lamps, copper containers and the silver plate we had picked up in second-hand shops and at auctions on Sauchihall Street. Fortunately, because Grizzo had come to Canada with us, I could take my time finding new furnishings. Her responsibilities, however, were light in our new home so she was able to enjoy her new surroundings, and both Rai and I noticed how quickly our simple "Scots lassie" picked up the latest Canadian fashions without losing any of her charm.

Since Roger, aged five, had already been at school for two years in Glasgow, grade one in Thornhill bored him, literally to tears, so we took him out of school. Heather, aged ten, was thought at first interview to be ready for grade five, but she had difficulty with some of the social changes and Canadian educational methods and found herself demoted to grade three. This was an understandable blow to her self esteem. But all was not sadness. The children's plea for animals was answered, first

167

by the SPCA, where they each found the perfect cat, and then at the Toronto and North York Hunt Pony Club where Heather began riding lessons. Rai and I, remembering our wartime dogs at Down Place, discovered a pair of Weimaraners that needed homes. And Rai's Toronto family became our family again, especially the children's favourites, Aunty Bea and Uncle Lint, who were more than happy to closely re-connect with us.

Rai, meanwhile, had taken on a huge challenge, but he was filled with new enthusiasm with such a bright future shining before him. Of course, it didn't hurt that the pay was far better than at STV and that one of the perks was a company car! Having returned to a familiar environment, he quickly connected with old friends, so it was no surprise to me that some of them joined the production staff at Baton Aldred Rogers. These included Dick Fonger, who had worked with Rai in his CFRB radio days, and Ev Staples, who had–until my riding accident–partnered me in the early days of the Canadian Army show as well as taking charge of wardrobe. It all seemed to me like such good fun to see them working together again.

Rai was able to lure tall, dark and delightful Murray Chercover away from CBC-TV to work with him as executive producer. Like Rai, Murray was experienced in legitimate theatre, radio and television and, although trained in New York, had worked in both Canada and the United States. Rai also hired producer Alan Shalleck from New York and producer David Main and director Graham Ford from England. To Lorne Freed, a Canadian who had been one of Scottish TV's top camera directors, Rai offered a similar position at CFTO, and Lorne soon became an executive producer. Rai also brought Robert Ash, a one-time circus performer he had hired in Scotland, to be a floor manager; later, as "Uncle Bobbie," Ash became the much loved host of CTV's long-lived children's program. And Rai's now grown-up elder son Brian, a graduate of Ryerson University who was by this time working for the CBC, joined CFTO as a floor manager, making this the first time that father and son had worked together. Ultimately Brian moved up through the ranks to become a senior producer/director at CFTO and later headed his own broadcast company. I had come to know Brian during our early New York days when he and his sister Brenda, still youngsters in their mother's custody, had come to visit Rai and me.

But while Rai was happy with the production team he was gathering around him, almost from the beginning he had serious misgivings about management. Bassett, who as chairman of the board had at first seemed to be so "with it," had now, along with the other shareholders, agreed to hand over the presidency to Joel Aldred. But Aldred had no particular qualifications to serve as president; though flamboyant, gregarious and self-assured, he had no management experience and soon showed himself to be vain, overbearing and heavy-handed. As president he had a free hand to hire all personnel except for those in Rai's production department, and he immediately brought in several of his close friends, including Charles Baldour as CFTO's station manager. But while Baldour had theatrical and production experience and Rai liked him, Rai questioned Aldred's wisdom in making him station manager because this was such a critical position. To the position of senior vice-president finance, Aldred assigned his pal Burgess Kayajanian. The legendary sports broadcaster and hockey promoter, Foster Hewitt, another of Aldred's (and Bassett's) friends, was named first vice-president.

During construction of the CFTO building, which took most of 1966, the station's primary offices remained in the Toronto Telegram building, while production planning and stockpiling of prerecorded shows went ahead on a horse ranch in Kleinburg. However, Rai and I visited the new studio site during construction and couldn't help but see that the executive offices on the second floor were spacious and elaborate. When the staff finally moved in, these suites had been expensively furnished–apparently they were all equipped with "casting couches"–and all of them were assigned to Aldred and his friends. Although Rai was also an executive, he and his production people were assigned comparatively cramped quarters on a lower floor, well separated from administration.

169

At midnight on the last day of December1960, CFTO went on the air with an 18-hour telethon which Rai, Murray Chercover, Charles Baldour and Joel Aldred had put together. A fund-raiser for the Ontario Association for Retarded Children, (awful as it now sounds, that was the advertised title), this frantic, but spectacularly successful production was followed immediately by a full schedule laid out by the director of programs.

For the first few weeks after the station's opening, Rai could take credit for a job well done, though even more importantly to his self esteem, this time he appeared to be finally well set and in good company. But although he always felt he had the support of Bassett and Bassett's lawyer, Eddie Goodman, it wasn't long before Rai found himself at odds with Aldred, who began telling him how to run his department. He interfered with equipment, show budgets and programming, announcing what shows would be cut and what replacements he and Bassett had agreed upon. One of Aldred's worst interferences was to summarily "pull" (after only a few weeks and before it could possibly build up an audience) a bound-to-be-popular "remote" called *Barn Dance*. This broadcast came directly from the glamorous Mart Kenney Ranch in Oakville and starred Mart with his wife, Norma Locke, and the "Western Gentlemen," the very best of the "down home" square-dance callers, and a wealth of competition-quality dancers in colourful regalia. We were staggered that Aldred could not see its potential. To Rai it was just one more sign that Aldred wanted to take over production and, even worse, it began to seem as if he had Bassett's approval to do it.

I think by this time Rai must have been aware that Aldred was fiddling funds allotted to the production department. I remember him telling me that Aldred "saw dollar bills in Bassett's eyes" and that, having gathered his friends around him and given them executive positions, he had gone on a colossal spending spree. When discrepancies began to show up, Aldred insisted to Bassett that Rai was a wastrel and trouble-maker and that Rai's production department was responsible for the huge overruns. For some time Bassett actually believed this.

170

My job during this period was to get the children settled and make a comfortable home where Rai could bring his business friends. It pleased Rai, who loved a party, that I could "put on a good spread." As in New York and Glasgow, as soon as we could, we invited members of the production staff and at times some of the executives to our home. Knowing or personally liking people didn't necessarily influence our invitations, and in the early days when the conflict at CFTO remained below the surface, it didn't prevent executives and heads of departments from joining members of the production staff for drinks or dinner at our home at our expense. (As in Scotland, Rai and I were the only people who cared about the social life of staff members and establishing a good rapport among them.) My recollection of Aldred and his Californian imports when they showed up on these occasions is that they always wore California casual clothes in muted shades–what we called "ice cream suits"–or came dressed all in black with expensive loafers on their feet. It quickly became quite obvious to Rai and me that they all liked the high life, and for some reason Bassett didn't seem disturbed by this. I remember feeling supernumerary among the senior executives who came to our home to drink and talk television with equal intensity, and so, aware to some degree of Rai's personal frustration, I stayed aloof when they came and simply did my job as hostess.

As Aldred and his group took more and more control of CFTO's operation, I could see Rai's freshly bolstered self-esteem begin to shrivel. Though he didn't tell me about it at the time, he was also upset that Aldred had summarily fired several of his production people. And then less than two months after the station's opening, Rai himself–ignored by Bassett–was forced by Aldred to sign a letter of resignation rather than be fired, which Aldred was in a position to do. Strangely enough, Rai had never become political nor had he learned how to fight, even though he had served seven years with CBS-TV and had three years at STV as programme director, weathering all kinds of ups and downs with them, and had come to this new company with an enormous amount of technical knowledge and television experience.

However, Rai's ousting from CFTO and the string of production department firings that followed didn't go unnoticed. Nathan Cohen, the arts and general gossip columnist for the Toronto Star, a strong competitor of Bassett's Telegram, apparently suspecting problems at CFTO, had been waiting to pounce, and pounce he did–though not in time to save Rai. On February 27 Cohen wrote that "evidence of the station's predicament occurred last Friday when 14 people received official, but unsigned, letters informing them their services were terminated. . . . It was explained that the people concerned had been hired as temporary office help, etc., and knew that there was no chance of permanent employment .... But among those let go last Friday were technicians, studio directors and two producers .... From the viewpoint of qualification and experience, the two producers who were let go were probably the most experienced men in the production department. David Main ... had been a network producer for two private stations in England. The experience of Alan Shalleck ... included work in New York." Cohen then went into much critical detail of the mess before discussing Rai's mysterious disappearance from the station:

> One of the key men of the CFTO operation, in finding a production staff, drawing up a program schedule and finding ways and means of honouring the promises regarding the encouragement of Canadian talent made by the Baton Aldred Rogers Broadcasting Ltd. when it applied for a licence to the Board of Broadcasting Governors in March 1960, has been Rai Purdy, Channel Nine's program director .... Even before the station went on air differences developed between Purdy and the board of CFTO regarding station policy, because of his insistence that pinch penny methods and short cutting from the pledges made in the original submission would be to break faith with the purpose of

making the programming, as chairman of board John Bassett originally promised, the heart and soul of the station's existence. In that fight, which became much more strident since the station opened, Purdy has been virtually alone as far as high-level support applies.

Cohen then remarked on the fact that no one at the station seemed to know where Rai was and that when he had asked Aldred, he had been told that Rai had taken a vacation. But Cohen was sceptical:

On the record then Mr. Purdy is still on vacation and still program director of CFTO. But the two producers dismissed on Friday were men he himself had hired; the decision to retrench on the local shows now on the air does not jibe with his views; . . . The policies that are now being given the go-ahead signal are in diametric opposition to those he holds. In short, the crisis at CFTO goes much beyond the to-be-expected adjustment problems of a new station.

The day following this attack, Cohen reported that "CFTO president Joel Aldred denies any crisis at the station."

I remember the look on Rai's face and the slouch of his shoulders when he told me he was leaving the company. Though he had hinted about some turmoil in the administration, I had no idea of the scope of the dramatic changes Joel was making. Now we experienced the same frustration we had both suffered back in New York when Rai had begun to lose his joy in working for CBS, and again our disappointment and sadness when his great success in developing STV had appeared to be of no importance to Thomson. In retrospect it is clear that Rai's personality and aspirations were never geared to the reality of the television business where it was always a case of promise fine programming, start with a splash, make a good impression then cut to the core! Rai's lasting successes and greatest personal rewards had resulted from owning his own company where he built successful shows, maintained them within budget and kept the quality consistently high.

Control room STV Glasgow

CHAPTER 13

Vancouver

Neither Rai nor I had ever considered my home town as a possible location for his broadcast interests. However, because I had always leaned that way, after the CFTO debacle he now looked west with me and chose to relocate Rai Purdy Productions (this time as a limited company) in Vancouver. So it was that in the spring of 1961, having moved house thirteen times since our marriage and changed countries three times on account of Rai's career, I was glad to call British Columbia home once again.

Rai's son Brian was left to look after our unsold Toronto home when we headed west. This move was taken without Grizzo, a huge sadness to all, but as luck would have it, she had been offered a position looking after the children of one of the T. Eaton families. (To this day, we are in close touch with her and her husband John Davis who now live in England.) On arrival we based ourselves temporarily at Sleepy Hollow, and the children, with their grandmother in charge, were registered in nearby schools. My job was to drive about with an agent looking for a house, while Rai bought a car, rented an office-with-telephone for his re-activated company and began calling the ad agencies.

Rai soon realized that broadcasters from coast to coast knew about the CFTO upheaval, were aware that he was not the culprit and were glad that his remarkable talent was again available. Thus, from the day he reopened RPP Ltd. in Vancouver, it was made clear to him that his theatrical acumen was highly marketable. One of his first moves was to contact his old friend, the legendary arranger/conductor Dal Richards. Together they threw around ideas for a weekly musical show, which he then offered to his Toronto buddy Spence Caldwell for his new Canadian Television Network (CTV). Within weeks, Caldwell had commissioned Rai's company to produce 26 episodes of West Coast, a half-hour show featuring Dal Richards and his orchestra with Richard's glamorous wife, Lorraine McAllister, as vocalist. At the studio where it was taped I was given the job of taking care of Lorraine's elegant gowns, and the two of us giggled as I snugged her into them, a feat made possible by her weekly weight loss of several pounds, thanks to diuretic pills, and the miracle of lastex corsetry.

But we had been barely settled in Vancouver when Rai received an apologetic personal call from John Bassett, begging him to return to CFTO as director of programs and, as such, to testify on Basset's behalf in his coming court case against Joel Aldred and several others. It is understandable that for the sake of his morale and reputation, Rai was sorely tempted to accept the invitation to return. Before making a decision, however, he talked with Basset's and CFTO's lawyer, Eddie Goodman, who explained what a bitter fight it was going to be. Later, Goodman would tell author Susan Gittens, when she was researching her book, CTV: The Television Wars, that "Purdy was terrific. He's the one guy who got screwed in all this."

Although it had been of some comfort to Rai to hear from Bassett himself that the men who had tried to become powerful while nearly ruining CFTO had already lost their jobs, Rai listened to my plea. "Too many times you've let people trample you," I told him. "You are better on your own. Why take on such a battle now? Remember, Bassett wasn't there for you when you needed him." I was greatly relieved when he said "no" to Bassett and chose to put all of his energy into building his own business. Rai and I knew the producing and performing sides of show business inside-out and knew how to give from the heart (often without remuneration), but it takes an entirely different technique–one that some of us fancy dancers never learn–to compete in television's "big business" arena.

As it turned out, the Bassett-Aldred battle never reached the courtroom. It was resolved later that year by Bassett buying out Aldred and Rogers for an undisclosed amount. The latter two then purchased CHFI, Canada's first FM station. Though few people had FM receivers at the time, Rogers began manufacturing inexpensive sets, thus making the investment in CHFI a financial success. Bassett, the winner in this battle, speaking to a Victoria Times reporter in December 1961, admitted that "he'd had his fingers burned in the first year's operation of CFTO." The report continued, "His first approach to TV was, he says, 'light hearted.' His present approach must be described as hard-headed. He. . . now spends his mornings in the Telegram office, his afternoons on television business. . . ."

In writing this story and attempting to put the CFTO pieces together, I spoke to many of the station's early employees, but none of them had clued in to the station's real trouble at the time. Murray Chercover, who had been Rai's executive producer, explained that he had been too far down the line to know anything about the conflicts at the upper executive and ownership level. He had been shocked by Rai's sudden departure and inundated with work when he was abruptly asked to handle many of Rai's responsibilities as well as his own. And although he had been aware of some of the California contingent's shenanigans, it also came as a surprise to him when just weeks later it was announced that Aldred was going on a protracted vacation from which he would not return to CFTO.

Apparently, at a meeting after Aldred left, it was discovered that there were many employees on the books who never seemed to have specific jobs. The task of cutting large numbers of employees, some of whom were working productively, could not have been fun. Michael Nolan, in his book CTV: The Network That Means Business, writes that:

177

Brian Purdy

View from Pasley Island

The following period saw the removal of the senior finance officers [including Burgess Kayajanian], station manager [Charles Baldour] and sales executives, etc., which explained why Bassett assigned a senior Telegram VP to the station until replacements could be found. It was during that time that Murray Chercover was promoted to VP status and program director for the station In fact, without Chercover's talent following the debacle of 1961, the station would have gone under. It was too late by then for Rai and other hard working employees that Aldred had sacked, but once the real problem came to light and Aldred and his friends had been discharged, quiet but strong Murray Chercover, as the new program director, took charge and built the station up, until CFTO became the key in the CTV network.

It was heaven for me to be back on the Pacific Coast, and once we were established there we borrowed Mum's cottage on Pasley Island on several weekends. Our children–Heather now eleven and Roger six–became instant water babies. Rai, despite our adventures on Loch Fyne, still wasn't keen on salt water and never swam, but he showed he was keen to handle small motor boats. On those weekends he met many of my cousins and was welcomed by other families who had cottages on the island, it being no longer exclusive to members of the Bell-Irving clan as it had been in my grandfather's day. The children found new companions and thrived on the feeling of belonging. In fact, we all felt much more at home in BC than we had in Ontario.

My quest for a home ended that summer when the Purdys settled into what we expected to be our permanent residence– an attractive, many windowed West Vancouver house almost at the top of mountainous Eyremount Drive in the British Properties. Its expansive view took in the harbour, the city, the Fraser River Delta and, beyond that, the American coast.

179

To the southeast on very clear days Mount Baker's snowy peak appeared to float above the curve of Lion's Gate Bridge.

We had only lived on Eyremont Drive for about two months when Brenda, by now a qualified children's nurse, came home from Scotland. She was wearing an engagement ring, and she showed us pictures of her handsome fiancé, John Knox, an ex-compulsory RAF trainee who, thanks to her financial help (through Rai's support), was soon to arrive in BC. Bren explained that she had met John in a dance hall in Glasgow. When I frowned, she assured me this was customary in Scotland where–with or without a partner–many young people gathered in huge dance halls under the supervision of chaperones. While she waited for her young man to arrive in Canada, I did my best to introduce Brenda to people who might employ a trained children's nurse, and I was excited when psychiatrist Dr. Jim Frazee offered her a position as a mother figure in a home for youngsters with emotional difficulties. But Brenda told me, with all the melodrama of the young, that she was not in the least interested. Her dream was to get married and have a family.

When John did arrive, we quickly understood what sort of bright, ambitious and upwardly mobile Scot she had been attracted to. He was well-spoken with very little Scottish accent until he lapsed into his natural way of speaking with Brenda; the thick Glaswegian brogue was an altogether different language. Though born in the Gorbals, the poorest part of Glasgow, John had thrived during WW II on the free supplementary rations provided for all British children. As a result, although his living conditions had been appalling, he had grown up healthy. And while his parents appeared never to have enjoyed a single luxury of any kind or had feelings of worth or confidence, John was bright and self-assured, and he obviously knew what he wanted; while serving with the RAF, he had taken several university courses (offered free to servicemen), one of them being Russian language and another Scottish law, since he intended to make his living doing business with an American company in Russia.

Though it seemed to me he was ambitious in a different way from our family-oriented Brenda, despite my misgivings, they were married in a simple but elegant ceremony in our beautiful new home, and John quickly adopted my Vancouver family. Short weeks later my uncle Duncan, having chided me for not introducing John properly, gave him a job with Bell-Irving Insurance Company, a job that came to an abrupt end because John could not keep the details of the family's personal insurance policies to himself. But he quickly found another company to work for, and by the time they had their second child John and Brenda Knox had bought a house on a double property in Dundarave village.

Early in 1962, Rai learned that, in light of a scandal over the legitimacy of a New York television show called *The Sixty-Four Thousand Dollar Question*, one of the show's producers, Dan Enright–also the executive producer of Screen Gems (New York), a division of Columbia Pictures–was looking for a Canadian company to handle another serial show that he and coproducer Jack Barry owned. They had already tried the format for this show, called People in Conflict, in the US, using real people in real-life conflict situations, but while it had worked, it had been taken off the air because the emotional content, developing spontaneously as it was bound to do, ultimately became too painful to watch.

Rai contacted Enright, for whom he had directed several CBS-TV series during the 1950s, and offered to talk to the people at CTV about airing a Canadian version of the show. As a result, Enright came to Vancouver to discuss Rai's ideas for taping Conflict here, using slightly altered but actual conflict situations with carefully chosen ordinary citizens to play the characters. Auditioning would be one vital key to success, writing clear-cut biographies for the actors to assume another. Having stated their problems as they understood them after being carefully prepped, the people (actors) in conflict would, according to Rai's plan, respond to questions from a panel of experts–a lawyer, a social worker, a sociologist, and a minister. Then, as the plot unfolded, they would allow themselves to express whatever emotions arose (often amazingly volatile). Ultimately, the specialists would explain

181

the problem as they saw it and offer their individual solutions. Because he trusted Rai's expertise, Enright gave his approval to this modified concept of his original idea, and to complete the package, Rai was able to tell him that Spence Caldwell's CTV network was keen to air *People in Conflict* five days a week.

Rai immediately hired Heidi Freya Sohnel, who turned out to be the perfect production assistant for *Conflict*; a talented young organizer, she had previously worked in radio, television and advertising in Vancouver, San Francisco and London, England. Rai next met with Ray Peters, president and CEO of Vancouver's first privately owned television station, Channel 8 or CHAN, which later became "British Columbia Television" (BCTV). Peters accepted Rai's offer to produce *Conflict* at CHAN's new state-of-the-art facilities in Burnaby, and by September 1962 a contract had been arranged between CHAN-TV, Screen Gems, the CTV network and Rai Purdy Productions Ltd., which set the show on its way for the first three years of its long life.

From noon until ten pm one day per week during the winter and spring seasons, Rai and the CHAN crew used the company's fine Burnaby studios to record a whole week of half-hour Conflict shows, then fed them one by one to the CTV network. On other days much of Rai's and Heidi's office time was devoted to studying new Conflict scripts as they arrived from the show's three writers, consulting with a lawyer and other panel members and casting the series. Month after month hundreds of other BC citizens–as well as all the people we knew–turned up for auditions. Because of the show's success, its permanent moderators–H.A.D. Oliver, QC, sociologist Dr. Gordon Bryenton, social worker Rosemary Brown, and Dr. Phillip Hewett, a Unitarian minister and board member of Family Services–became household names.

From that time on Rai relied almost completely on CHAN/BCTV to supply the studios and staff needed to make his show concepts into reality. This valuable connection provided the perfect facilities for RPP Ltd. to produce a weekly musical with flautist Paul Horn, a gourmet cooking show with James Beard and a beauty salon show with stylist David Ansen. He also created new formats for shows such as The Wasserman Show and Magistrate's Court.

However, during the summer months, although television was still his forte, Rai's past experience with big theatrical productions encouraged him to create pageants. Having put together a successful military tattoo in Empire Stadium for the Pacific National Exhibition (PNE) in the fall of 1962, he was offered a contract by the Exhibition to oversee all their outdoor stages and to handle all theatrical entertainment on the fairgrounds year round. As a result, that same year he became the man in the control booth atop the stadium for a concert by the Beatles with all the insane hoopla that entailed. But it was one time when he questioned his own sanity because he invited his smitten and screaming teen-aged daughter to watch the stars from that safe distance! RPP Ltd's contract with the PNE also included staging the annual Miss PNE Beauty Pageant, which took place during the last three days of the summer holidays, and for the next thirteen years the PNE paid Purdy Productions to hire me to choreograph this pageant. Though the PNE contract was mostly seasonal, it gave Rai plenty of summer work, introduced us to new and influential friends among the officers of the PNE, and provided a bonanza of free passes for our children to all the rides and concessions. But managing PNE events also brought other contracts to Purdy Productions; a quote from a newspaper article published following Rai's death and written by David Catton, a friend from his early Toronto theatrical days, describes the climax of another of his shows:

> Approached by Stuart Keate, then publisher of the Vancouver Sun, [in1967] Rai Purdy produced a spectacular party at the Pacific National Exhibition's Empire Stadium to celebrate BC's 100th birthday. There were several hundred performers and several thousand spectators in the stands watching the finale when Stuart Keate, who chaired the event, arrived on the field atop a motorized airplane staircase and, with a

flaming torch, personally lit 100 candles carried by 100 dancers circling an enormous birthday cake. Other parts of this same show took place in several locations within Stanley Park.

CHAPTER 14

Horse Heaven

Two years after our move west, Heather, by then a pushy thirteen-year-old preparing to enter West Van's brand new Hillside Secondary School, announced she had changed her name to Heath and would be needing a weekly allowance like the other girls who had fancy hairdos, wore lipstick and dressed in knee-high black leather boots. "They go to movies on Saturdays," announced our daughter. Rai and I became so alarmed at the materialistic attitude of the girls her age that, despite my family connections and his business obligations in Vancouver, we agreed we must take the children out of the city. When John Rennie, the comptroller at the PNE, and by now a good friend of Rai's, described a property he planned to buy in Fort Langley close to that belonging to the PNE's head of agriculture, John Farrow, we put Number 14 Eyremount Drive on the market and began to look seriously in the Fort Langley area. It seemed as though we had caught from each other an old-new kind of excitement: something truly mutual about our pasts, something that had to do with animals and the out-of-doors, and something to do with Heather (now Heath) and horses. And in the end it was probably because we saw the Farrow children riding upon English saddles in the field right next door to it, that Rai and I acquired the very first piece of land we were shown: 9.9 beautiful acres with stables and a house! The price was $15,000 and, with great good fortune and in the nick of time, I learned that my service with the Canadian Army still entitled me to a Veteran's Land Act mortgage at 3.5 percent!

Without letting Heath know, we enquired of our new neighbour where we might get the right sort of animal for our horse-keen daughter and learned that John Farrow had for sale a half-Arab yearling of the perfect size and temperament. Obviously delighted with the whole idea, Rai made an immediate deal with John to buy "Simbo." Clearly he wanted this new way of life as much as I did.

On the summer day in 1963 when we Purdys took possession of our new "estate" (home number 15!), Rai led his family through a gate between the two properties and far across John Farrow's field to where Simbo, a shining bay pony, stood waist deep in grass and flowers watching us approach. Rai asked Heath, "Would you like to have your own horse?" Then, without waiting for an answer, "Would you like to own this one right now?" Heath couldn't speak, but as she looked at her Dad, her blue eyes filled with tears. Then she turned and with her hand out palm upwards walked toward her new heartthrob. For years she had been saving for her own horse—no chewing gum, no lipstick, no hair ornaments. Simbo's price was a hundred dollars. She could pay ninety. Her dad offered to make up the difference and the sale was complete.

When Rai and I had first looked at the property—rolling fields close to the Fraser River—we had barely glanced inside the house because of what lay in the hollow below it, just beyond the garden fence: a sizeable barn with two box-stalls, a loafing area and a hayloft. And, 50 yards to the east across the crest of a hill stood a long, two-storey chicken house which seemed to invite immediate remodelling into a stable. Something in our blood had set us on a course to horse heaven.

"Better get a pony for Roger," Rai said. "And what about you, Mum? Are you going to ride again?"

His suggestion came as a surprise, but I answered positively,

"Why not? I'd love to, wouldn't you?"

On later inspection we were glad to learn that the kitchen in our old but very ordinary farmhouse was large and that the basement, although unfinished, was dry. There were bedrooms enough for the time being, and we could put in a fireplace, add a master bedroom and make all sorts of other improvements later. But first we must replace sagging fences and see what could be made of the chicken house. Simbo would have to remain at the Farrows' until our place was animal-proof.

In the early days at the farm, we had to rely on the willing help of neighbours who must have laughed at our amateur efforts to build fences and fix gates, but John Farrow put us in touch with local builders, introduced us to Bill Rogers, the feed man, whose son, David, also rode "English" and to Dr. John Gilray, the top veterinarian. None of the materials or services was cheap, and we were soon running accounts at the lumber mill, the feed shop, the tack shop and with Doctor Gilray. Thank goodness for the PNE contract and for People In Conflict, which Rai continued to produce one day a week at the Burnaby studios. On other weekdays he drove into Vancouver to work with production assistant Heidi Sohnel on commercial projects. He provided TV coverage of the Liberal rally in Vancouver and the back-to-back federal election campaigns of April 1963. Even with all this on his plate, Rai did try to share himself with his family, though this was never predictable. For one thing, because he often came home late and tired, he slept most weekday mornings, which meant keeping the children quiet till they left for school. Thank heaven for school buses. Sadly for all of us, he also slept some weekends, which made planning things with the children difficult, and his cheery Sunday 2:00 pm inquiry, "What would you like to do this weekend," was apt to fall a bit flat.

Meanwhile, because of our children's interest in animals, they and the Farrow children quickly became friends. John believed in teaching his kids about life in the most natural way possible and included our children—in fact, all of us—whenever a cow was about to calve. No matter what time of night, he would

187

give us a call and we would troop over to his cow barn. Rai, too, if he was home. As the five children of the two Scottish doctors, Mike and George Nielsen, also rode English style, it was natural that the Nielsens became our family doctors.

As soon as our fences were secure, we asked veterinary Doctor Gilray where we should look for a mount for Roger. He sent us to Sue Mills at Southlands, the place long recognized as the heart of Vancouver's horse world. A delightfully natural and obviously knowledgeable horsewoman, Sue asked us questions about ourselves and the children as well as about our stable while showing us various child-sized mounts. In the end she recommended "Burnish," a well-schooled, well-aged, copper-coated range-pony with blonde main and tail. The pony, Sue said, had a mind of her own, but promised she would be perfectly safe. When the animal arrived a few days later, Roger, not yet nine and lightly built, was hesitant about riding her right away. She seemed so big. Indeed, she was maximum for a pony–fourteen-two hands at the withers. But this pleased his sister. Since Simbo was still too young to be ridden and was as yet unbroken, Heath happily started riding Burnish regularly with a group of youngsters who were taught by Pamela Arthur. In the meantime, we bought an affectionate half-Welsh pony called "Wee Boy" that was exactly right for Roger. Within a few months, several of the local riders, including our daughter, entered a weekend horse-show in Duncan on Vancouver Island. Burnish travelled with the other children's ponies in a big horse trailer while Rai and I and our children brought along her tack, hay, grain and cleaning equipment in our top-down yellow Acadian. I don't suppose there was ever a happier bunch of farmers than the Purdys. To top it off, Heath placed first on Roger's pony–thanks to Burnish's earlier training in junior equitation–and brought home a red ribbon.

While Heath and Roger enjoyed their after-school riding in our fields and along the nearby verges or with friends on their properties, none of our fields was spacious or level enough for practising equitation or learning to jump. So, very early in the game

188

Farmhouse

Strath Ahshling

we realized we must put in a riding ring. Margo Parker, who had designed the best riding rings in Southlands, told us exactly how to level and drain and fill our own competition-sized practice-ring. She didn't tell us how much it might cost as we seemed to be oblivious to that sort of thing. In fact, for the first few months at Fort Langley, only Rai and I knew how really close to the wind we were flying. Although RPP Ltd. was making good money we were, as usual, spending it even before we had it. It wasn't until RRSPs became popular years later and Rai's accountant showed him the tax benefits that we ever had a penny's worth of savings.

Work began on the ring at about the same time we started turning the 80-foot-long, two-storey chicken house into a stable. After securing the upper floor with stalwart posts down the centre of the building, workmen removed the front half of the upper floor to achieve enough height for eight 10 foot by 10 foot box-stalls. The remaining back half of the upper floor could hold ten tonnes of hay, leaving space directly underneath it at ground level for feed-storage bins. Along the front of the building, the eight stalls were given two by ten-inch board flooring, sliding doors to the inside hall and Dutch doors to the outside. They were ultimately equipped with hay-racks and automatic water-troughs. All this, plus setting up a tack room and fencing separate paddocks and fields, took about six months.

As though in a fever, we bought another horse, "Mr. Chips" or "Chipper" for short, as well as riding clothes, tack and boots of every description. We ran up more vet bills, feed bills, and farrier bills as well as more lumber bills to modernize part of the old barn into a recreation room. We even set up lighting for night riding in the ring, greatly increasing the electrical bill. Rai and I were equally enchanted with our project and though it put considerable stress on Rai's income, that aspect didn't stop us. Neither did it stop us from hiring a lad from a nearby farm to help with stable cleaning and feeding. Ross Bowling was a queen's scout, good at everything he tackled and totally reliable.

At about this time we applied for a building permit to renovate the farmhouse and, as the plans went forward, Rai and

I discussed possible names for the property. Although we really thought the place was heaven and swore we'd never move again, we wanted to avoid the hackneyed End-of-the-Road or Final-Resting-Place sort of names that came to mind. I suggested "Glen," which admirably suited Fort Langley's position among the mountains, and "Strath," the Scottish name for the low land beside a river. But this reminded Rai that his sisters had traced the Purdy name back to the kings of Munster, and he said he thought we should look for an appropriate Irish name.

A day or so later, as I brushed my hair in the bathroom, my attention strayed to a small green bottle that my cousin Elizabeth had brought me from a recent visit to the birthplace of her brilliant and funny Irish husband, Darmuid O'Cadlaigh. It contained perfume, but I, having lost my sense of smell as a result of my riding accident during the war, hadn't bothered to open it. There was, however, an odd name on the square bottle and, at Liz's suggestion, I had turned it over to read in gold lettering a fragment of Ireland's political history. It spoke of the period when poets, forbidden to mention their homeland by name, had written instead about "Aisling" which, to the Irish, means a beautiful dream. Liz had also told me how to pronounce the word correctly with a soft "aahsh" sound at the beginning. Here, I could see, was an honestly Irish partner for honestly Scottish Strath. I rushed out to the stable where Rai was grooming Chipper and explained how I'd learned the Irish word for a beautiful dream. "How about Aisling?" I said the word softly. "How about Strath Aisling? Half Scottish, half-Irish, but we'd have to change the spelling or no one would say it properly." Rai thought for a moment. I said it again, Ahsh-ling and spelled it out for him, A-H-S-H-L-I-N G. (Much later I learned that, by adding two Hs, I had changed the word from Irish Urse to Scots Gallic!)

Rai grinned. "You've got it! I really think you've got it," said he, evoking the song in My Fair Lady. "Strath Ahshling. That's perfect!" And so, when the renovation was complete, an elegant green-lettering-on-white sign hanging from a lamp post near the house welcomed friends to Strath Ahshling. Another sign at our double gates further along Allard Crescent read, Ahshling Stables. (I remember how hard I swallowed when later, at a swanky event, someone addressed me as Mrs. Ahshling)! By then we had acquired several cats, one dalmatian we called Stripes and another wearing such a wonderful facial mask we called him Kelly after the famous clown, Emmett Kelly.

Although Heath seemed content at the local high school, Roger was less than happy at the elementary school. Rather against Rai's wishes, I asked Mum if she could finance Roger as a weekly border at Vancouver's St. George's School for Boys where long ago Dad had been a master and each of my brothers in turn had attended. This she did. Fortunately, the Purdys could share the transportation load with the Nielsens since Mike junior already attended St. George's.

Rai moved into farming with relish, never griping about his tedious, almost daily, commute into and out of Burnaby or Vancouver. He made friends with Dr.Gilray who explained at length over mugs of coffee about feeding and caring for horses. He bought the right shovels and wheel-barrows and wore the right kind of boots when mucking-out. He learned quickly how to mend fences and enjoyed building and hanging gates. And all of this endeared him to my mother who visited regularly. She fit into life on our horse farm as though born to it, visiting the horses in their fields, talking to them as friends. Often on a Friday, if it was his turn to collect the two boys at St. Georges', Rai would also pick up his mother-in-law or Brenda in West Vancouver.

Once, when he brought Brenda to Ahshling, she seemed depressed and complained that John had been rough with her. Both Rai and I assumed she was being overly dramatic and dismissed the conversation. But Bren must have felt badly let down because she never mentioned John's misbehaviour again, and as our own lives were full, we made no further enquiries.

Bill Irwin, the young man whom John Gilray had recommended to keep our horses' feet in shape, became like a member of the family. Not just a farrier, he had the perfect temperament to handle and train horses and was just the teacher Heath needed to break and train young Simbo. However, Irwin never used the word "break." The whole thing, he told us, was about gaining a horse's confidence, rewarding it with affection and never getting angry when it didn't understand what you asked of it. He told us what Heath would later need in the way of harness and driving lines, but for the time being he explained how she must use her hands all over him, keeping her body close to him until Simbo trusted her, even let her pick up his feet.

Sitting up on the ring fence, Irwin would talk to the two of them. After Heath and Simbo had really made friends, he showed her how to introduce the pony to potato sacks, to rub them on his neck, cover his eyes with them and rest them on his back. Black plastic and white plastic and newspapers came next, followed by cardboard and wood and metal on his back, on his rump or touching his tummy. It took several weeks of this daily work before the young animal was ready for a bridle of sorts, then a saddle, next the driving lines and lunging whip. Finally Simbo was ready to learn the voice aids. Irwin was always there on the fence, but Heath did the training herself, and one day, having quietly tacked up her pony, she led Simbo over to Irwin, handed him the reins and climbed up on the fence beside him. That was the day she put one leg over her horse and gently lowered herself into the saddle. Simbo's ears twitched but he didn't move a foot. Carefully she released the stirrups and put her feet into them. When she gathered up her reins, made the clicking sound he now understood, and squeezed him slightly with her legs, he moved forward, one step then another. When she shortened one rein and pressed her leg against his ribs on that side he began to turn in that direction, and when she evened the pressure on his mouth and pressed in with both legs equally, he walked steadily toward the centre of the ring. Backing Simbo–that is, teaching him to accept a rider–was as simple as that. He learned rapidly and was only two-and-a-half when Heath entered him in the Abbotsford Horse Show in the green pony class. (Foot-note: Bill Irwin's careful teaching led Heath much later toward a business of buying, training and selling horses through her own company, Ahshling Stables.)

One weekend in 1964 when Mother was with us, I saw a new sparkle in that old girl's eye as she discussed with Rai the purchase of a well-trained half-thoroughbred he had been offered by Vancouver's Mounted Police squad. Although this particular gelding's conformation was perfectly balanced, he hadn't come up to size or weight for police work. Rai wanted the horse for himself, but Mum said, "If he's a size that both you and Heath can manage, and you'll let me ride him now and then, I'll pay for half of him and give that half to Heath for her birthday." And so she did. Because none of the names Heath suggested, such as Kanga or Baby Roo (she thought he was bound to jump well), appealed to her grandmother, the fine little chap became "Watch-a-ma-call-um?" or Watchum for short, a catchy name for a horse that actually did turn out to be a fabulous jumper and won many hunter-jumper classes for our daughter.

On weekends off, Roger had started riding his own pony, Burnish, even though she was pregnant, having been bred to a pure Arab stallion (we had all been there to watch this carefully choreographed event). However, Simbo wasn't trained enough for Heath to ride seriously, Rai was taking lessons on Watchum (he really needed them as he was terribly tense despite his bravado) and I needed a mount. The result was, several more ponies and horses came to live with us: Anglo-Arab Bonnie Gay seemed just right for me, though a bit *dancy*. (But weren't we both fancy dancers?) Cricket was a scruffy but brave little bay mare who had in her youth weathered the cruelty of having a rock tied into her forelock to stop her from running away. Just because we couldn't resist him, we also offered a small sum and got Dyllan, a pure Welsh pony. These purchases, plus three welcome boarders, brought to eleven the horses and ponies we now must feed and care for, five of them stabled at night while the rest sheltered in the loafing-barn. Sometimes of a dark evening all four of us Purdys would troop up to the stable to check the stabled horses. They would whinny when they heard us climb the outside stairs and, looking down on

194

Heath on Burnish

Tony Popplewell teaching Heath how to open the gate
without dismounting

their often steaming backs, we'd throw them each an extra sheaf of hay. This *is* horse heaven, I thought, and Rai said, "It doesn't get any better, Mum. Thank you for bringing me here."

Although we all ate and slept horses and our vocabularies became laughably splattered with horse language, we did have other interests. Music was always important. Rai and I had records of all the Broadway shows as well as classics and stuff that was "beyond the fringe." Roger didn't get into music until later, but every other week I drove Heath into Vancouver for a double-length piano lesson from a UBC graduate, a handsome young man who kept her keenly focused. Without too much prodding she practised regularly, finding it easier and much more fun once she got into the Conservatory's grade ten book.

After breakfast one lovely, peaceful Saturday, Rai, up surprisingly early, was chatting with me by a window in the living room, remarking on the delicious undulations of our sun-splashed Fort Langley property. Before us, a path slanted down through our small orchard toward a gate in a rustic fence. Just beyond the gate a little bridge spanned the creek that divided our private garden from the old stable and the stable yard. The creek then angled away to the east to water John Farrow's fields, enhancing the sweep of our view. To the west was our own home field. Across the top of the hill above that, the new stable obscured our two top fields from sight. At this hour of the morning, Heath, who spent all her free time in and around the stable, would turn the horses out to graze in various fenced pastures. It was always a pleasure to hear them at play, galloping and snorting, racing each other along the fence lines. But although no horses were in sight, what we heard right at that moment was more than play. Something else was happening! Scared by the deep sound of many pounding hoofs, I felt my throat tighten and my heart thud. Suddenly, there they were, galloping across the home field and the stable yard below us.

"They're stampeding!" I cried. The horses were galloping, every last one of them—our own, several boarders as well as the ponies—straight across the stable yard and out through an

196

open gate. And the Dalmations were right in among them, flying! As we watched, they all veered left and raced away from us. And suddenly we saw that Heath was herding them, guiding Burnish bareback with nothing on him but a halter. She was in shorts, her own bare feet flying. Oh, the fool!

We rushed outside to call our daughter (fourteen by this time and fearless on any horse) to stop her crazy adventure.

"She'll break her neck!" Rai sounded really frightened.

"She's mad!" I echoed, but I was catching the thrill of it. I grabbed his hand. "Oh, don't stop her, please," I begged him. "Don't. She's okay!"

We stood, riveted on the crest of our property, caught by the flow of the crazy dance. As the animals thundered up the long hill opposite, I could feel the anxiety in Rai's taut hand and I was breathing hard myself. Wheeling left, Heath herded them through another open gate onto the top field. With manes and tails flying they pelted across that field toward the big stable and disappeared from sight somewhere down the back slope.

Then they came again from behind the building in a flood straight down the roadway toward us. Left turn across the stable yard, out of the gate again and back up the hill. Full circle on the big field at the top. The small Welsh ponies, faster on the turns, were out in front ducking under the necks of the horses. "Beat you, slow pokes!" We could feel them laughing. Rai, catching the joy of it, let out a long "Oh-h-h God . . . what fun!" For a moment or two the herd disappeared again behind the stable. Turning to each other, we grasped both hands remembering long ago times when we would have done it ourselves. When they came back into view this time, the animals had run out of steam. Trotting lightly down the road they spread about in the home field. Heath circled and they followed her up again, disappearing. After that we could relax and watch as our daughter, still mounted, put the horses and ponies away in their own fields, carefully securing each gate. Then, with head flopped down and arms hugging the pony's neck, she steered Burnish in our direction. Sliding off near the bridge, she slapped the pony on the rump and headed for the house. Noticing us for the first time, she climbed the gate and hurried up the path.

"Oh, Dad," she said, "did you see? Oh, Mum, if I could only play piano like that!"

December 1964 gave us ten days of such heavy snow that the local roads became un-driveable, but the views were rich in every direction with the low winter sun throwing deep blue shadows from fence posts and trees and buildings. Luckily Rai had no obligations in Vancouver, and Mum, my sister Moira and my cousin's daughter, Chantal, had already arrived to spend the holidays with us. All the horses we owned by then seemed perfectly content in their thick winter coats to plough around the property with the white stuff up to their bellies. They and the neighbour's ponies obliged the youngsters by cavorting in the riding ring while the kids, who were shrieking with laughter, clambered on bareback and fell off into the snow. Next day, one after another, our four-legged creatures behaved like angels when attached by long lines to Rai's home-made sleigh. Each one of us, even my mother, whizzed off on several bumpy but safe journeys halfway to Fort Langley village and back. Ours was the perfect white Christmas.

Come spring 1965, the valley was green again and fresh bark-mulch covered the stable yard, which had by then become the popular gathering place for local riders. It was then, remembering joyful Pony Club experiences in England during my youth, that I decided to start a local branch of the Canadian Pony Club. Though the district of Langley had hundreds of riders, of which by far the majority rode in stock saddles, this club would be for those youngsters who rode in the English style. When I learned from Dr. Gilray that he still belonged to the Toronto and North York Hunt Club as well as to their Pony Club, and that he had been the Toronto Pony Club's district commissioner, I realized he was just the man to draw up the plan. He was also delighted to become an integral part of the administration so long as I would do most of the footwork. I immediately sent to England for horsemanship manuals and the examination rule-book. After that, largely through Dr. Gilray's clients, word quickly got around about Ahshling's riding ring and the possibility of a new branch of the Canadian Pony Club.

Within a few months our club had a strong executive committee, mostly parents of the riders (they made me Langley district commissioner), and several excellent instructors. Pamela Arthur gave mounted equitation lessons in the ring and John Gilray lectured on conformation, breeding, feeding and stable management. Champion dressage rider Dodi Watney came (for free, as did all the instructors) and brought her famous black Arab, Arabi Ba, on which to demonstrate her skill. Dave Esworthy, the hunter judge from Southlands, taught jumping. Canada's Olympic dressage rider, Inez Fischer-Credo, instructed in her own speciality and various other professionals came to encourage and guide the members of our Pony Club. As soon as we had enough events taking place in the new riding ring as well as movies (there are wonderful equestrian films in the UBC library) and regular lectures in the new recreation room to prove that we were up and running, I applied for official sanction from British headquarters.

Meanwhile, I had been enforcing among the youngsters a strict code of impeccable personal behaviour and kindness to animals. The committee supported my wish that the Langley branch take on the official British Pony Club colours, light blue, purple and gold. Our hunt-cap covers, shirts and sweaters, tack-boxes, tack-markers, water-buckets and horse-blankets became highly visible at local horse shows and we quickly gained a reputation for our meticulous stable management, smart turnout and good manners.

In September our already sizable club received approval from British PC headquarters, and cap badges and ties, which had already arrived, could now be distributed just in time for our first competition with the Maple Ridge branch across the river. Uniformly dressed in grey pleated skirts or flannel trousers, light blue shirts and PC ties, our "D" team crossed the Fraser River set to win. Not only did our club members rise to their feet when addressing the adjudicator but, to everyone's surprise, they spoke clearly, repeating each question before answering it. We outshone our competitors, and to my delight Rai was able to be there to witness it. He was so impressed he promised to attend whenever he could.

By November, several of the youngsters, including Roger, were ready to take their "C" level exams. (These exams start at "E" level and go up to "A.") When I added the teaching of tack-cleaning and stable management to my agenda, every day became chockablock for me. Then, though we Purdys already had our heads and our hands full enough, Rai purchased for himself a dark bay, almost thoroughbred gelding, well boned and kindly. He was quickly named Horatio. Measuring 16.2 hands, he was a special horse. On the same day from the same stable we acquired a beautiful Welsh-thoroughbred cross, dark grey with black legs that looked like the boots on a guardsman. He needed a home, so we gave him one and called this little beauty Spit and Polish.

By the age of fifteen, Heath, having passed her "B" test, was one of the Langley Pony Club's most competent riders and a fearless regional competitor when riding either Watchum or Horatio (on occasion both in the same class). Rai was responsible for her nickname: "Heathio the Greatio on Horatio." She was as fastidious about her own turnout as she was about grooming and tack, and she and Mike Neilsen, who had also passed his "B" test, were invited to join British Columbia's "B" team when they flew east to compete in the "A" level National Rally in Ontario. Although the Westerners had to ride on borrowed horses, and Heath had an injury to an ankle which meant she was riding bootless on that side, our BC team won the jumping and cross-country classes and brought home the trophy that year. Heath personally won the highest marks in the written test. Rai and I were immensely proud of our daughter, though sometimes I wished she'd chatter less at a horse show with her teen-aged friends, and pay more attention to the course-plan before entering a hunter or jumper class. It also worried me when she became clever about positioning her horse so as to be noticed by the judge. In Pony Club language, "judge-watching" is considered to be in poor taste.

As district commissioner I had become paranoid that I might

show favouritism to either of my children, so without discussion with Heath, when the time came to choose the members of our club's "B" level team for our own upcoming Langley rally, I voted to select another rider. Of course, because she had passed her "B" test and had every reason to believe she would be on the team, she was deeply disappointed. This and her angry reaction to the situation caused the beginning of a rift we both found difficult to erase. Still, the Pony Club with its high expectations had taken over and was colouring our world. To non-horse-lovers, we must have sounded like a broken record.

How could anyone have stables and paddocks, a recreation hall, a lighted riding-ring and an active Pony Club and not operate an equitation school? Rai and I couldn't resist the temptation. We wrote to my brother Sedley, always an ardent horseman, who was at that time breeding Welsh hill-ponies as well as sheep farming in Wales, and asked him to advertise in Britain for an experienced equestrian who needed a sponsor in Canada in order to emigrate. By the end of August 1965 we had bought a small trailer, which we furnished for comfortable living, and installed it behind the big stable where we had put in a septic field and built a little washroom-with-shower. All we needed now was our pro.

Tony Popplewell arrived with his wife and child in September. A red-headed whipper-snapper with a freckled face, he was barely taller than I and had a hippy-age London accent even I found difficult to understand. Though his clothes were trendy, he was hardly well groomed; as a horseman, however, he showed absolute genius. He came to us from the "King's Troop," the company of men who train Britain's Household Cavalry, where he had become expert at show-jumping. He used the "Ritchie Wriggle," and we soon discovered that this bum-circling method of pushing one's mount—four, three, two, one—into a jump, worked like magic. As well as impressing adult students who very soon flocked to the Ahshling Stables School, Popplewell took a real interest in Pony Club activities and willingly shared his professional knowledge with our members. Of course, he had to have a quality horse to ride himself and, knowing a good mount when he saw one, he quickly commandeered Horatio who was to have been Rai's horse. However, as Heath had already fallen in love with this handsome and powerful hunter-jumper and they made a wonderful pair, for Tony Popplewell we found Knik, a 16.3 hands black thoroughbred. Together they won almost every class he entered in regional registered equestrian competitions.

Popplewell's charming and capable wife, Margot, was a qualified mental health nurse, and their very small child was Katrina. All three seemed happy to begin their Canadian life at Ahshling Stables, and I grin whenever I think of those volcanic but vibrant, infuriating but laughable, exhausting but wonderful years with Popplewell. He and his family managed to exist in, if not wholly enjoy, the trailer long enough for him and his students, including our two, to bring home ribbons from dozens of shows and to make quite a name for Ahshling Stables. But I also remember how my insides burned with indignation when Popplewell, while instructing a client in the ring, shouted at me, A Bring me another lunging whip. This one's 'ad it." He must have been accustomed to an endless supply of expensive tack in the royal stables for he had absolutely no respect for our pocketbook. He broke whips, lost bits, lent halters or just gave them away. But even though he was rude and impudent, I pandered to his vanity. One day he came up to the house wearing skin-tight, white leather britches designed to be buttoned below the knee. (They had been swiped, he told me, from the King's Troop.) His calves were bare and he wore running shoes. He said he needed the legs of the breeches lengthened. Despite being stretched to dry on his body–"You don't believe me?" says he. "Feel'em, they're still damp."–they had shrunk so much in the wash that they now barely covered his knees and certainly wouldn't close below them. By luck I had a piece of bleached chamois which, cut in half, was just enough to cover the hairy gaps between britches and riding boots. Hoping not to draw blood, I attached the extensions there and then with linen thread forced through the eye of a curved tack-mending needle. The seam wasn't perfect but who could tell? The strap of his black boots would cover the join. He wore those breeks for many a show, but in future when they needed a wash, I think Margot put her husband into them before scrubbing.

Popplewell was supposed to keep track of his pupils and record their lessons, but his book soon became a jumble of indecipherable notes. And whenever I asked him why things weren't done, his answer was invariably, "Oi din''av toim, did Oi?" Since he "din' `ave toim," I took on the business side of the school and quickly learned that his salary, which Rai paid each month, was considerably more than the school was bringing in. Then as Popplewell, competed in more and more shows, winning awards and becoming important in the local horse circles, he became less interested in the school and more and more brash and arrogant. I even heard him shout at his wife, who one day confided to me, "I love Tony but I don't always like him."

Ahshling Stables' only steady income came from the boarders. These horses, which occupied the eight big loose-boxes, mostly belonged to Popplewell's students and he was supposed to keep them clean, but to spread these chores onto other shoulders, he gave free lessons to several senior Pony Clubbers who came to clean stalls after school and on weekends. Though these youngsters made capable and willing "working-students," he expected a lot from them and wasn't always patient. When they came to my kitchen to appease their healthy appetites, they sometimes needed mothering more than food. On weekends when Roger was home from school Popplewell pushed him (through tears, I must admit) into having great confidence in Burnish, and the boy and pony became inseparable. Because of her age and solid understanding of correct behaviour in the show ring, Burnish took Roger to first place in junior equitation and pony jumping on several occasions. Many of our Pony Club members entered some or all of the local shows, and some of us trailered long distances to compete in professional events.

The competitions at horse shows are bigger today, and the jumps more expensively painted and decorated, but every time I watch a rider gather the elements of each particular obstacle for himself and his mount, check his progress so far, plus the challenges ahead (to which he hopefully adds his past experience and determination to win), the feeling in the pit of my stomach is just the same. The rider may look calm, but I feel his stress. I know some of the possible mistakes in judgement a rider can make, not to mention the weariness of the animal, which, despite its willingness, can by the third or fourth round affect the outcome. Back then, time and again I bit my nails to the knuckle for other people's children and, when it came to my own, I often felt sick with anxiety.

Years later Heath told me how gut-wrenching it had been for her, too, especially if she hadn't taken quite enough care in the warm-up, or if she had become cross and lost her cool in the practice ring. She knew better. Still, kids will be kids! She knew she was good and so did I, and I really wanted her to shine, but on her way to winning those coveted awards she often managed to infuriate me, showing off, talking too loudly, criticizing others, judge-watching. "Smart-assing," Rai called it. She got angry at me for expecting too much, but she also wanted a lot herself. She wanted to be seen as capable. But occasionally, just when everything looked rosy, she'd forget her course and be disqualified, and sometimes she had crashes. I remember the time at the International, as Horatio came to the last fence on his fourth round, clear with no time faults, his back feet shot out behind him on take-off. I saw Heath fly into the air as he dove straight into the fence and demolished it. There is a picture of her upside-down, head about to hit the ground and feet pointing skyward. Rai was in the control booth and I was halfway up the Agrodome seating. For an instant I froze, then flew from bench to bench between people, leapt the wall and ran to her. The jump stewards were rolling her over. She was out cold. It may have been five minutes, but it felt like forever before her eyes opened. Rai arrived just as someone caught Horatio who had found his feet, and the stewards were helping Heath up. She was all right. We were lucky. Some people's children get badly hurt in jumping events. Not ours this time, thank God.

Back at Ahshling with the Pony Club well established, excellent volunteers handling lectures, equitation and stable-management instruction, I turned our basement into a winery. Having failed endless times to convince Rai that we could save money by making our own wine instead of serving hard liquor to our many visitors, I felt vindicated when one of his dearest theatrical friends, Jimmy Johnston, served us a delicious red wine when we dined with him and his wife Cathy at their Vancouver home. Rai couldn't believe Jim had made it. I learned that he also made "saki" for which he gave me the recipe. Rai agreed we should try it as long as I promised to do the work. Since it was simple and cheap, we bought equipment–a five-gallon crock and a five-gallon fermentation bottle with a valve, a siphoning hose and the makings: sugar, rice, and raisins. I was happy to accept the chore of regular stirring, which went on for several weeks, before siphoning the liquid from the crock into the fermentation bottle. And sometimes I got a midday high from swallowing a gulp when I had to re-start the syphon owing to the tube's having sucked up a raisin! And luck was with us. Even the first brew was remarkably smooth, and future batches got better and better.

At first we served it hot in some minuscule jade saki-cups we had been given in New York. But that was fussy and didn't please the real drinkers. Next we tried highball glasses with ice. Because this tipple produced such a delightful atmosphere without any negative after-effects, our saki became extremely popular. Finally we ended up ladling the golden brew from an antique, flower-painted "hand-basin" in which we floated dozens of frozen coloured balls to keep it cool but not dilute the alcohol. At a dollar a gallon we could afford to be generous, but the demand became such that we upped each batch to five 5-gallon crocks. Our neighbours and friends collected old wine bottles for us, and Rai built extensive racks for holding them flat when filled.

Of all our various married experiences, this period of horse-farming, Pony Clubbing and wine-making topped them all for Rai and me. But in spite of being so busy at Ahshling, in 1967 we managed to commence the building of a Panabode cottage at West Bay, Pasley Island, on the property-share Mum had given us. Later, when our house was finished, Rai bought a 12-foot Davidson fibreglass dinghy. In those days everybody had a Davidson with its oak stem, transom and gunwales. In fact, there were enough of these bright little boats around that, during the annual mid-summer Pasley Island Games (PIG), there was a sailing class just for Davidsons. They came in red, blue, yellow or green and the fibreglass was so clear you could see sunlight through the hull. Ten-foot was the smallest that was really useful, but a 12- foot had the option of becoming a sailing dinghy with removable mast and centreboard. Our 12-footer was deep marine blue and usually wore a 25-horsepower Mercury outboard, which the whole family learned to operate.

Although I had never tried it, I remembered as a child watching the big boys steering their outboards standing up with an oar attached to the tiller. And though this had intrigued me, there was something else I'd seen them do that I really wanted to try. So one quiet evening, all by myself, I set straight out from our dock at West Bay–full throttle but stern heavy. Barefoot and being careful to leave the steering dead centre, I nipped forward over the two thwarts to place my feet evenly on either side of the stem. The boat remained on course. Now, as I moved my weight gently to port, she curved left, then I leaned to starboard and she came with me. It worked! No hands! Each time I moved, she altered course! So I experimented first with wide curves and then full circles. It was like skating! Absolutely fabulous!

Setting out to encircle the island, a good nautical mile, I rounded North Point, and the Davidson and I danced our way right across North Bay. I hoped someone would be watching. Heading for East Bay, we hit a bit of a swell near Pirate Rock, not enough to be dangerous but even more fun to manoeuvre in. Now I used my knees as well as leaning sideways. We flew on across East Bay, then South Bay. Minutes later, curving into our own West Bay again, I slipped to the stern to slow the engine and make a quiet landing. Rai was waiting for me. He had seen me leave and gave me hell. "Don't you have any sense of responsibility–for your children if for no one else?" I stayed grounded for the rest of the weekend. But when on Monday morning Rai left the island in another fellow's boat to attend to business in Vancouver, leaving the children and me in the new house, I couldn't resist showing our daughter, Heath, my new trick. She had no fear, and loved it as much as I did.

Once the Purdys were established at Pasley, we invited some of our West Vancouver and Fraser Valley friends to visit us there, among them Raymond J. Peters and his new wife, Heidi Freya (nee Sohnel) whose wedding we had recently attended. The four of us took an elegant picnic to Summit Rock and right then, the Peters decided they wanted a piece of this magical island. Since the Preston property was available, the Peters became our neighbours.

Late that year Rai was invited by Charles "Chunky" Woodward, John Gilray, Dave Esworthy and other members of the horsey set who now considered him a bona fide "gentleman farmer," to produce the prestigious Vancouver International Horse Show which was to open the PNE's new Agrodome. For me, working with Rai on choosing music for the show felt a bit like "Rhythm Rodeo" all over again. For Heath and several of her friends, who were in their last years of high school, these were halcyon days of competitive horsemanship with her dad at the helm.

In my youth the enthusiastic horse-loving English and Scottish cousins who had initiated me into Pony Club in Scotland had also introduced me to the sport of fox hunting, which now seemed to be the appropriate next step for our thriving Langley Pony Club. With the proviso that we respect crops, livestock, fences and gates, the executive committee invited farmers in the Langley area to support us by giving our riders access to their properties. In this way, we figured, long safe rides away from traffic might become available. The farmers' cooperation was extraordinary, far more than we could have dreamed. They even made sections of fence safe for jumping and bulldozed and cut brush where streams had to be navigated. Our riders had strict rules to follow. And they did. In the end we had permission to cross farms for a distance of 20 miles without retracing our tracks, enough for a

Langley pony club

The first Fraser Valley hunt

fully fledged drag-hunt. So, with the blessing of all the farmers over whose land we would ride, we planned to do just that.

In hunting country it is usual for an established hunt to support its own Pony Club in order to bring along young riders and instil in them the spirit of sportsmanship and consideration for others while preparing them to become members of the hunt. In our case, the procedure was reversed: our Pony Club planned to raise the money to establish the Fraser Valley Hunt Club (FVHC), long a dream of the Southlands crowd and of many Valley equestrians. This new hunt club was to be based in Southlands, where Vancouverites' still keep horses, play polo and hold horse shows, and where the club could raise and train a pack of hounds. In order to fund and launch this venture, our PC executive planned to stage a fully fledged drag-hunt within our new territory in October. Now a drag-hunt needs no fox, but it does need the scent of one which the hounds recognize and follow, and when asked to assist us, Stanley Park Zoo attendants were intrigued enough to set up a urine-salvage system in their fox pens. Half an hour before the riders are ready to set off on the chase, "the fox" (a Pony Club member with a fox-brush flying from the back of the hunt-cap), rides over a planned but secret course, dragging behind his horse the scent of a fox–that is, a urine-soaked sack on a long rope.

Our hunt would be preceded by a "hunt ball" par excellence at Fort Langley's Municipal Hall. The Pony Club executive set up hunt ball committees to deal with invitations, ticket sales, music, decorations and food. Invitations to the ball would be formal and include the mention of miniatures (mini-replicas of service medals from WW II). Although we planned to ask all the Fraser Valley riders, at John Gilray's suggestion, our first invitation went to the members of the Washington and Tacoma Hunt Club–including their horses, of course. These great people not only accepted our invitation but also agreed to bring their pack of foxhounds to inaugurate the Fraser Valley Hunt. Other replies came by return mail. Very quickly we had almost 200 individuals eager to attend our Langley Hunt Ball, and arrangements had to be made to billet out-of-town guests and their horses. Sleeping accommodation and stabling was immediately offered. Parking of horse-trailers was arranged and numerous people planned pre-ball gatherings. It was expected that tails, white gowns, long gloves and even tiaras might come out of hiding.

However, with the party only weeks away, one major hurdle stood in our way; how to beautify the site of our ball. Anyone looking at the aged Fort Langley Municipal Hall could see what sort of challenge faced the Pony Club's decorating committee. The building is set back from the main street about 50 feet and the route to it in those days took you through potholes in a gravel track that curved through a bumpy field of grass and garbage, passed the front door and curved back to the street. The building itself was, and still is, a shapeless blob. Back then, no one took the least care of it, and it was covered with peeling pink paint. With three windows on either side of central double-doors and six more to match above them, the only saving graces to a boring design are the two stubby pillars on each side of the entrance. Inside, at the end of a gloomy hallway banked with panelled doors, a tall and surprisingly wide wooden staircase leads upward to a huge echoing reception room with a stage at the far end. The woodwork was, at that time, badly in need of paint and polish.

Had there been any other venue choice we would have taken it, but nothing smaller would hold the crowd expected to attend. However, not everything was as depressing as it first appeared. Having explained to the municipality why we wanted to rent the hall and with careful political manoeuvring convinced them that it was time to spend money to refinish the rough floor, they even promised to polish it. That was when I learned, to my surprise, that the old floor was properly sprung for ballroom dancing!

It was imperative that we create a good first impression for those attending the ball and that, once inside, their attention should be directed toward the staircase which, with carpet, lighting and baskets of flowers, could be made to look inviting. The outside, however, called for nothing less than a complete face lift! Cover it with greenery was my immediate decision.

210

Measuring the height of the pillars and the size of the windows, I estimated we'd need at least 1,500 feet of thick cedar garlands to create a disguise. I arranged a meeting of mothers and friends and, after describing to them what I felt we needed, we worked for a whole morning attaching cedar boughs to lengths of garden twine with short pieces of wire. As soon as we got good at it and knew how fast it could be done, each of my volunteers left, having promised to deliver "x" number of yards of garland on schedule.

Once I had my own dinner party planned (we would be twelve), the last big job–the floral decorations for the hall–would be mine. And this was a job I loved. I had been noting the progress of autumn and knew exactly where to pick long branches of rose hips, blackberry vines with unripe berries on them, coloured leaves, snow berries and holly. I knew every garden that had hydrangeas and chrysanthemums and had gained permission from their owners to pick. I knew who had big pots and vases, baskets, copper buckets and other suitable containers. And I also lined up several helpers for collecting and arranging. Tables around the dance floor were to be opulently decorated with flaming cotoneaster and, where the masters of the hunt and Pony Club officials were to sit with their ladies at the table of honour, I could visualize as the central decoration a scenic arrangement of fences with Thelwell ponies, and their coat-tail-flying-riders approaching and jumping impossible obstacles and landing precariously. This, I knew, would be brilliantly executed by Marni Nordman, a non-riding but artistically talented club member.

With the cooperation of the Pony Club boys, volunteer members of Scouts and Rangers as well as the fire department (who brought their long ladders), the job of wrapping the pillars and swagging the windows took the first shift of volunteers only one night. By morning the second shift were ready to scythe, mow, then rake the grass, as well as fix the potholes. With additional lengths of cedar ropes, we created a canopy which swooped out from the front doors to two posts dug into the turf and topped with torches. And we borrowed more torches, popular at that time, to provide clusters of them out by the street. Flood lights placed on the grass gave body to the decoration so the pink of the building was lost in feathery shadow giving the old place an aura of enchantment. The lights also illuminated an impressive grid of white jump-standards and *cavaletti* (small jump poles) which we borrowed from riding rings and set in a curve outwards from either side of the front doors to offer a grand approach.

The final touch to the grounds was added on the day itself when "Chunky" Woodward of Woodward's Department Stores (a keen supporter of the hunt) had his garden shop driver deliver a whole truckload of the potted trees that had just been used to decorate the jump courses at the International Horse Show in Vancouver. We placed them along our freshly manicured circular driveway and from there, caught in the flood lights, they cast tall shadows up the face of the building.

Even with its rejuvenated dance floor, the inside of the building had been a challenge, but the pulp and paper division of MacMillan Bloedel had responded to my request by providing enough reject print roller pads, soft grey/green in tone, to completely carpet the entrance hall, the stairs and the foyer. To lower the ceiling, my masculine volunteers had strung wires from end to end of the ballroom and hung lengths of light pink, yellow and green cotton borrowed from Woodward's Spring fashion show. Woodward's had also provided extra cotton strips to disguise the customary black velours curtaining the stage.

Rai had arranged with his old friend Mart Kenney that he and his famous Western Gentlemen would play for our dancing, and Mart had agreed that his music should include waltzes, polkas, Schottisches and reels as well as current dance music and that he would close with his signature tune, "The West, a Nest, and You." When the time came, handsome Dr. John Gilray emceed the entertainment which included our guests in pogo stick races, a difficult feat at the best of times but the cause of great hilarity when our formally dressed contestants raced across that slippery floor. The horse-headed pogo-sticks which I had found at an exposition also had swishing tails. But the most interesting skill-test that evening turned out to be the horn-blowing competition.

212

As if by magic, no less than six old polished instruments had appeared: a posting horn, a coaching horn, a French horn and three English horns–and it was astonishing how many men and women were familiar with the hunting calls and pressed their embouchure (lips) to the horns. Several of the Americans sounded like seasoned huntsmen, but the contest was won by our own Popplewell, who turned out to be a truly talented trumpeter!

The ball was a huge success, as formal and well dressed as any ball at Victoria's Empress Hotel but probably much more fun, and the festive and friendly mood was enhanced by the anticipation of the morrow's hunt. Though they'd had plenty to drink, the guests left at a reasonable hour so as to be in good shape to ride. Next morning dressed in their best,–"pink" coats very much in evidence–109 mounts and their riders, including Heath on Horatio and Roger on Burnish and other members of our pony club, as well as a huge crowd of spectators (called hill-toppers), met at ten at the Fort Langley sand field near the Fraser River. The day was glorious. The American hounds behaved impeccably. Photographers, having stationed themselves to get good coverage as the field moved off, had a fine time recording the event. After welcoming speeches, stirrup-cups and much well-wishing for a good hunt, the hounds were put to scent and within moments streaked off down the dyke. Away! Away! The Tacoma huntsman's horn and the "tongue" of hounds were soon lost amid the clatter of horses. What a day to remember! And there are pictures to keep the memory fresh. One of the outcomes of that weekend was that as soon as the new Hunt Club was registered, they began their breeding program with one "couple" of hounds from Washington and several "couple" from Ontario. Weren't we pleased with ourselves!

During all this horse business, Rai's television career was continuing in Vancouver with numerous exciting assignments. One of these occurred when in 1968, during Pierre Elliott Trudeau's campaign to become prime minister, he appeared in a TV interview broadcast from Vancouver. The interviewer was our old friend from Scottish television, newscaster Jack

Webster, and by lucky chance, Rai, who in addition to his role as a producer, was also one of the very best camera directors in the west, was chosen to groom P.E.T. for the broadcast. Not quite by chance, our Heath skipped school that day to be in the CBC office with her Dad. As was his style, Pierre greeted our teenager warmly, bestowed one of his kisses and tucked her under his arm as he listened to Rai and Jack discuss the show. He took Heath with him when he and Jack crossed the studio floor to the set. Heath remained with them until Rai was ready to roll and called her into the control room. It was in ways like this that he could bring his family into his career.

As the years went by, although Rai continued his heavy schedule in Vancouver, we Purdys still participated in everything to do with young people and horses that took place within reach of our horse-trailer, including the International Horse Show, and with Rai in charge, enjoyed the wonderful friendships that were the result of all our energies. However, though we had sworn we would never leave Ahshling, the time was nearing for us to move on. Heath had registered for UBC, Roger had important football games with his school on weekends, and Rai really needed to be nearer to his work. As my knee had gone out of joint while I was loading a bail of alfalfa into a station-wagon, I couldn't handle that sort of heavy work any more.

Except for Horatio, all the animals were gradually sold or given away. I know Burnish went on for several years making other children happy and winning ribbons. Tony Popplewell took Dyllan for his daughter Catrina, now four years old, and Wee Boy went to another good home. The others were bought up quite quickly because all the horsey people knew them to be well fed and well trained. We sent Horatio to a stable at Southlands because Heath was still riding competitively, and that season she managed to win five zone awards which made her top junior for the year. We all attended the celebration at Southlands riding centre.

The sale of the farm was ultimately clinched by our basement full of saki, once the buyers–a British couple, who had drunk saki while they lived in Hong Kong–had tasted ours and passed it with flying colours. In the spring of 1968 we said goodbye to Ahshling with heavy hearts and moved back to Vancouver. But our hearts were also full of gratitude. In little more than five years our family had packed into their lives enough wonderful horsey experiences to serve us in memory for all our days.

CHAPTER 15

Back to Vancouver

After leaving Fort Langley, Rai, Roger and I took an apartment on Point Grey Road in Kitsilano. Roger continued at St. George's as a day boy and Heath chose to stay on the UBC campus. Rai was relieved to be closer to his work, which was by that time very demanding.

During our stay in the apartment I was able to spend time with my sister Moira who, miserable from the effects of chemotherapy, was failing rapidly. One night as Rai and I struggled to make my sister's ancient record-player (which we'd brought to her hospital room) provide a reasonable volume to fill her ears with her favourite requiem, Moira, who had lain unconsciousness for several days, came back to awareness complaining, "What's all the fuss about?" I tried to explain we were changing shift, and she said, "Why don't we all have a good long sleep?" With that, she closed her eyes and breathed her last. When the mirror test satisfied the nurse that my sister was no longer alive, she drew the sheet up over Moira's face and left the room. I must say I welcomed Rai's great sense of timing in that particular situation. As I removed the sheet to look one last time at the face of that dear person who had supported me selflessly all her days, he shook his head gently and said, "She doesn't look at all well, does she?"

"No," I said, and smilingly accepted his understanding hug.

That fall after Moira's death, my life took a new direction. Hoping I might find a niche in Continuing Education's Theatre Arts program, I applied and was accepted at Vancouver City College. I attended lectures there for the next two years, the only senior schooling I ever had, but I loved every class and got good marks, too. My courses were English, French, social sciences, fitness, swimming and drama.

I was not far into my second term, however, when I had to take time off. Rai had received a call from the police telling him that both Brenda and John were patients at Lion's Gate Hospital in North Vancouver, one suffering from a car accident, the other from head wounds. John was unconscious and within 48 hours he died. Bren was released from hospital two days later and Rai drove her to West Vancouver to collect her children from neighbours who had been caring for them. He then brought Bren, five-year-old Karen and three-year-old Sandy to our two-bedroom apartment.

Hot chocolate and raisin-toast calmed the children. Rai offered Bren a drink but, pasty-faced and shivering, she wanted only tea and a hug. I was ashamed to realize how little sympathy or caring either Rai or I had shown Bren and her family, too busy with our own lives to recognize John's problems and too critical of Bren's simple emotionalism to pay attention to her cries for help. But the beatings she had hinted at had been real and John's drinking and philandering had become serious. This time he had tried to kill her, was holding her on the kitchen floor face down and beating her head with a wooden toy, when Sandy had appeared at the kitchen door and screamed. In that moment, Brenda had squirmed free and shouted at John, "You don't want the children to see this. Stop! Stop!" He had rushed out of the door, jumped into his brand new car and roared up the driveway. Brenda, bleeding profusely, had managed to telephone for help. She had arrived at Lion's Gate Hospital emergency just minutes before John had been delivered, comatose, to the same department. He had driven out along the Upper Levels Highway and crashed full speed into a rock face.

Rai slept in the second bed in Roger's room so that Bren and the two little ones could be with me in the big bed. After the children had fallen asleep and I held a sobbing Bren, I heard much more of the Knoxes' sad story. It all came out: John's pretence of loving her, his arrogance and belittling, his physical cruelty and her efforts to appease him. She showed me, under her dark, dishevelled hair, some of the 48 stitches that had closed her surface wounds. What terrible disappointment and sadness for her, for Rai, and for John's family. Nothing I could say would soften the iniquities that had befallen Brenda from the beginning of her life. The best I could do was listen and look for ways to comfort her and to nurture two little people who couldn't comprehend what had happened. A memorial service in the Unitarian chapel, collecting John's ashes, and writing letters to his sisters in Scotland seemed all that I could help with. After two weeks, Rai returned Bren and her children to their empty West Vancouver house.

Shortly after that I was forced to have knee surgery and took to crutches, but it wasn't long before I limped back to college. Rai's business life flourished, but he complained he felt cramped living in an apartment after the freedom of Ahshling, so as soon as my knee was strong enough, I found us a little house on Blenhiem, closer to Roger's school. It was good for entertaining and convenient to Rai's office, which was an apartment in a downtown hotel.

During the 1960s and '70s, telethons were the "in thing" for raising large sums of money for charity, and in October 1966 Rai had produced the Variety Club's first ABC Show of Hearts," a fund raiser for children with disabilities. Contracted by BCTV, these Variety telethons were at first televised from the Vancouver Playhouse, though in later years they were moved to the Queen Elizabeth Theatre. Rai was no stranger to Variety, a theatrical charity organization as he had belonged to it in Ontario. Neither was he daunted by the marathon that was standard telethon programming; he had launched CFTO with this format in December 1960. His ability to deal with hundreds of acts interspersed with pledges and station breaks while keeping the show on time brought him enormous respect and popularity among fund raisers across the country who booked him several years in advance.

Because he knew I loved the backstage scene, right from his earliest days with telethons he had asked me to give him a hand, and over the years I worked with him on many occasions, not as his production assistant but simply as his runner. I attended auditions and met the performers. I became familiar with their material and where in the program Rai had placed them. I knew which dressing room was allotted to whom and for how long, and I kept tabs on where else in the building I might find MCs or hosts between appearances. There were times during those shows when Rai needed someone to communicate personal information to a performer or to take special instructions to the show girls who constantly raised the totals. Those were the times when I moved in a hurry, having discovered early on that running was generally faster than checking in with the stage manager on head phones.

Mainly because most telethons ran for 20 hours, I also made it my job to look after my husband, the producer, who hardly took a breather once the musicians entered the orchestra pit. Rehearsals began at ten on the morning of the show in preparation for an eight pm on-air performance. With all the technical people in place and attached to each other and the control booth via head phones, the stars, one after the other, had time on stage to discuss their introductions with Rai and perform at least part of their acts with the orchestra. Then, after the (union) musicians had departed for a break until show time, local performers, using their own musical accompaniment, checked openings and closings and tempi with the conductor. While non-musical acts took instructions from Rai about entrances and exits, the technical crew checked lighting, sound and any special effects those acts needed. Aside from talent, literally dozens of service club representatives had to learn how, when and where they were to present their gifts and tell the audience about their involvement in fund raising. However, important as these people were, it was imperative they keep their presentations short, and this was no easy task as all were introduced by fanfares and

220

spot lights which encouraged them to "hog" the microphone. It usually took until about five pm to get through the whole script, leaving Rai an hour to check his notes. At six pm he would move his stool to centre stage and gather around him the entire technical crew as well as the music conductor–perhaps 40 people in all–plus anyone who had a question about running order or his or her particular job. As I stood on the fringe of this eager group listening, ready to do his bidding, I was always amazed how calmly and quickly Rai went through his list of comments to the various department heads and answered the multitude of questions in high humour as well as with understanding and precision. It was like being in the eye of a hurricane, I thought. Everyone respected Rai, and he knew they'd give him their best.

I kept him nourished through the night with easily digested snacks plus juice or milk, and did the same for anchor people such as the brilliant puppeteer Shari Lewis, whose personality set the tone for Variety Club telethons and who for several years was largely responsible for their increasing popularity. As each huge cast gathered to create cohesive and appealing presentations, they also took on the serious challenge of encouraging generosity in the hearts of audience members. During the long night hours, ever-changing casts continued to build excitement as the big dollars rolled in, each contributor hoping his or her donation would prove record-breaking. Thus, during these years, in addition to being known as the producer/director of Conflict and other highly successful series, Rai became known as the Telethon King.

By 1970, a bit bored with telethons (not that he stopped producing them) and having decided to freelance as a TV movie maker, Rai gathered several of his old actor-friends and teamed up with a photographer named Roseboom. "Life begins at sixty for R.P.," wrote Jack Wasserman in his theatrical news column. It was about this time that Rai hired as his production assistant Fiona Jackson, a dynamic young Irishwoman, and she joined the crew that worked out of his downtown office. For their first TV movie effort, Rai chose a script based on George Axelrod's 1967 book, *The Taming of the Canadian West*, which was well documented with photographs of nineteenth-century paintings by artists such as Paul Kane and A.J. Millar and wood cuts by John Webber. As well as filming live scenes with local actors, he used what was then a new technique–moving slowly across an artist's depiction of a buffalo hunt, for instance, with voice-over by an actor in character. He was excited when he saw rushes of the film, which starred several of his friends, but the CBC criticised both the book and the show as being patronizing toward Native people and refused to buy it. This came as a shock to Rai, but it didn't put him off movie-making. Paul Rockett, a cinematographer newly in town from Hollywood, joined the production team on a second film about Canadian confederation which used BC actors and a good deal of film footage taken around Pasley and other islands in Howe Sound.

By this time I was very concerned that Rai was out of his depth. I felt sure he hadn't the knowledge to handle history and politics, and I wasn't surprised when this effort didn't get far either. Rai's disappointments sent him home pretty disheartened, but though I hadn't the knowledge to help him, I listened while he poured out his frustration and did my best to cheer him up. Strangely enough, in Rai's down times when he needed my encouragement, we were good pals. He would take better care of me. We would discuss our differences and vow to be kinder to each other. Always sure his next idea would fly, he would tell me about his newest dreams, then together, with real excitement, we'd foster their development until one of them intrigued a buyer and his business surged again. But as his career once again consumed him, he no longer needed to be patient with me nor restrain his drinking. Feeling less than important to him, I deliberately took myself away on several occasions, once as far as England to visit relatives. Each time on my return he admitted he had missed me, and each time we made a new start. We actually studied Scot Peck's *Road Less Travelled*, took therapy and just talked, trying to bridge an increasingly persistent gap. But I had long ago given up trying to be the pal who would keep up with him drink for drink night after night, and when talking

222

no longer made any difference, I had to look the other way and find interests of my own.

However, although I struggled through this period of Rai's career without much compassion–indeed, with considerable despair–his assistant, thoroughly educated and totally Irish Fiona, who ultimately occupied all the official and unofficial positions on Rai's staff, took his company's ups and downs without surprise. From her point of view, Rai was forging ahead in a burgeoning industry, pushing all the boundaries and taking disaster in his stride. From the beginning I liked and trusted Fiona who quickly became family. She and I collaborated on several shows and always had fun.

Though Rai and I lost touch with her several years later, I now realize–through unexpected letters from her–that in those days she had been considerably more aware than I of Rai's outstanding talents in the still fledgling television industry of which she was a bona fide member. In 2003, this is how she described their first meeting:

I had recently made my own first film about the late Blanche MacDonald. It was through working at her school/ talent agency I met Rai. . . . I had attended a meeting of the BC Film Industries Association, dragged there by a filmmaker, and had sat through what seemed like hours of whining and complaining, which horrified me. Bravely I stood up and asked if there were any solutions to be mentioned or if one merely stated problems. I spoke of my excitement about the talent we represented at the agency. I also spoke of the difficulty of getting that talent recognised. . . .

At that point a very dapper gentleman stood up. He wore a trench coat, had the sort of moustache I recognised as belonging to a certain sort of man (having been raised in the British Isles myself). His voice had a musical quality. He introduced himself as Rai Purdy and said he was a producer who was always willing to hear from or about actors. He said if I ever wanted to go into production to give him a call. . . .

223

Fiona went to work for Rai in his downtown apartment-office which she later described as: "a marvellous space filled with film cans, scripts, typewriters, books and papers."

My title [at Purdy Productions] was flexible. Depending on the job of the moment, I was production assistant, executive assistant, continuity girl, clapper board girl, camera assistant, casting director, writer's assistant or production manager. No film school on earth could have matched it for hands-on, do-or-die adrenalin. He introduced me to Chief Dan George, with whom I worked occasionally over the ensuing years in film and feel so grateful to have known. Being introduced by Rai meant I met a "man" and not a celebrity or an "other". . . .

He taught me everything . . .

On the Empire Stadium project, Rai had me co-ordinate representative costumed dance groups from every ethnic group in the province. This introduced me into a mind-boggling new world of ethnic politics where Estonians would not dance with Lithuanians, who had to have the same allotted time as the who-knows-who. What an education for me! I, of course, was well prepared for all of the politics, my being Irish and also the daughter of an activist mother who brooked no interference with what she perceived to be just and true. When, after weeks and weeks of meetings and hullabaloo, I got them all agreed and sorted out, they then decided, as a group, that they could not participate unless the Native people were given equal time. I still remember my perplexity at that one, suggesting to them that since the Native people were indigenous and Aboriginal, perhaps they might not take kindly to being invited to join the ethnic minorities. . . .

It is an eye opener to me now how clear Fiona was, so long ago, about racial discrimination. In another letter she wrote:

What was so rare about Rai, which I intuited then and which hindsight proved, was his personal spirit. He just went on, did things, if they didn't fly, did other things. He did not wring his hands, whine, complain, combust–as do most of today's producers. His vision was huge because his experience was huge. Not alone was he a pioneer of international television (surely one of the most profound of 20th century changes), he had been to war, met people of every stripe and social class. Fundamentally, he enjoyed his work.

But I wonder, Verity, is it lonely at the top? What might it have been like on a stormy night, far off in the pacific northwest when the centre of your working universe is thousands of miles away? No peer group to share the fears and unnameable dreads.

Little older than my daughter Heath, Fiona's youthful wisdom came as a surprise to me. For the first two years after leaving the farm, Heath had lived in residence at UBC. Her major was music, her minor linguistics. But her keenest interest remained in horses. With Horatio stabled nearby in Southlands, she had entered and won several hunter-jumper classes in important shows. Concerned that she wasn't planning to finish her education, I suggested to Rai we register her for a year at Ecole Superieur, a fabulous language school sponsored by Canadians in Neuchatel, Switzerland, and since Heath seemed interested in becoming fully bilingual, Rai agreed. So, right after her 19th birthday party at the Blenheim house, we shipped our first-born to Neuchatel, hoping to broaden her vision and spark her interest in returning to UBC. So as far as speaking the French language was concerned, Heath did brilliantly. Within a year the was totally fluent in everyday conversation and, returning to UBC, registered for second year French with a view to teaching. By then she shared an apartment with her Fort Langley friend Marni Nordman. On her first practicum, facing grades nine and ten students (grade nine boys being notoriously difficult to teach French), she nursed every one of them through their exams without a failure. Her method of teaching, however, was strictly Heath. But while it didn't please the faculty that she sat on the desk, swinging her legs, and kept her class in stitches–fancy dancing in French, of course–she passed her practicum

225

without trouble and moved in with her steady beau, George Gudewill. In her third year, faced with French literature, her luck failed. Not the least academic, she figured fourth year French would be out of the question and got herself a well-paid job instead. Looking back, I can understand the feelings of unworthiness she must have suffered, but that same year George Gudewill cushioned the blow when he asked her to marry him.

At about that time, despite a lull in his business, Rai and I fell for (at what seemed even then a very low price at $75,000) a once grand old mansion on Laurier Street in Shaughnessy and straightway began to update this, our sixteenth home. Having given up his downtown office, Rai had fun setting up his desk and cabinets, installing lights and hanging pictures in his own comfortable space (with bar) on the lower floor. There for a short while he held production meetings before a sudden rebound in his business forced him to hire more staff. The space then being too small, he moved Rai Purdy Productions Ltd. to the Queen Elizabeth Theatre building.

Although we had only owned the Laurier house for a few months, when Heath told us that she and George had become engaged and planned to be married in November, Rai and I were equally excited about arranging the wedding. We knew the house could be ready in time because the drawing room had already been painted to show off a stunning fireplace faced in jade-green tile ,and we had chosen fabrics for renewing our old furniture. We had wallpapered the hall, carpeted the grand staircase and bleached the panelling in the dining room. We'd trimmed the hedges, rejuvenated the lawns and painted every inch of the big old place on the outside including pillars and verandas. However, unlike our usual style, this time we'd arranged for other people to do the work. Having lived in and refurbished so many homes during our marriage, we felt quite confident as decorator-contractors. Beneath a smart black roof, the exterior was now a muted battle-ship blue with white inner and black outer trim at the windows. I had chosen mustardy-greenish-yellow paint for the broad front stairs and veranda floors.

Inside the house, however, work had come to a halt at the swing door leading to the pantry. Because we'd been extravagant on the rest of the house, the kitchen was obliged to remain old-fashioned, and the renovation of bedrooms plus the almost-turn-of-the-century bathrooms–huge tubs, separate loos–must remain on our wish-list. Never mind! The reception areas were perfect for a wedding: the staircase was ideal for taking pictures and the impressive dining room awaited speeches and cake cutting.

When their engagement was formally announced, I promised myself that Heath's wedding would shine with all the delightful embellishments mine had lacked. It would be one super Purdy Production and we had three months in which to make it all happen. I don't think Heath had ever been to a wedding, and she seemed surprised and delighted that her parents would arrange everything. Rai took on the production part of it–sound system and recording, photographs and transport. Champagne and other libations were also on his program and I worked with Heath on the lengthy guest list.

Doctor Phillip Hewett, the counsellor on *People In Conflict*, was happy to marry Heath and George, and I knew he would lead a dignified but refreshingly simple service in his Unitarian Church. I also knew the church would be filled with glorious music and friendly people. I wanted the whole thing to be generous as well as formal. My fun jobs were to make the bridal gown and do the flowers and my head swam with decorating ideas. A November ceremony called for rich colours.

Despite the fact that my mother didn't approve of her granddaughter's behaviour–cohabiting with her fiancée before marriage–and warned me she would not attend the wedding (which saddened but didn't really surprise me)–she did remind me of the yards and yards of off-white velvet which hung from its selvedges, carefully covered, in one of her closets. This fabric, prewar and made of pure silk, had belonged to my late sister. Around 1950, recognizing a bargain, Moira had bought the velvet and put it away for her wedding–which never came. Although she had been Heath's godmother, a responsibility she had taken rather too seriously so that it caused a cool relationship between them, Heath was overjoyed to accept this sentimental gift along with other treasures such as the pearl girdle from her granny's wedding dress. Mum also lent Heath an heirloom tiara of pearls and a double string for around her neck.

Heath and I settled on a dress design, long-sleeved and high-necked with lace at wrist and throat, and I took up my task. While I sewed every stitch by hand, my thoughts were on flowers: for the bride, three bridesmaids, (her cousins Chantal, Lila and Ginny), her maid of honour, (Marni), and her flower girl (Brenda's daughter, Karen.) There were to be "button holes" for George, his best man, for Roger and his cousin Campbell, for both the dads and ten other men. And for a dozen ladies small corsages. I also needed flowers for the house, the cake and the church. For all this I wanted and set about finding sources for, exotic hellebores, (Christmas rose), one of my favourite flowers.

I knew two people in Surrey who cultivated Hellebores (Christmas roses) in their gardens and I had heard about several old estates on Southwest Marine Drive where they grew wild. On my walks around Kerrisdale, I peeked into gardens and noted the numbers on the streets where the shiny leaves of these particular plants looked encouraging. One by one, I phoned or visited the property owners during September and October, inviting them to contribute to the beauty of my daughter's wedding. "Not now," I would say, "but about the second week in November when, with luck, hellebores will be in bloom." If the people seemed intrigued, I'd hurry on, "Could I ask you to cut them on long stems at a slant and immediately put them into a deep container of hot water? They then have to cool out-of-doors, be stored in a cool place and you'll see, they'll hold their shape and last indefinitely!" Not everyone was interested, but a surprising number kept in touch with me on the progress of the flowers. And we *were* in luck; buds pushed up early that year.

Meanwhile, the station wagon and I made the rounds to talk with gardeners in charge of the planting around hospitals and other public places where landscaping featured cotoneaster,

228

holly, oriental red maple and pyracantha. At the Red Cross headquarters on Oak Street, the cotoneaster bushes were ten feet high and laden with berries. The caretaker there agreed with me that the bushes were badly in need of pruning. He told me to bring clippers and fill the wagon at my convenience. "Take all you can use." This kind of generosity was great for decorating the church, which was spacious but rather stark. Huge arrangements of cotoneaster would be elegant without looking too showy. The bridesmaids, whose long Elizabethan-style dresses were being fashioned in deep green silk shantung with sashes of scarlet velvet, would wear circlets of berries in their hair, and carry cascading bouquets of berries with ivy. But who would create these important arrangements?

I'd heard there was a Dutch girl somewhere in Kerrisdale who had a special knack. Searching along 41st Avenue, I found nothing, drove all the way to Dunbar, turned the corner to head home and there was her shop. Just meeting Olga gave me confidence, but would she want to do all that work and not sell me flowers as well? You bet she would! Olga was almost as excited as I was. "Just bring me the makings and tell me what you want. I can provide wire and anything else we'll need."

"Mixed with Christmas roses and holly," I told her, "I want daffodils and white freesia in the dining room, and I shall need more freesia for the cake. I've located long strands of twin-flower leaves under the snow on the trail up to Hollyburn," said I, pointing in the direction of that mountain, "and I've found a good source of fine ivy, too. Can you think of anything else we should have?" Olga was grinning at the way I waved my hands about, but I felt sure she understood.

The week of the wedding, my helpers set out to collect the many basins, buckets, jars and boxes of Christmas roses–at their best as had been promised–their ivory petals wax-like, palest green and pink-tipped, their stems in water as I'd requested. The containers half-filled a cool room in our basement. Then came the greenery. I'd found tall new shoots of bamboo to arrange in an old copper milk carrier. They were just the colour my own taffeta gown was to be, hardly green at all. I phoned Olga. "Right," she said. "Keep it all cool for two more days, then bring it to me. You said hellebores for fifteen button-holes, didn't you?"

As was customary at that time, the mothers of Heath's bridesmaids were asked to be responsible for producing gowns for their daughters, and the groom's family knew they were expected to pay the florist's invoice. The girl's dresses turned out most professionally, and on the wedding day when the flowers arrived, each package revealed more of Olga's talent. Berries literally tumbled over rich winter green for the bridesmaids. Each lady's corsage held several Christmas roses but was otherwise varied in character, and Heath's abundant bouquet was so breathtakingly gentle, I nearly cried.

On that day, Ray Peters arrived wearing a proper chauffeur's cap as our radiant daughter, in her velvet wedding gown carrying an armful of Christmas roses, appeared at the head of the stairs on the arm of her proud and dapper Dad. With all the swish in the world, Ray held open the door of his blue Mercedes for them, then whisked them away to the ceremony. "Trumpets and Fanfares" were to accompany them down the aisle.

For some months thereafter Rai and I attended services at the Unitarian Church. It was the only time Rai had ever shown interest in a formal service. We both enjoyed listening to Philip Hewett.

The following spring the celebration for Roger's graduation from St. George's School was a very different kind of party, but the Laurier House was again ideal, especially Rai's old office which had the bar in it. About twenty boys and their girl friends drank copiously, danced to loud music and devoured beef dip, popular at that time. If the level of noise indicated enjoyment, they had a very good time.

But after grad, Roger didn't stick around Laurier. That summer he went into the bush as a choker man, put the money in his pocket and then for a few months apprenticed himself to a shipwright. Next, he worked his way on a Norwegian freighter to England where he looked up relatives and revisited Loch Fyne, scene of his youth, before hitching a ride across the

Heath

Roger

English Channel. On the French coast, he made a little money when he found a yacht-owner who needed a shipwright. After several rewarding months in Europe testing his high school French and German, he came home thinner and wiser to a prettier and greener land than he had remembered.

While Roger was away, the pattern of Rai's moods and behaviour, which, according to the ups and downs of his business career, had habitually fluctuated, became clearer to me. Although I had enjoyed sharing his limelight when he was on a high, it was then that he drank more and an ugly streak of self-centredness, indeed arrogance, showed up in him. As a result, I had discovered I actually liked him a lot more when he wasn't wearing a crown. Now, except for entertaining his friends and helping him on telethons, he needed me less and less. Since the children had become independent, there had been several occasions when I'd felt so servile and used that I wanted with all my heart to be free of him. On one occasion I faced him squarely and said I'd leave if he didn't change his egotistical attitude and his drinking habits. This obviously shocked him into silence. A few days later, though we had been barely speaking, he took my arm as we crossed a downtown street. It felt as if he cared for me. A feeling like electricity went through me. I was desperate for some genuine attention and could have died for him at that moment, but I couldn't respond, and we walked on in silence. Finally, to prop up my own self-esteem, I signed up for a typing course and after that joined the Chelsea Shop of interior design.

By that time Rai had become interested in getting a licence to operate a new private TV outlet, so we moved to West Vancouver to be near the planned station. Roger joined us in the new house above Gleneagles and overlooking White Cliff Marina and Howe Sound. Rai spent long hours at the site of his new dream, a moribund film studio on Panorama Ridge where the new broadcasting tower was to be built. He spent even more time in the city with lawyers, investors and broadcast technicians who were setting up the company. He was full of energy and optimism. Never before had he been so close to owning something this BIG, and he thrived on it. Despite the fact he had literally no money coming in, we were both excited and geared up by his great hopes. In spite of his new interest and my new job, as usual we planned renovations to our new home, and the year passed swiftly.

Rai was happy to have Roger living at home and was willing to support his first year at Capilano College; our son, however, wasn't much inclined to fit into our pattern. During that year, his part of the house was one hell of a mess and he never let me know if or when he or his friends wanted to eat, bathe or use the laundry. When he turned 20, after having spent the summer instructing kids at a camp, he told us quite casually that he wasn't going back to college. Distressed, though hoping he might change his mind, we told him bluntly that, unless he attended college, cleaned up his own mess and showed some consideration for our lives, we no longer felt obliged to extend free room and board. Although it seemed to come as a shock that we would consider turfing him out, Roger gathered his belongings and left. We saw very little of him for several years.

Faced with making a living, Roger's bright brain, his strong physique and his green jalopy took him to the BC Parks branch at Cypress Bowl where he learned about chain saws, tree felling, carpentry and chair-lift engines. He made enough to pay for an apartment and enjoyed free skiing, too. Then, he headed for the Alberta oil rigs and put money away in order to travel by motorcycle down the west coast of the USA. In Southern California he got a job doing yacht repairs. Back in BC, he apprenticed again to a shipwright for several months before becoming a deckhand-engineer so as to learn about radar and sonar and Loran navigational systems. All this new technological information didn't help much, however, on the trans-Pacific adventure that followed.

Responding to an ad they had found in a Vancouver paper early in September, Roger and a seafaring friend agreed to deliver the 24-foot sailboat, Simply Super, to Hawaii for the young woman who had sailed it single-handedly all the way from Britain. Jill Baty, a top navigator from the Royal Yacht Club, had recently crossed the Irish Sea and the Atlantic Ocean to Newfoundland, sailed down the American east coast, through the Panama Canal and up to Vancouver. But it was November when Roger, his friend, and two young women (who had little sailing experience) set out from Vancouver's inner harbour with no radar, no sonar, and no engine—nothing more, in fact, than the sails, a chart, a shortwave radio, a sextant, a compass, the sun and the stars to get them to the big island of Hawaii.

The journey took 29 days and nights, some of them battened down with buckets overboard on the ends of extended ropes acting as sea anchors to steady her as Simply Super rose and wallowed in brutally rough weather. Other days, forced by southwest winds, they found themselves moving back toward Alaska. Roger spoke to me later of one particularly scary night when he was on watch, while the other three huddled below deck trying to rest. Each time the boat rose to the crest of a great wave and crashed into the trough of the next, he thought it would be their last. It felt, he said, as if the little craft would break apart. Clutching the tiller with both hands, he had been fighting with all his strength to hold her bow into the wind so that she wouldn't roll over, until he remembered a talk we had had. Out of my own concern for their safety as they prepared to set sail, I had said to Roger, "Should you find yourself in trouble, and the problem you have is too big for you, remember you are not alone. Turn it over to that friend." I didn't know from where this wisdom came, but Roger told me he heard my words that night, and felt himself relax. As he softened his grip, Simply Super responded by rolling with the waves instead of fighting them. She didn't turn turtle, and when the sun rose again, she was still afloat.

Both sea and forest appealed to Roger. When he came home, he bought an old but beautiful wooden sailing boat and cruised among the islands in the Strait of Georgia. He chose to stay on Cortes Island where he had many friends because it offered a simple, uncritical way of life and the opportunity to use his forestry and building skills, as well as to sail, fish, sing, dance and play music among other considerably less idyllic pastimes.

234

Several years went by when he seldom called. Twice, Rai and I went to see him in the meagre but colourful dwellings he shared with one or another of his pleasant country women friends during those "hippy" days. Lean and bearded, he was glad to see us and showed us the property he hoped one day to buy. In time he came back to the city, but he wasn't yet ready to settle down.

Roger was never a tough guy nor was he without artistic leanings, and live theatre interested him. A job at CBC-TV doing set construction led him to spend a summer in Stanley Park with "Theatre Under the Stars" where he focussed on sound and lighting in the technical department. The director even gave him a singing part. I was surprised what a pure voice he had developed and how well he projected it. When his dad asked if he'd like to try television, Roger worked a whole season as a production assistant (including five telethons across the country earning $3,000 for each of them). The job was demanding and the backstage politics were cruel enough to convince our son he wanted no part of his father's business, but by this time he knew he must return to university. Without Rai's financial help, Roger completed four years on the UBC campus at the BC Institute of Technology and two more at the University of Victoria which gave him a teaching degree in Industrial Arts and made his life rich and valuable.

Meanwhile, Purdy Productions had become one of the three finalists selected from the CRTC's first hearings, and Rai was convinced they would give him the licence following the second hearings. However, after another hectic year of preparation for it, Rai Purdy Production's Biggest Ever Dream collapsed. None of the applicants received a licence.

Now in order to pay off our mortgage on our Gleneagles house, I asked Mum's permission to sell our Pasley share. I was grateful for the years we had been able to enjoy the island and surprised how easily I resigned myself to the final loss of it. Just as I had always done, when things went wrong for Rai, I managed to stay strong largely because his failures brought with them his deep neediness and a gentle humility. But as usual, his depressed mood didn't last long. Purdy Production's business picked up again and we stayed for five good though volatile years at Gleneagles. Neither of us ever having put down deep roots, next to New York, it was the longest we'd stayed anywhere.

I had been glad to be near Mum who, though still living on her own at Sleepy Hollow, was getting on in years and spent a few days from time to time in hospital having fluid drained from her lungs. I would pop in on her on my way to and from my job at the Chelsea Shop. But at 7:30 am on the morning of November 29, 1973, I telephoned her instead.

"Wasn't it a great show?" I said, when I learned she too had been awake in the wee small hours to watch the moon's eclipse. Then I told her that since I was running a bit late, I couldn't visit her on my way into town.

"Quite all right," she said. "You brought me good things to eat only yesterday."

"I'll see you on my way home," I promised, but at about 1:00 pm I had a call at work from my aunt, Pye Bell-Irving, who told me she had just taken a casserole to Mum.

"You'd better get over here," she said brusquely. "Your mother has had a fall."

"How badly is she hurt?" I asked.

"She's dead," said my aunt.

By the time a member of the staff had driven me back to West Van, two undertakers from the First Memorial Society were waiting for my arrival before taking Mum away. Our family doctor was also there, standing in the kitchen where Mum had been preparing her lunch. Dr. Robin Bell-Irving gave me a hug and told me she couldn't have suffered. "Her heart must have stopped," he said, "before she fell. Even though she cut her head on the counter, there was no blood."

"Did you want to see the body?" asked one of the men in black.

"We put it in the bedroom." Of course I wanted to see her and took myself to Mum's familiar squirrel's den filled with pictures and letters. Turning down the coverlet, I was surprised to meet her feet! When I found her dear face, I knew she was no longer

236

there, but we'd both seen the joke. Nearby she was laughing with me.

Rai was understanding about the time and attention I gave to settling Mum's estate, and I was grateful he refused to become involved in the division of her belongings. Instead, he began taking an interest in our Gleneagles garden, turning poor turf into a beautiful lawn, though he complained that it now grew too fast and he was faced with constant mowing. Later, while he built trellises and arbours, I planted rich herbaceous borders. As always with a project on hand, we worked well together.

But while I had the garden and exercise classes, my job and study courses to keep me interested, and we had lots of friends who came to our parties, our personal life continued to be fraught because of the disruptive influence of alcohol, Rai's constant desire for intimacy, and my reluctance to cooperate under the circumstances.

Fed up with me, I suppose, he was also becoming negative about other people—drivers on the road, ferry staff, unions, do-gooders, even about people who had worked for him faithfully and generously, and I thought this was despicable of him.

Some time during 1974 I told him I wanted out. After another round of therapy, this time in Seattle, Rai agreed that before making a decision about a separation, we would deliberately avoid all acrimony for six weeks then talk about it. Though he became even more negative, I did my best to give him the benefit of the doubt. While often biting my tongue, I remained sunny and uncritical. Neither of us mentioned the agreement but I assumed it was on his mind. After six weeks it occurred to me he figured I'd changed my mind. Seven, then eight weeks went by during which, though boiling on the inside, I became silent.

That autumn, after a telethon when Rai's exalted opinion of himself had become exasperating, I finally faced the possibility that my aching legs and feet might be caused by something other than being his runner on shows. I decided to attend a spa in Zurich. Though Rai knew that I needed to get away, he couldn't believe I would go in December. "How could you go at Christmas?" he asked, then complained, "What will I tell people?" But I couldn't face Christmas parties and said I really didn't care. I told him I wasn't going to write to him and that I'd rather he didn't write to me. This was a traumatic decision to make, but I couldn't go on blaming myself for not being a good partner in bed and for not being able to forgive his drinking himself into an unsteady blob night after night. If he could quit smoking when he chose, stay sober while he worked–which he always did–why couldn't he stay sober the odd evening for me?

The diet at the Bercher Benner health clinic seemed appallingly bland and the vegetables horrendously overcooked, but there were a few compensations. In the mornings we had exercises in the music room, followed by an art class. There I met Marta Rebel, a frail but charming German woman who spoke English and knew the clinic well. We spent a lot of time in her room once we discovered the similarity of our likes and dislikes. With me, she blossomed and showed her true spirit. We have been friends ever since.

Marta introduced me to Yehudi Menuhin's sister, Yalta. She told me that the Menuhin family regularly took health treatments at the clinic, and Yalta used the grand piano in the music room to practice. On Christmas Eve, everyone was treated to her carol service. According to each country from which we patients had come, Yalta played a suitable melody, but for me, because she had heard that I was a classical dancer, she played Chopin instead. After that, up two broad steps from the music room, two wide white doors were opened into an anteroom to disclose a glittering Christmas tree decorated from tip to floor with hundreds of lighted candles. Yalta played "Tannenbaum, O Tannenbaum."

Having settled the date for home-going, I sent Rai a note addressed to Purdy Productions with no personal greeting, signed only V. Shortly thereafter, his friendly but questioning answer noted my lack of affection but assured me he'd meet me in Montreal. In the intervening weeks we had both looked at our lives and decided to work harder to resolve our difficulties. His letter had ended with: "I adore you, Sweetie." Both Rai and Roger met me in Montreal where they had just finished a successful telethon. They were happy

238

working together and I felt better about my relationship with Rai who seemed to have cut down on his drinking.

CHAPTER 16

The Sunshine Coast

Two years after Mum's death, when I had a little of my own money, and because I really did hold some resentment about having lost the Pasley inheritance, I pressed Rai to look for a small piece of waterfront where we could build a cottage to leave to our children. He liked the idea. He also knew a real estate chap who had a boat and dealt in country properties. The Sunshine Coast, reasonably accessible to Vancouver, was the obvious choice. It was as though real estate and the challenge to create a beautiful living space–interests we shared equally and amicably–was taking over from show business.

Tucked into the rounded rocks of Halfmoon Bay, barely visible from passing boats yet taking advantage of the fabulous westerly view, there grew a woodsy but elegant country house, cedar-sided to melt into the landscape. It had vaulted ceilings, open beams and a great granite fireplace. No Pasley cottage, to be sure. Camping there at weekends, we both worked long hours on the interior finishing. Energised and happy, Rai sometimes even forgot to mix a drink before dinner. We were getting mighty good at this sport of ours but we couldn't afford two homes so we put them both on the market, which was good at that time, and let the market choose for us. The Gleneagles property sold quickly and well, and the new owners allowed us three months to prepare for our move to the Sunshine Coast.

This created the perfect opportunity for Rai and me to visit Pamela, that dear friend of my childhood whom I had last seen in New York. She now lived in Lima, Peru, with her new husband, Orlando Orlandini, the charming paediatrician she had met aboard the ship that was, she thought, taking her and Louis Stumer's furniture from San Francisco to their new home in Peru. Not so. Louis had flown south toward Lima, but detoured to Reno on the way. There he had divorced Pam and married another woman. Multilingual, Pam had survived and supported herself during her first year in Lima with a Spanish language radio broadcast for women, La Hora Pamela, before she opened a travel agency there. Now she and Orlando had a fabulous ranch in the mountains where they lived with llamas and parrots, servants, high fences and watch-dogs.

Having obeyed the notice on their great gate: "Wait to be introduced to the dogs before entering," Rai and I were shown to a guest house by Orlando. There he gave us a key and warned us to lock our door on departure. It appeared the Orlandinis didn't even trust their own servants. Pam had a grin on her face when she met us outside the main house and showed us to a splendid feast spread in the shade of their vine-covered patio. As she lavished hugs and kisses on us, a parrot fluttered in under the greenery to settle on her shoulder. The whole place seemed to me like a lush movie set.

We learned a great deal about Peru, its government and its people during the next few days, quickly getting a picture of extreme differences between the "haves" and the "have-nots." It became obvious that men like Orlandini, an Italian Peruvian, educated and trained as a physician in the States and Canada, were of particular value to members of the socialist government. In fact, he and Pam had raised funds amongst their capitalist friends to build a children's hospital which served those families well. In return, the Orladinis received such privileges as extra gas for their cars, freedom to travel and permission to send their son away to school.

It had been Pam's idea that while visiting Peru we should see Machu Picchu, and we had taken her suggestion to book a room in the small tourist hotel at the top so that we might wander about on our own after the crowds left. But first we spent three days in Cuzco, fifty minutes from Lima by plane and 13,000 feet above sea level. We had been told that because of the swift change in altitude we must, upon arrival, carry no baggage, eat nothing, but should drink "matte tea" and then rest until our systems became accustomed to the thin air. Although Rai wasn't affected, I reacted as expected, quite unable to say the words that were in my head. In fact, to my surprise, while trying to order an evening meal, my struggling brain produced remnants of long forgotten French, learned as a kid from my Aunt Doffie. Characteristically vociferous, she often used that language for swearing but, try as she did to tutor me, I picked up little more than her cultured French accent.

After Cuzco, we made the journey by train to visit Macchu Picchu, the substantial ruins of an ancient Inca city. Where the incline was steep, the railway tracks zigzagged upward and the train moved as though shunting–a mile or so forward, then switching track, it travelled backward but gained altitude with each zigzag to reach a pass between the peaks, then it did the same descending. The trip was punctuated with stops at picturesque native villages where we were offered freshly cooked corn-on-the-cob, carried in the seller's apron-pouches and sold through open train windows. On the final stretch, the train zigzagged downward for a thousand feet or so into a valley. There we left it and crossed a river by foot-bridge to waiting buses which climbed on a precariously narrow road with one-after-another hairpin bends up the face of Machu Picchu. For a couple of steaming hours our guides, speaking many different languages, directed separate large groups through the ruins until lunch was served on the spacious veranda of the minute hotel. There, up a narrow staircase, we located our room with its two casement windows and spectacular view. At around 3:00 pm all but the two of us departed Macchu Piccu and returned to Cuzco.

In the stillness when the air cooled and dusk descended, Rai and I–together but wonderfully alone–set out to explore the many layers of an ancient society. Soon I began to see and feel this empty Inca city as it must once have been, full of life and colour. Remembering what we had read and been told of a people lost to history, they still seemed vividly present in their art and architecture. Judging by the way their stonework came out of and blended into the natural curves of the landscape, I felt sure they must have been a happy people though the reality of ritual sacrifice of animals and children was deeply disturbing.

Rai seemed unusually quiet as we wandered again into the Chapel of the Moon. I saw him touch the stone altar thoughtfully. When he stood by one of the oddly-shaped windows in the stone wall–typically narrower at the top than at the bottom–looking out over the darkening terraces, he appeared more moved than I had ever seen him. Later, I looked at Rai in amazement when he spoke of this exploration as a religious experience.

Next morning, though Rai slept, I opened my eyes into an eerie mist which had clearly entered our bedroom through the open windows. I soon realized it must be part of the cloud which shrouded the whole mountain. When that cloud lifted, the clear air brought other mountains across the valley so close that it felt as though I could reach out and touch the orchids that clung to the sheer rock face. After breakfast we had plenty of time to explore the lower agricultural terraces, then we climbed well above the heart of the city to get a map-like view of it before the next load of tourists arrived.

After a couple of days spent in the ancient and beautiful, but hauntingly all-white city of Arequipa (where dogs howl all night), we flew north to Caracas which was such a contrast with its huge American hotels and glass-covered malls. Nearing the airport we had seen shanty towns spread in all directions, but we deliberately closed our eyes to them, choosing to wallow in luxury at Hotel Tamanaco. We even danced to Latin music on their marble terrace, danced so well we found ourselves

244

alone, dipping and swirling while others watched from the shadows. It felt wonderful. Our personal world was at peace.

We came home via Grenada where we spent several days with the Wilcoxes, friends from New Rochelle who now lived (and Bill painted) in a sugar-mill-with-swimming-pool in St.George's. The four of us sailed for several days among the Caribbean islands on a heavily built, creaking delivery vessel. From a distance the ship had looked enchanting, but as we climbed onto her crowded deck carrying food and booze, I had my doubts about the whole idea. Once the sails were up and the wind bore us out of the bay, the barefoot, sparsely dressed, Spanish-speaking crew navigated through rough seas from one island to the next, dropping off people, mail, sheep and chickens–all but the animals' heads tied into sacks–and taking on other livestock and travellers. The ship was frankly filthy, it stunk, and the head was unusable. Once as the craft ploughed through mighty green waves, I watched from my seat on a heap of rope as a sailor, obviously oblivious to the angle of it, scramble up the loosely stepped mast to mend a sail. Some men fished off the stern. Others barbecued what had been caught.

After one drink ashore on Saint Lucia, Ernest Hemingway's favourite island, I took to my bed with something like food poisoning and missed the tales–Rai filled me in later–of the great man's writing and debauchery there. After two more days we went home.

Still awash in the ambience of our travels, the move to the Sunshine Coast went easily. Because I had measured carefully, the furniture fit the house. Rai now had fewer shows to take him into Vancouver–a couple of annual telethons and the once weekly *Magistrate's Court. People In Conflict* was no more. Rai had produced it for about 10 years in black and white, but when CFCF Montreal bought colour cameras, Dan Enright had moved the production east. Rai decided not to commute to Montreal and two members of the show's panel simply couldn't. In Quebec the quality of production suffered and the show quickly folded. Rai now spent his time working on new outlines in a separate cottage-cum-office built on our property. The first year hurried by as we finished the interior of the main house, planted rockeries and made friends with near neighbours. That September I began teaching classes for Continuing Education in interior design, colour and exercise for seniors. We had a few really good parties and people came from all over to rave about the view from our guest room. Heath and George brought their baby, Erica, and when Roger started his career as a teacher at the local high school, he found a place to live nearby. This was a bonus as we had seen little of him since he left home.

Still looking for personal challenges, I became involved with the Festival of the Written Arts and the Community Arts Council. Then I opened my own dance school. Though few of my students had professional aspirations, through teaching in various locations I collected a good crop of keen youngsters. This kept me busy and healthy, but the sad fact was that Rai, now nearing 75, had too much free time. He began to drink heavily again, partly I believe, because I had found interests outside the house but also because he was being offered fewer shows and was making less money. The demand for his expertise had diminished to the degree that he failed to move, as other producers had, toward fresh telethon formats. "If it's not broken, don't fix it" had become his motto. Though he said he didn't mind, more than likely he resented my interest in activities such as social workshops and the local dream group.

During the next few years, feeling the pinch money-wise, becoming restless again, and prompted by a boom in the market, we sold at a good profit, bought, refurbished and lost money on another rather ugly house before setting out to build the perfect small house on a view lot we had found near Gibson's Landing.

An architect whose work we loved drew up the plans, but six months later when we had expected to move in, our new project was far from complete. We put our stuff in storage and moved into an appliance-free, lamp-lit summer cottage. Unfortunately, the only available builder turned out to be a fancy dancer who not only changed the plans but kept the invoices for materials in his back pocket, absconded with the salaries of his crew and took a week off to get married! Rai went to the police who said they would "look into it." He consulted his bank manager who said, "Not to worry. He's okay. He's unconventional but reliable." So we carried on. The guys on the job knew Rai and liked him but needed the money they were owed. Finally Rai borrowed from his friendly bank and put enough in our joint account to finish the house then gave the builder the advance he asked for. And it was nearly finished when Rai had to go east for six weeks, taking Deb Carswell, his occasional production assistant, to produce a telethon for the Lion's Club. I was left to encourage the recalcitrant builder to bring to completion this latest bit of wishful thinking that Rai and I were into, and I was alone in the cottage one November night when the foreman knocked at my door. He'd come to tell me that the electrician had refused to connect our new house to the hydro pole because the builder hadn't paid him. He said he'd had to bring in gas heaters to dry the dry-wall, and if I didn't pay the electrician–indeed, all the salaries–and daily oversee the operation, the work would stop.

Next day and the next I took yellow-eyed "Bloop" (our big Doberman cross) to the site and asked a lot of questions to show the men I knew what should be happening. After a few more days on duty, I wrote the following note to Rai. It turned up years after his death, among letters which had followed his memorial service.

Hi Luv,

Here's a birthday greeting and a hug - a quiet meaningful hug - for each day that you are away.

I wish that the telethon will come together with ease and exuberance, and be fun and satisfying, and that lots of energy, yours and a great many Lions, will combine to make it the best one yet.

Bloop and I will do our best to be ready on your return to greet you with the lights on and a fire in the new hearth, so that we can quickly forget the struggles and frustration this adventure has caused.

"Take care of yourself" you say to me, and I repeat "Take care of yourself." Keep fruit available, bananas are valuable food and cantaloupe and apple juice–if you can't get pears–and order extra veg and salad.

I'm grateful Deb is with you. She will be a tower of strength.

Three weeks seems like forever at the moment, but this will pass and we'll be okay and get our enthusiasm back and put some new joy into each day.

Love and caring,

Me.

That last home we built was a gem, full of light and soft colour, but it had cost us half again the original estimate and we couldn't afford it. Within eighteen months we sold it for all that it had cost and then for a comparatively small amount, bought a big, dark place with a tennis court that Rai thought was grand. Though not my taste, I didn't argue because he had agreed to retire entirely from show business in two years at which time we would find an unpretentious cottage on an island.

"Promise," he'd said. But just then someone asked him to take on the presidency of the Gibson's Landing Theatre Project, a plan to turn an old fire hall into a modern theatre in this tiny resort town. Rai was delighted. "Now this is more like it!" he exclaimed.

From the outset the project frightened me because I could see that Rai had notions of bringing New York to Gibson's Landing. And at first there was a lot of enthusiasm, and Rai answered the phone dramatically, "This is the president of the GLTP." Many meetings were held in our house, and he and the friends he gathered to work with him planned big time strategies. He had persuaded artists to create expensive brochures and sold several big companies on the idea of supporting the new theatre. Their promises appeared to convince the provincial government to match these sponsorships and Rai flew high. But this approach ignored the local people who might have volunteered to help. I could feel tension growing among his committee members as it dawned on them he was dreaming in another world, and

248

when someone finally disagreed with him, Rai's own frustration brought him to tears. Then one day he read in a Vancouver newspaper that the promised government money was to go instead to a Native band to build a theatre in Sechelt, the town just north of us. Ironically, the band had not asked for the money.

When Rai's expansive project fell through, he became depressed and angry. But this time I really couldn't prop him up. I watched myself stand back and observe him without pity. Neither could I drink with him, not even one drink to be sociable. Sad evening after sad evening passed without reasonable conversation and after a time of many silences, I withdrew into a vacuum. He wasn't the only person suffering.

CHAPTER 17

May 1990–Last Dance

Remember how we danced? I whispered. "We really danced, you and I, that night in Caracas. Had the floor to ourselves!"

Wanting no one else to hear, I leaned over my husband's hospital bed and spoke softly, close to his ear. If I could reach him, I wanted him to go on his way with a happy thought.

"Wasn't that marble floor smooth and wonderful? Wasn't the music irresistibly sensual? Yes, we had good times. Those times stay clear in my memory. Nothing can spoil them." But he was far away, didn't flutter an eyelid, didn't move the hand I held.

I had been with Rai almost continuously for the four tense days since the dawn when he stood in his blue dressing gown in my bedroom doorway. "I can't breathe," he wheezed. I flew out of bed and guided him to a chair in the living room. Gasping and shivering, he grasped the arm of the chair and tumbled into the seat.

"Hold on, I'll get you a cold cloth." Rai coughed and tried to spit.

"Good Christ! it hurts," he said, holding his chest, then he scrambled to lie face down on the floor. But only for a moment. "It's no good," he rasped, pulling himself back into the chair. "Jesus! What's happening?"

"Try to relax," I coaxed him. "Take slow breaths. I'll call the hospital."

Having managed to provide the correct information, I wet a towel and went back to Rai. He was ashen and sweat covered his face. I held the cold towel to the back of his neck and whispered, "You'll be all right. The ambulance won't be long. They'll help you. Could you drink some water?" He didn't speak but sat still, breathing in short gasps, not fighting. I left him long enough get my dressing gown.

It was perhaps ten minutes before two men were in the house, putting an oxygen mask over Rai's face and lifting him onto a stretcher. I pulled on a pair of slacks and went with him in the screeching ambulance to Sechelt Hospital, following the stretcher into Emergency.

Very soon I was sent away while they "stabilized" him, whatever that meant, and when I went back he could talk to me. "Why the hell did they shove this tube up me. Jeez, it hurts." A nurse explained that they needed to get rid of fluid. At least Rai was breathing better and feeling less pain. A few minutes later, someone told me I'd have to leave. They said they must prepare him for air-lifting to Vancouver. After half an hour someone took me home. I called our son Roger, who was working in Burns Lake, stuffed a few things into a bag and still caught the 8:30 am boat to Horseshoe Bay, arriving at Shaughnessy Hospital a few minutes after the helicopter had delivered Rai to intensive care. There was still time to call my brother, a nurse said, before I would be allowed to visit my husband.

By the time I saw him, Rai seemed barely conscious. The medics had already hooked him up to several machines arranged around the head of his bed which ticked and flashed signals. When he heard my hello, he said, "Hi, Honey," and lifted the fingers of the hand with the intravenous in it. When a doctor came in and asked how his patient was doing after such an insult, Rai showed anger in both his face and voice. "Insult, indeed!" he hissed.

"You are breathing better now, yes?"

Rai managed "Thanks," then he asked me, "Did you call Roger?" I nodded. "Good," he said and closed his eyes. After that he became peaceful. Next day Rai smiled at me, said a few words to Roger when he arrived, and listened on a cell phone when a call came through from Brian, his first son, in Toronto. Brian did most of the talking but Rai's face showed that he was listening. He even chuckled.

On the third day Rai seemed to remember that he and I had discussed parting company. Roger said later that he had noticed a sudden change in his dad's attitude toward me.

The medics kept Rai alive on the third and fourth days until Heath could be there to say good bye to her father and give the signal to remove life support. By then my brother Roger and his wife and daughter had joined us as we watched the images slow and flicker. During the next hour Rai's breathing stopped and started again several times, but each time the spaces between grew longer–until it didn't start again.

Heath shed a few quiet tears, but she was the only one. When we left the hospital, Roger and Heath and I followed my brother and his wife and daughter back to their place in Shaughnessy for a cup of tea and then a stiffer kind of drink. We were standing about in their kitchen when I was suddenly overcome. It was the only time I cried, but that time I cried for all the chances of happiness we had missed, for wizened dreams and fallen castles. I cried for the emptiness we'd both suffered and the pettiness of the differences that had from the beginning marred our relationship. Lately I'd watched him– "puffed up" I had thought then–walk slowly round and round "his" property. But perhaps he had just been looking, seeing and loving. There had been times in the past when on our walks he had pressed me to stop rushing, to stroll–something I'd always found difficult. Maybe even then, he had wanted to enjoy each thing of beauty. Or because of his high blood pressure he may also have been in physical pain. "He rests now," I told myself.

Roger stayed close to me for the next several days and the two of us, with help from dear Doctor Hewett, planned a memorial service at his Unitarian church. For Rai's sake, it had to be a "production," and when Rai's son Brian, still a broadcaster, came from Toronto, we took him to meet and talk with Doctor

Hewett who, quite aware of Rai's antipathy toward formal religion, spoke of him as his true friend. He agreed with both Roger and Brian that they should arrange to record the ceremony.

Then, on May 22, from the pulpit of his elegantly simple church on 49th Avenue, the Reverend Doctor guided Rai's service. On that day, his packed congregation included many show people, some of whom had volunteered to take part in the proceedings. For the man whose family and colleagues now gathered to bid him farewell, Phillip asked for peace and rest for those closest to Rai and gave thanks for the powerful creative energy which he had shared throughout his career. It was then that Mart Kenny on his Selmer Clarinet, subtly accompanied on the piano by Bud Henderson, took us back through the strains of "Sunrise Serenade" and "Lola" to the days when the "Western Gentlemen" were very young. "The West, A Nest And You" never sounded so sweet. David Catton talked about working with Rai in their Ontario Drama Festival days and spoke of Rai's long years on the cutting edge of broadcasting. Budge Bell-Irving who had, in place of my late father, given me away when Rai and I were married, commended the showman for having put a lot of polish on the Pasley Island Games. Other Pasley people attending the service understood exactly what Budge meant. Bud Henderson played nostalgia from Broadway musicals with great charm until Phillip Hewett brought the service to a close in a way that connected Rai's colourful life to his numerous and valuable undertakings in many communities, often under stressful conditions. And then Dal Richards gave us a haunting medley of saxophone tunes familiar to everyone before "playing us out," Pied Piper-style, with "Seventy-six Trombones." Rai would have loved it.

EPILOGUE

Journey to the Sea

B rian was still with us several days later when, having returned to the Sunshine Coast, he and Roger, and Heath and her daughter, Erica, came with me to spread Rai's ashes in a place he had especially loved.

Cliff Gilker Park is an ancient fir and cedar forest that lets in little sunlight, except where Robert's Creek flows through it and catches a glimpse of sky as it curves through deep gullies. Among old growth trees, foot paths lead up and over steep hills and down to cross the creek in various places on rustic bridges. Rai's favourite spot in this park was a quiet stretch of the creek just above a broad waterfall.

The creek was down to a mere trickle on the day we took Rai's ashes there, and I noticed, as we climbed up the path beside it, that the breast of the falls, the great, smooth stone over which the rushing water usually passed before dropping 30 or 40 feet to a swirling pool, was literally dry. Indeed, we could walk out onto it, which we did, stepping carefully across little cracks which still carried water. Here it was bright. As they crossed the rock, miniature rivers ran into several small pools from which they overflowed into lower crevasses leading to the very edge of the fall. It seemed perfectly natural that each of us should choose a pool and sprinkle a handful of ashes into it, watching as the glittering dust filtered into the water and was born away. One of the little rivers ran strongly enough to carry the three stems of gladioli I'd brought–palest yellow, green tipped–tied with ribbon. The posy started and stopped and went on again till it reached the edge, paused as though looking down, then tumbled over. We watched it circle slowly three times in the pool below before a current caught the blossoms and hurried them out of sight into the darkness of their journey to the sea.

Fare you well, Horatio.

1923905

Made in the USA